DEC Is Dead, Long Live DEC

DEC Is Dead

Long Live DEC

THE LASTING LEGACY
OF DIGITAL EQUIPMENT CORPORATION

Edgar H. Schein

with Peter DeLisi, Paul Kampas,
and Michael Sonduck

BK

BERRETT-KOEHLER PUBLISHERS, INC.
San Francisco

Berrett-Koehler Publishers, Inc.

235 Montgomery Street, Suite 650
San Francisco, CA 94104-2916
Tel: (415) 288-0260; Fax: (415) 362-2512
www.bkconnection.com

Ordering Information

Quantity sales. Special discounts are available on quantity purchases by corporations, associations, and others. For details, contact the "Special Sales Department" at the Berrett-Koehler address above.

Individual sales. Berrett-Koehler publications are available through most bookstores. They can also be ordered direct from Berrett-Koehler:
Tel: (800) 929-2929; Fax: (802) 864-7626; www.bkconnection.com

Orders for college textbook/course adoption use. Please contact Berrett-Koehler:
Tel: (800) 929-2929; Fax: (802) 864-7626.

Orders by U.S. trade bookstores and wholesalers. Please contact Publishers Group West, 1700 Fourth Street, Berkeley, CA 94710. Tel: (510) 528-1444; Fax: (510) 528-3444.

Berrett-Koehler and the BK logo are registered trademarks of Berrett-Koehler Publishers, Inc.

Printed in the United States of America

Berrett-Koehler books are printed on long-lasting acid-free paper. When it is available, we choose paper that has been manufactured by environmentally responsible processes. These may include using trees grown in sustainable forests, incorporating recycled paper, minimizing chlorine in bleaching, or recycling the energy produced at the paper mill.

Library of Congress Cataloging-in-Publication Data

DEC is dead, long live DEC : the lasting legacy of Digital Equipment Corporation / by Edgar H. Schein ... [et al.]
    p. cm.
  Includes bibliographical references and index.
  ISBN 1-57675-225-9
  1. Digital Equipment Corporation—History. 2. Digital Equipment Corporation—Biography. 3. Computer industry—United States—History. 4. Computer industry—United States—Management—Case studies. I. Schein, Edgar H.
HD9696.2.U64D543 2003
338.7'61004'0973—dc21   2003041788

First edition
07 06 05 04 03   10 9 8 7 6 5 4 3 2 1

Project management, design, and composition: BookMatters, Berkeley;
Copyedit: Mike Mollett; Proofreading: Janet Reed Blake; Index: Ken DellaPenta

JAN 5 2004

Contents

Illustrations

Preface

My collaborating authors and I have, from the very beginning of this project, struggled with the question of who is our audience and who might benefit from the lessons that one can glean from such a story of one company. We have identified many possible audiences—founders and entrepreneurs; investors; executives who are trying to change their companies to become more innovative, or perhaps more efficient and less innovative; management theorists interested in the growth, evolution, and death of an organization; organizational consultants; students going into business and wondering what sort of a world they might be entering; professors interested in teaching about leadership, organizational culture, and technology; and, of course, Digital Equipment Corportion (DEC) alumni, many of whom are still wondering what happened and why.

My own answer to the question of audience is that we are writing to the *thinking* and *reflective* person in all of the above categories. Too many of our business books just focus on what to do. They make glib assumptions about a situation that an organization might face and propose a few action steps to solve the problem. The DEC story should make you think and reflect and make you aware of the tough choices and trade-offs that have to be made in the real world all the time. The DEC story illustrates that every company's evolution is unique but that certain kinds of events are universal because they derive from the inevitable consequences of success, growth, and age. What DEC should have done, what another company in the same situation should or might have done, what you should do in your unique organizational situation requires some deep thought and insight into the dynamics of organizational evolution.

As I hope the reader will see, the implementation of even the simplest prescriptions like "Have a strategy," something all management books agree on, becomes quite complex in the context of a particular company, with a particular history, and with particular personalities that create a certain kind of culture.

My contributing authors and I have had many arguments about what are the "lessons" to be learned from the DEC story about governance, leadership, entrepreneurship, technology, innovation, strategy, marketing and, perhaps most important, organizational culture. What makes the DEC story both so interesting and so complicated is that there are lessons to be learned about all of these things, but they don't fall out nicely into ten principles, or five things to avoid, or seven steps to business success.

One of our interviewees who spent most of his career within DEC kept reminding me that "DEC was a coat of many colors, so don't try to write a simple one-dimensional history of it. It won't work." He was, of course, correct, and we found this out the hard way in our own discussions of how to write this book because each of us saw DEC from our own perspective, drew our own lessons, and our his own biases in how the story should be told. We tried to integrate these points of view, but just as DEC failed at many levels to integrate the agendas of its various subgroups, so we also failed in this task and have, therefore, a story that is itself also a coat of many colors.

This preface is written in the first person because I felt that ultimately my outsider perspective and my interest in organizational culture and leadership added a dimension to the analysis that is missing in most books about organizations and management. I have tried to learn from my supporting authors and have encouraged them to write their own views to be included wherever possible, but in the end I tried to write what seemed to me to be the aspects of the story that are typically not told by insiders, either because they are not of interest to them or because, by being insiders, they cannot see their own culture sufficiently clearly to understand its power and ubiquitousness.

So we have here a book about culture and leadership, a book about technology, innovation, organizational success, and failure. The DEC story is to me a story of how technology, organizational growth, and business functions such as strategy, marketing, and finance not only interact with one another but are deeply colored by the cultural forces that are at play in the organization. To grasp this *interplay* requires something from the reader—some thought and reflection. The lessons are there for all the audiences mentioned above, and we try to bring them out as clearly as possible, but none of these lessons are simple because, in the end, real organizations founded and run by real people are not simple. This book is an attempt to pay tribute to those real people who were solving difficult real problems and to identify how their efforts left an important legacy.

Edgar H. Schein
May 2003

Acknowledgments

My collaborating authors, Peter DeLisi, Paul Kampas, and Michael Sonduck, not only contributed directly to various chapters of this book but were also invaluable in helping me to think through how to tell the DEC story. They each had different experiences and different biases but our long discussions and exchanges of phone calls and e-mails gradually enabled me to think through how best to tell the story. The Sloan School of Management's research committee generously supported this three-year project, and my colleague John Van Maanen provided helpful comments on the final manuscript.

My most heartfelt thanks go to Ken Olsen, the founder of Digital Equipment Corporation. Not only did his willingness to keep me around as a consultant for thirty years enable me to perceive what was going on in DEC in a way that most outsiders never have a chance to see, but his support for this book was unflagging. He has spent many hours in the past couple of years giving me his thoughts on what happened and why, sent me many documents, and encouraged me to reveal to the world how his vision of science and technology created a unique kind of organization and culture.

I am also greatly indebted to Rod Sutherland, who turned over to me twenty years worth of DEC reports, management memos, and other materials that he had accumulated in his marketing role. I sent out general inquiries through the DEC Alumni Association and thank them for helping me to locate many of my informants. Gordon Bell was particularly helpful in structuring the technical side of this story and in providing his "final words" on what he thinks really happened. I am also especially grateful to Tracy Gibbons for offering to write a chapter on how DEC contributed to leadership development. We also received great help from Reesa Abrams, Debra Amidon, Crawford Beveridge, George Chamberlain, Jeff Clanon, Jim Cudmore, Denzil Doyle, Pier Carlo Falotti, Bob Ferrone, Jay Forrester, Steve Frigand, Sam Fuller, Rose Ann Giordano, Bob Glorioso, Bill Hanson, Win Hindle, Bea Mah Holland, Michael Horner, Ann Jenkins, Bill Johnson (BJ), Jeff Kalb, Peter Kaufmann (now Peter Chipman), Andy Knowles, Ed Kramer, John Leng, Jesse Lipcon, Sue Lotz, Kevin Melia, Bob Metcalfe, Stan Olsen, Dave Packer, Jamie Pearson, Bob Puffer, George Roth, Grant Saviers, Willow Shire, John Sims, Ron Smart, Jack Smith, Bill Strecker, and Bob Supnick. I also want to thank the many people who volunteered to help but were in the end not called because I ran out of time. I do not pretend that I have captured the whole DEC story, and I apologize to those who feel they have crucial insights that I somehow overlooked or ignored.

My publisher, Berrett-Koehler, and Steve Piersanti in particular were most helpful in formulating how to present this story. The five reviewers who saw the first draft were outstanding in providing both general comments and detailed suggestions. I found that I used most of what they suggested.

I have thought about the lessons of the DEC story for many years and have worked on pieces of this book for a long time. My DEC experiences were crucial in helping to formulate my concepts of consultation, organization development, and organizational culture. For this I will be forever grateful to Ken Olsen; his trust in people allowed me full access to all of DEC.

Producing this final manuscript has been difficult because there are potentially so many materials and stories to be processed. As the reader will discover, I ended up leaning heavily on my first-hand experience because I found that materials and stories always had some degree of spin in them that was not always easy to decipher. To ensure that I was not too far off in my accounts I sent various chapters to select people, and I thank them for their responses and corrections.

As always when I go into a writing funk my wife has to deal with my psychological absence. I am forever grateful for her patience and support during those times. I have also sworn never to write another original book based on historical data.

Edgar H. Schein
May 2003

one

Purpose and Overview

The story of Digital Equipment Corporation (DEC) is fundamentally a forty-year saga encompassing the creation of a new technology, the building of a company that became the number two computer company in the United States with $14 billion in sales at its peak, the decline and ultimate sale of that company to the Compaq Corporation in 1998, and the preservation in its many alumni of the values that were the essence of the culture of that company. (The company's official name was Digital Equipment Corporation, and its logo was "D.I.G.I.T.A.L." or "Digital," but common usage around the company was typically "DEC," so we will adopt that usage throughout this book.) That culture was an almost pure model of what we can think of as a "culture of innovation." It created the minicomputer revolution and laid the groundwork for the interactive computing that today is taken for granted. The managerial values and processes that were at the heart of that culture produced an almost uniformly positive response in DEC employees throughout its history.

The DEC culture emphasized—to an extraordinary degree—creativity, freedom, responsibility, openness, commitment to truth, and having fun. Not only were these values central in its early formative

1

years but even when it was an organization of 100,000 people and over $10 billion in sales, these values held firm. DEC's management model empowered the people who worked there, and most of the employees internalized these values and expressed them in their careers with other companies.

In choosing the title of this book, we thought about the British Empire, which disappeared as a major political entity yet instilled its values in the former colonies that eventually became stronger than the parent. DEC disappeared as a company, yet former DEC engineers and managers populated the computer industry and became major contributors to other companies. The DEC culture lived on in the "colonies" that it spawned or helped to develop.

WHAT IS TO BE LEARNED FROM THE DEC STORY?

The lessons to be learned from this story are many. In our effort to learn from it, we will be asking the following questions:

1. How is a culture of product innovation created, and how does it evolve?
2. What are the essential ingredients of such a culture in terms of the managerial values and practices it displays?
3. What contributions did DEC make to the growing technology of computing and to management practices?
4. How did the "genetic structure," the DNA of such a culture, produce extraordinary results without containing what can be thought of as a pure commercial or "money gene"?
5. How were the traditional business functions handled in such a culture of innovation?
6. How did success, growth, and age create particular organizational problems that had to be managed?
7. How did technical progress create changes in competition and in the marketplace that required cultural evolution?
8. How was that cultural evolution inhibited by the very success that the organization experienced?

9. How is it that essential elements of a culture survived, while DEC, the economic entity, disappeared?

Why is it important to learn more about these nine issues? Primarily because every organization as it matures goes through developmental stages that require the making of choices, and these choices often involve difficult trade-offs between conflicting values. Yet these choices determine the future of the organization. The DEC story is a unique opportunity to study in some detail how the choices made at various developmental stages had both desirable and undesirable consequences. Entrepreneurs, investors, consultants, managers, and organization theorists can all benefit from seeing how complex these choices can become when one looks at one organization in detail and over a long period of time.

WHY IS DEC AN ORGANIZATION WORTH STUDYING?

DEC as a Classic Case of Entrepreneurial Leadership

One of the key values in the DEC culture was "Do the right thing." In emphasizing "Doing the right thing," the DEC culture created a unique climate that stimulated leadership at all levels. The DEC story is therefore also a story about the triumph and, in the end, the "tragedy" of technical, organizational, and social leadership. Warren Bennis, the eminent researcher of leadership, has pointed out that the difference between leadership and management is that managers "do things right," while leaders "do the right thing." In DEC "Do the right thing" was a license both to insubordination and to leadership. As we will see, DEC, more than any other company of its size and scale that I am aware of, created leaders at every level of its organization. And, as we will also see, a culture built around leaders creates its own turmoil and difficulties.

The DEC story is about leadership not only in technical innovation but also in management practice, manufacturing, community relations, affirmative action, sales and service practices, and, perhaps most important, human development. Ken Olsen, DEC's founder, articulated values that are frequently touted as being the essence of what a good organization should be, and it maintained those values for thirty-five years. Those same values created in the end an economic problem that led to disaster for the company. But the DEC story leaves us with two huge questions. Would it have been possible to save the economic entity without giving up those values, that is, without destroying the culture? And, in the end, what is more valuable—the culture or the company?

Fundamental questions also arise as to whether DEC's ultimate contribution was to technology or to management practice. Did the technological vision dictate a certain management style, or did a certain management style enable extraordinary technical achievements? Was it Ken Olsen's technical vision that created DEC's successes, or was it his organizational genius that fostered what came to be known as a world-class engineering organization under the leadership of Gordon Bell? Was it the culture that Olsen created that attracted talents like Gordon Bell and made possible the building of an organization in which world-class engineers wanted to work? Or was DEC's success the product of the interaction of Ken Olsen's and Gordon Bell's visions and management practices?

A Classic Example of Organizational Culture Dynamics

Why focus on culture? Culture creation and culture change are a constant source of preoccupation these days for entrepreneurs and executives. Hardly a day goes by without seeing a newspaper story or a book announcement about an executive who is "changing the culture" or "creating a new culture" in his or her company, usually to stimulate innovation in a rapidly changing technical environment. We see calls for "service cultures," "cultures of empowerment," "teamwork cultures," "cultures of openness," "trust cultures," and, most recently and emphatically, "cultures of innovation." Everyone seems to want to know how to create innovation, especially in older companies that seem to have lost their innovative edge. And it is increasingly recognized that culture creation and culture management are the essence of leadership.

One of the main preoccupations of entrepreneurs and company founders is how to "create the right culture" or "preserve the culture that they have created." Yet little is known about creating or preserving a culture. Leaders in more mature companies seem to believe that announcing a culture of innovation from a position of influence is sufficient to make it happen or that they can "change" culture to fit the new requirements of the market. Few of these executives question whether cultures of innovation formed around products, processes, or management systems would actually solve the particular business problems that they are encountering. Few of them question whether certain cultures should be retained even if they produce economic difficulties.

We don't have a coherent theory or set of concepts for culture "process." We don't understand well enough how culture works—how it is created; how it evolves; how it changes; and how it influences strategy, structure, and business processes. It is precisely this absence of knowledge that makes executives nervous about culture as a concept. Culture appears to be something that is difficult to control; hence, it is often avoided when strategy and process are discussed. Yet as we will see, in a mature organization culture pervades everything, even the most fundamental economic decisions that the board and senior executives make. A better understanding of cultural dynamics in relationship to technology and organizational evolution is therefore not a choice; it is a necessity.

One can write about how culture and leadership work in the abstract, providing case illustrations as one goes. I have done this in two of my previous books, *Organizational Culture and Leadership* (1992) and *The Corporate Culture Survival Guide* (1999). What remains to be done is to look at one or more of these cases in greater depth to appreciate the subtle dynamic processes that are at work in organizational cultures and to show how these processes explain the rise and fall of organizations, particularly ones that seemed to be on the road to success yet could not sustain themselves. And it is especially important to understand better the role of leadership in the creation, maintenance, evolution, and ultimately destruction of a given organizational culture.

One of the most dramatic of these cases is DEC, an organization my contributing authors and I came to know intimately as consultants or employees or both from 1966 to 1992. DEC virtually transformed the computing landscape and rose to be the number two computer maker with a $14 billion sales volume in 1992, which put it in the top fifty corporations in the United States. Ed Roberts in his seminal book on high tech entrepreneurs calls DEC "the most successful MIT [Massachusetts Institute of Technology] spin-off company" (Roberts 1991, p. 12). Ken Olsen was called by *Fortune* magazine in 1986 "arguably the most successful entrepreneur in the history of American business." DEC's economic rise was accompanied by a myriad of contributions to technology, to management theory and practice, to production processes, to the utilization of women and minorities in industry, and to community relations. Common to all of these contributions was a set of cultural dynamics that made extraordinary things possible. What can these cultural dynamics teach us?

Culture works its influences in many ways. First of all, DEC was created at a time in U.S. society when social values were moving toward more individualism and where technology was facilitating this trend. Not only was Ken Olsen, the key architect of the company, brought up at a time when certain postwar values were salient, but the whole design thrust of DEC's products toward distributed interactive computing reflected decentralization, rejection of formal authority, empowerment of the individual, and, at the same time, the networking of individuals for greater efficiency. Peter DeLisi, coming from IBM, noted immediately that the IBM mainframe was symbolic of authority and centralization, while DEC's time-shared and networked computers were symbolic of individualism and freedom (DeLisi 1998). In other words, product design does not occur in a vacuum; it reflects social trends and social issues. When DEC appeared on the scene, social norms supported and stimulated the kinds of products that were designed.

DEC as One of the First Dot-Coms: A Knowledge Company before Its Time

As the world gets more complex, organizations are more than ever dependent on knowledge workers and knowledge management. Many observers and analysts of DEC saw it as one of the first and most vivid examples of a knowledge-based company with a culture in which knowledge creation and management were highly valued and in which networking and open exchange of knowledge was a central management principle. (Debra Rogers Amidon noted this in a 1991 management memo that is reproduced in appendix C. Two of the first books on networking as a business organization concept were published by DEC employees Jessica Lipnack and Jeffrey Stamps [1993, 1994]. Debra Amidon has also published two books on the "knowledge economy," based on insights first gained at DEC [Amidon 1997, 2003]). Several alumni have pointed out that because of DEC's early use of networking, it was one of the first companies ever to be assigned a "dot-com" address by the U.S. government. As we will see, there are many lessons to be learned from DEC, both about how one creates an effective knowledge-based company and what managerial dilemmas and dysfunctions can arise in such an organization as it gets larger and more differentiated. Even though DEC failed as a business, the management systems and principles it instituted around networks and knowledge management are seen by many as a blueprint for how future organizations will have to be designed and managed. In particular there are lessons for decision-making theory. Knowledge workers operate from different premises when they have to reach consensus in a network in the absence of hierarchical authority.

DEC as a Classic Case of Values-Based Management

Much is written these days about values-based management and the need for management to clearly articulate its values. DEC is a classic case of an organization that was built on its founder's very clear set of values. Ken Olsen's values were written down, articulated throughout DEC's history, used explicitly in the training and socialization of new employees, restated explicitly in company documents of all sorts, and adhered to with a passion right to the end. In most organizations there is a disconnect between articulated values and actual management practices. In DEC, to a surprising degree, the values were reflected in actual work practices and became thoroughly embedded in the culture. Many DEC values had a strong moral imperative, which gave them stability and which makes it possible to see both the strengths and weaknesses of this degree of values-based management.

DEC created what would, by any definition, be thought of as a strong corporate culture. The basic question then is to what extent such a culture can evolve as technology and organizational requirements change. An even more fundamental question is whether such highly valued managerial practices should evolve and change. Should values change to support organizations, or are organizations an expression of human values? And if they cannot sustain those values, should organizations die?

DEC as a Classic Case of Technological Evolution to Commodification

The DEC story illustrates clearly the difficult challenge of modifying an organization to adapt to changing market conditions as its own technological innovations create new markets. Especially difficult is the move from a culture of innovation, based on one set of managerial values, to an organization geared to producing commodity products that typically require a different set of managerial values and practices. As Paul Kampas's analysis in chapter 9 shows, the failure of DEC's culture of innovation to coevolve with changing market conditions lead to inefficiencies and ultimately to economic failure. The very success of the early innovation created competitive forces that changed the nature of the innovation, stimulated disruptive technologies and market demands, and therefore created a need for organizational transformation. That transformation may have been beyond the organization's ability or will to manage, even if the leadership recognized the need. Could DEC have survived? We will see that the answer to this question is fraught with complexity and lessons for both young and mature organizations.

Was DEC a Case of Strategic Myopia or a Case of Deliberately Diffuse Vision?

In its early years DEC had a clear technical vision built around high-quality, new, and innovative products. The market supported this vision and started DEC on a thirty-five-year path of financial success. Eventually, though, the market evolved, and DEC found itself in strategic turmoil. Some argued that DEC needed to focus and stop trying to do everything, while others argued that DEC's ability to continue to produce powerful innovative products across the board was precisely its strength and that therefore it had to continue to support a wide range of innovations.

DeLisi feels that this issue was complicated by the lack of a strategic process that would resolve the dilemma and enable the company to set priorities, as he points out in appendix D. Olsen and other senior executives always believed that DEC had a strategy, but, according to DeLisi, they did not in fact understand what business strategy really is, how one forges it, or why it is needed more and more as the organization grows and matures. Most managers use the concept of *strategy* glibly without considering how one actually formulates strategy and what functions it must perform for an organization at different stages of growth. And then the question arises: what is "strategy" in a peer-to-peer network such as DEC attempted to maintain, even on a large scale?

DEC as an Illustration of Classic Problems of Entrepreneurial Succession, Governance, and the Role of the Board

The recent rise and fall of dot-coms highlights the problem of how investors and entrepreneurs can and should relate to one another. How long should an entrepreneur be in control of his or her company? When is an optimal time to go public and, if successful, how should the founder relate to an outside board of directors? When should a founder be replaced by professional management? What are the problems of governance at the different stages of an organization's evolution? How do technological changes create new dilemmas of governance?

The DEC story bears directly on these questions, especially on the role that the initial investor plays in controlling who is on the board even after the company has gone public and the role that the founder plays in selecting board members. As we will see, the relationship between General Georges Doriot in the venture capitalist role, the board members he selected, and Ken Olsen as founder and chief executive officer (CEO) created a complex "governance system" that had both strengths and weaknesses. The DEC story raises questions about how a board can and should evaluate the ability of the founder to manage a growing and mature business, when and how succession problems should be raised, and what kind of manager should succeed a founder. In the late 1980s and early 1990s DEC faltered financially, which raised these very issues. There is much to be learned from how the scenario played out and how Ken Olsen's successor in 1992, Robert Palmer, managed in the years until DEC was bought by the Compaq Computer Corporation in 1998.

DEC'S FATE: THE RESULT OF ROOT CAUSES
OR A COMPLEX INTERDEPENDENT FORCE FIELD?

In the managerial world there is a great need to find simple explanations that will enable us to avoid the errors of the past, but simple answers are usually so abstract that they do not really enlighten us. DEC's demise has been explained very simply but not convincingly. One simple explanation is that Ken Olsen in his later years lost his vision, failed to take appropriate action, and stuck to values that were no longer appropriate for the business situation. This explanation turns out to be a gross oversimplification and is, to a considerable degree, incorrect. We will never know what might have happened if Olsen had left ten years earlier, but, as this analysis will show, what happened to DEC in the 1980s and beyond was predictable from events that could be observed already in the 1960s, and much of the difficulty that DEC ran into was endemic to successful growth and differentiation, based on a culture and management system that employees and managers alike really liked, valued, and wanted to preserve at all costs. The culture did not coevolve with the technology and the organization. We need to understand better all the forces that made the culture so strong and the forces that kept it from coevolving, and that takes us well beyond Olsen and his own behavior, as we will see.

Many other so-called root causes have been proposed to explain DEC's sharp decline. "Failing to see market changes," "arrogance," "failure to control costs," "lack of strategic direction," and other explanations abound, but the question remains: if any of these diagnoses are correct, why did these failures occur? What underlying cultural dynamics were operating to explain why DEC "missed the PC market opportunity," why DEC "chose to stay with a proprietary system" rather than embracing "open architectures," why DEC in its later years "was not able to achieve a clear sense of strategic direction"?

Paradoxically, even as DEC was declining as an organization, it was creating projects that led to state-of-the-art new products and organizations—AltaVista, the Alpha chip, and the Enterprise Integration Service Organization, to name just three. Ex-DEC executives were increasingly playing key roles in other organizations in the growing computer industry. When these DEC alumni tell you that they learned critical lessons about how to manage during their years at DEC; when they choose to get together in meetings to reminisce about the good old days at DEC; when they use their alumni directory to maintain contact with friends from the DEC years, it says something about the stability of the culture that Ken Olsen and the early leaders of the company fostered. What was so special about this culture?

The lessons to be learned here are about how culture works at different stages in an organization's life cycle. The very same processes can have very different outcomes at different times in the life of an organization. Culture is a complex force field that influences all of an organization's processes. We try to manage culture but, in fact, culture manages us far more than we ever manage it, and this happens largely outside our awareness. The most dangerous error in the analysis of culture is to overlook its tremendous yet invisible coercive qualities and its extraordinary stability. The DEC story provides an opportunity to examine culture as a complex force field and to bring to awareness forces that are often ignored.

THE "DATABASE"

Most of the DEC story will be told from the point of view of participants who worked in the company. I worked as a consultant to Ken

Olsen and the Operations Committee from 1966 to 1992. I spent many weekends with the entire top management of the company at the various Woods Meetings that occurred over the years and was involved in a variety of projects in different groups and functions within DEC. Though Ken Olsen was the primary client, his style made it not only possible but also mandatory to treat the entire organization as a kind of "ultimate client," which resulted in meeting many managers and employees from many functions over the years. As will be noted in various chapters, my experiences within DEC were also instrumental in evolving my own concepts of *organization development* and *process consultation* (Schein 1987, 1988, 1999b).

Peter DeLisi was recruited in 1977 from IBM into the role of a product line manager. He later held positions in sales, sales training, marketing, and as a consultant in Enterprise Services. He left the company in 1993. Paul Kampas's career at DEC spanned engineering, strategic planning, and competitive analysis from 1976 to 1994. Mike Sonduck worked primarily in manufacturing from 1976 to 1981 as an internal organization development consultant.

During 2000 and 2001 we conducted over fifty intensive interviews with senior managers and with key engineers around whom so much of the story evolved. I spent many hours with Ken Olsen in 1999 and 2000 reminiscing about past events and trying to make some sense of them. Olsen strongly supported this project because he felt that the real story of how DEC succeeded and what caused its decline had not been told. Olsen the scientist wanted a more "scholarly" analysis even though he realized that some of that analysis would involve criticism of him and some of his decisions. He wrote many memos articulating his managerial philosophy, and these will be liberally quoted throughout the text.

In June 2001 the Computer Museum of Menlo Park, California, sponsored DECworld 2001, a two-day conference attended by two hundred DEC alumni, including many of its former senior managers and engineers. The reminiscences, formal talks, and informal conversations provided valuable input to me in thinking through this project. Perhaps most remarkable of all was the high attendance and the great enthusiasm of the group in looking back over what they regarded as positive experiences.

Key executives such as Gordon Bell, Barry Folsom, Bob Glorioso, Win Hindle, Jeff Kalb, Peter Kaufmann, Andy Knowles, Ed Kramer, Grant Saviers, John Sims, and Jack Smith provided invaluable information. Consulting engineers, those who held DEC's top technical rank, such as Dave Cutler, Sam Fuller, Alan Kotok, Jesse Lipcon, Bill Strecker, and Bob Supnick supplied various points of view, reviewed some of the chapters, and helped with examples and incidents that illustrated some of the key points. I also interviewed board members and made material available to them for their comment. Invitations were sent out through the alumni network for ex-DEC people to write to me with their own analyses of why DEC succeeded and why DEC failed. As chapters evolved, these were sent out to various alumni for comment, correction, and elaboration, recognizing that the "coat of many colors" would not be easily captured in a single image. The ability to use e-mail to circulate chapters, get opinions, ask questions, and check conflicting points of view made the writing of this book a DEC-like networking experience in itself.

My contributing authors and I spent many hours debating various aspects of the DEC story in trying to make sense of the many events that occurred over the forty-year history. Peter DeLisi focused on strategy, marketing, and governance issues. Paul Kampas was most concerned with the technological evolution and its impacts. Michael Sonduck lived with the many transformations and innovations that occurred in the manufacturing world and in DEC's growing organization development function. My own concern was primarily with trying to understand the cultural dynamics and how these colored the other issues. Most of the book is presented from my own point of view, but when particular issues were of concern to my contributing authors, I quote them directly or insert their material into the text. We were also fortunate in having Tracy Gibbons, one of the many talented members of DEC's internal organization consulting group and an organization development specialist, volunteer to do a chapter on how the DEC experience influenced the leadership potential of many of its employees.

Other writers have analyzed the DEC story, so we also examined the theories of Roberts (1991), Christensen (1997), Utterback (1994), Rifkin and Harrar (1988), and others who have published their views of why DEC succeeded and failed. We incorporated their theories in our analysis, but the primary sources are our own experiences and our interview data.

Communicating the nuances of how a culture works is difficult. We will rely on a mixture of stories and analysis to bring out both the concrete detail of how things happened and the underlying implications of those events. We will supplement these stories and analyses with quotes from DEC employees and managers as well as with formal written materials from different times in DEC's history.

THE ORGANIZATION OF THE BOOK

The book's structure reflects three organizing principles: (1) chronological history; (2) the three evolutionary streams of technology, organization, and culture; and (3) the multiple points of view of the authors and other ex-DEC managers who made contributions to the manuscript. We have begun with this introductory chapter that lays out our purposes. Chapter 2 describes how to think about the three developmental streams and how to think about the concept of *culture;* it also introduces the metaphor of *cultural DNA* and the *money gene.* In part I we describe how the DEC culture was created. Chapters 3, 4, and 5 analyze aspects of Ken Olsen's beliefs and values. Chapter 6 describes the DEC cultural paradigm in a more formal manner. Chapter 7 by Tracy Gibbons describes the impact of this culture on a sample of DEC alumni, and in chapter 8 I show how DEC's culture impacted me directly and helped me to formulate my own concepts of *process consultation* and *organization development.*

Part II describes some of the events that shaped DEC's midlife and ultimately led to its death as an economic entity. In chapter 9 Paul Kampas analyzes this period from a technological evolution point of view and shows how DEC's fate could be expected as technology changed. Chapter 10 analyzes the organizational evolution that occurred as a result of success, growth, and age. Chapter 11 describes how DEC as a learning organization attempted to deal with the various issues that growth brought with it, and chapter 12 shows how those same issues continued to influence DEC's continued success yet eroded DEC's strength as an economic competitor. Chapter 13 describes how through the 1980s and early 1990s Ken Olsen and others attempted to remedy the deteriorating situation and how that period came to an end in 1992 with Ken Olsen's resignation and Bob Palmer's promotion to CEO.

Part III tackles the question of what it all means. In chapter 14 I examine some of the obvious and not so obvious lessons about innovation, leadership, culture, and social issues. Embedded in these lessons are some observations about DEC's ultimate role and some of its lasting impacts. Chapter 15 summarizes and elaborates on some of the legacies as seen by various alumni and outside observers.

The five appendixes provide details and enhance various parts of the DEC story. Appendix A summarizes for the more technically inclined reader the contributions DEC made to computing and networking technology. In appendix B Michael Sonduck reviews his own experiences as an organization development consultant in the manufacturing organization. In appendix C we reprint a 1991 memo from Debra Rogers Amidon to Ken Olsen showing how DEC was actually one of the first true knowledge-based companies. Appendix D provides an analysis by Peter DeLisi of DEC's strategic failure. The final appendix is entitled "What Happened? A Postscript," by Gordon Bell, who was DEC's primary technical architect. These appendixes sharpen and highlight the lessons and legacies by giving us more concrete data around various issues discussed.

two

Three Developmental Streams

A MODEL FOR DECIPHERING THE LESSONS OF THE DEC STORY

As we have seen, DEC was a coat of many colors, and there are many ways the DEC story could be told. In order to bring out the cultural dynamics that are the central part of the story, I will discuss DEC's founding and early history, its rise and peak years, and its decline and death. However, I will not present the story the way a historian would, with many dates and details. Two other books have provided such a historical perspective (Pearson 1992; Rifkin and Harrar 1988). Rather, the emphasis will be on the cultural eras and critical periods that highlight major trends and that enable us to begin to see why those trends were developing.

THREE DEVELOPMENTAL STREAMS

Organizations can be analyzed from three developmental perspectives. Although these perspectives are often treated as independent, they are, in fact, highly interdependent. The analysis of DEC will show how this interdependence works and what can be learned from it. The three developmental streams are

1. The technology stream: the technological environment in which DEC operated and its own contribution through its products to that environment;

2. The organizational development stream: the ways in which an organization working in this technological context begins, grows, evolves, and, in the case of DEC, dies; the structures and processes that result from success, growth, size, and age; and

3. The cultural stream: the founding values that are shared through early and continued business success and eventually become embedded as shared, taken-for-granted assumptions about how an organization should be run.

Technology evolves as a function of inventions, innovations, product developments, and market forces. An individual company such as DEC influences this evolution, but it is only one force among many. The organization's structures and processes evolve as a function of its own success, its growth, its age and maturity, and its geographical, functional, and product diversification. The broader societal culture evolves as social, political, and economic conditions change, and the organizational culture evolves as a function of its leaders and the degree to which shared assumptions enable the organization to solve its problems of survival, growth, and internal integration.

Difficulties arise when these streams do not converge, that is, when the technology, the market, and the organization's capacity to respond to changing technological and market requirements are no longer aligned because the culture did not coevolve with the other streams. Culture is, by definition, a conservative force; hence, failure of cultural evolution is potentially an organization's Achilles heel. What this story will reveal is how that lack of alignment can result from a kind of culture that makes organizational adaptation virtually impossible.

Why should you care about this complex set of developmental dynamics and their interaction? Because the things that can be managed and controlled, the structural components and processes of the organization, are deeply influenced by the technological and cultural forces that are less controllable. If those influences are not understood and taken into account, the organization becomes a passive victim of cultural and technological forces. If they are understood and taken into account, the organization can, to some degree, compensate for and locate those elements that are manageable.

The illusion that organizations can control their own fate stems from the failure to understand how technology and culture limit what is possible. We will see that as DEC pushed into new areas of technology, it had to make major trade-offs between developing innovations that pushed the technological limits and concentrating on commodities that were technically feasible. The cultural constraints entered the picture through the taken-for-granted assumptions and mental models of the founders and early leaders of that organization. Founders, investors, and leaders are not autonomous rational actors. Their own family, educational, and occupational backgrounds influence their values and assumptions. To understand the evolution of a particular company's culture, therefore, requires an understanding of both the personal backgrounds of the founders and leaders and of the technological context in which the organization was created. Organizational dilemmas arise when the external technological environment evolves and the organization grows and ages while the founders continue to operate in terms of the technological and managerial values that they grew up with.

General Doriot, as the initial investor, and Ken Olsen and Harlan Anderson, as DEC's primary founders, were all working in a technological and social environment that made certain things seem more feasible than others and that provided market opportunities that shaped how DEC evolved. Broad social trends and societal needs influenced their thinking. At the same time, Ken Olsen's background and personality led him to create an organization and a management style that deeply reflected his own family values and his engineering mentality.

To summarize, the evolving DEC story can best be understood if we consider that in the decades of the 1950s through the 1980s three things happened:

1. The evolution of the technology that DEC helped to create changed the market and created new competitive conditions that DEC had to deal with.

2. As a result of its economic success, the organization grew, aged, and evolved into new forms that had to be managed.

3. As a result of its economic success, the culture within DEC was strongly reinforced and was superimposed on a set of subcultures that evolved as the organization grew and differentiated. These subcultures reflected the core culture but developed other values that came into conflict with those of other subcultures and with the core culture.

The DEC culture did not coevolve with the changing technological context, with growing competition in the marketplace, and with changing consumer attitudes toward computing. Nor did the culture coevolve with the growth in size, maturity, and differentiation of the organization, thus creating organizational dysfunctions that, in turn, led to business failure. At the organizational level this failure has been described variously as

- marketing myopia in not seeing the advent of the personal computer (PC)
- arrogance in not seeing the need to adopt more open systems and in the attempt to compete directly with IBM
- strategic failure in not pulling together or aligning the disparate elements in DEC's product set
- leadership failure in not providing a unifying vision during a period of product diversification
- accounting failure in not identifying clearly enough which products or markets were or were not profitable
- structural failure in never making any business unit truly accountable
- human resource failure in not developing the management talent needed for divisionalization and to prepare for orderly succession
- governance failure in that neither the CEO nor the board acted effectively to correct many of the problems that were, in fact, highly visible and acknowledged

All of these explanations are true to some degree, but the big question to be answered is *why* these failures occurred. Why did an organization that was wildly successful for thirty-five years, filled with intelligent, articulate, powerful engineers and managers, fail to act effectively to deal with problems that were highly visible to everyone, both inside and outside the organization? Why did the culture not evolve? Cultural assumptions are a priori neither good nor bad, but they can become highly enabling of certain kinds of organizational evolution and highly dysfunctional or constraining for other kinds of evolution.

The ultimate managerial question, then, is how to simultaneously perceive, analyze, and manage the developmental stage of the technology and market, the developmental stage of the organization, and the developmental stage of the culture. If technological and market forces require a redesign of the organization, and if the culture constrains that redesign, then elements of the culture need to be encouraged to evolve in new directions or changed drastically to permit adaptive organizational evolution to occur. In order to manage such evolution it is necessary to understand that culture is a combination of many elements rather than a single entity.

Beyond this managerial question there is a broader social question. If economic survival requires an organization to compromise or abandon certain values on which that organization was built, should it maintain those values even if the organization as an economic entity dies in the process? Do economic organizations have the right to survive if important values are compromised? Or are organizations ultimately an expression of social values that if strongly held in a community, have the right to survive even if that means organizational failure?

HOW TO THINK ABOUT CULTURE AND CULTURAL DNA

Culture in an organization can be thought of as the organization's accumulated learning that becomes so taken for granted that it drops out of awareness (Schein 1992, 1999a). That learning covers both how the organization deals with its various external environments in accomplishing its primary tasks and how it manages its internal integration. If an organization is not successful in its early years, it will not develop a strong culture; on the other hand, if certain ways of think-

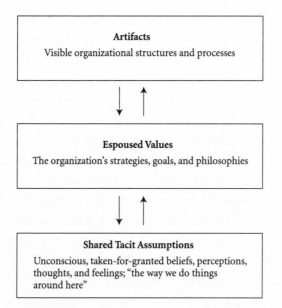

FIGURE 2.1. Three Levels of Culture. Source: Adapted from Edgar H. Schein, *The Coporate Culture Survival Guide* (Jossey-Bass: San Francisco, 1999), page 16.

ing, feeling, and behaving continue to work, they become taken for granted and eventually drop out of awareness except when they are taught to newcomers as the way to get along in that organization.

Once shared tacit assumptions have enabled the organization to succeed in its environment and to manage its internal affairs, they become very stable. They come to be taken for granted so much that efforts to change them are viewed as "crazy" because they are seen to be an attack on the very things that made the organization successful. This level of the culture is not only the essence but also the main source of stability that provides meaning and predictability for the members of the organization. Proposed culture changes are then inevitably sources of anxiety because they upset the ability of employees to predict what is ahead.

Culture can be observed at several levels (see figure 2.1). One can see and feel the overt *artifacts* of the culture in the behavioral patterns, physical layouts, rituals, and other manifestations that are clear but are not necessarily decipherable. We see what people do, but we may not know why they do what they do. When we inquire about these artifacts, we elicit the level of *espoused values,* ideology, and aspirations—what members feel are the justifications and rationalizations of what they do. However, those espoused values often do not match with what is observed behaviorally, so there must be a deeper level that is actually the driving force, what I have called above the *shared tacit assumptions* that have come to be taken for granted. Assumptions need to be distinguished from beliefs and values in that they are so taken for granted that they become non-negotiable and tacit. Once we understand some of these tacit assumptions, the meaning of the artifacts becomes clear.

What eventually become the shared tacit assumptions start out in the early development of a group or organization as the values and beliefs that the founders of a group bring with them. These are usually imposed on new employees or selected for in people hired in the first place. If the behavior resulting from those values is adaptive and leads to success in the environment, then the beliefs and values come to be shared. If the behavior based on them continues to be successful, they gradually come to be taken for granted and drop out of awareness. They can then be thought of as deeply shared tacit assumptions.

The pattern of these shared tacit assumptions within any given culture can be thought of as its DNA, with various specific assumptions constituting "genes" that will produce certain "body parts" and "processes." The DNA and its component genes will determine what the organization is destined to become, what it is capable of becoming, and, most important, what it is incapable of becoming and what its "immune system" will reject. Only if there are mutations or planned changes in the DNA can this inevitable growth process be altered. Such changes cannot be produced unless culture carriers are themselves changed (for example, top leadership, dominant coalitions) or if those carriers experience a major personal transformation themselves. Mutations can become sources of change, as when managers who are "creative individualists" or "role innovators" (Schein 1970) are put into positions of power (for example, Welch at General Electric), or can become sources of "cancer," as in the case of some of the executives of Enron.

The most basic genes in the cultural DNA are the non-negotiable values and beliefs that creators of organizations claim as the basis for the right of that organization to exist. In the case of a technical entrepreneur these genes can be thought of as his or her technical vision that is sold to investors and ultimately to consumers. In the case of a religious movement it is the humanistic and spiritual values and beliefs of the founder that are initially attractive to followers. In the case of financial entrepreneurs it is the rationale of the deal they are trying to put together. However, these initial values and beliefs do not become shared and thereby become part of the cultural DNA until the organization succeeds and builds a shared history. The "organization" can be thought of at this stage as the "dominant coalition," the network of executives, managers, and employees who share the basic assumptions and who mutually reinforce one another as the organization evolves. To decipher these key genes one must keep asking questions: What in the eyes of this dominant coalition keeps the organization afloat? By what right, in their view, does it exist? What is its primary task in the larger sociocultural context? What functions does it fulfill for society?

It is important to recognize that the culture as evolved by the dominant coalition is not necessarily accepted by every member of the organization. Subgroups will evolve and form their own subcultures, and individuals will be present in the organization who do not accept many of the basic values and beliefs. But they will be conscious of the larger culture even if they do not accept all of it. As we will see, among the important characteristics of DEC were the degree of unanimity around certain key values and beliefs, the organization's consciousness of its own culture, and the degree to which it explicitly taught that culture to newcomers (Kunda 1992).

The existence of particular genes, certain non-negotiable values and beliefs, determines what the organization wants to do, is capable of doing, and also what it will resist. The dominant coalition may recognize the need for certain new behaviors to adapt to changes in the technological environment, but if the learning involved challenges some of these non-negotiable beliefs and values, the leaders and members of the dominant coalition will not make the trade-offs necessary to acquire them. Insight and recognition are not enough to produce new skill sets if the gene demanding the outcomes of those skill sets is missing in the cultural DNA.

As is often the case in therapy, providing insight to the patient does not necessarily produce behavioral change or healthy adaptation. The pathological behavior may provide secondary gain in that it gets attention and maybe other kinds of rewards. Or the basic motivation to change may be missing because the learning of new behavior may seem too difficult or anxiety provoking. Sometimes people choose to live with their conflicts and pathologies because it is too "expensive" to give them up. In the same way, a mature organization with a strong culture can perceive accurately that it needs to change in various ways yet fail to make any constructive changes because the deep motivation, the will, and the skill to make certain trade-offs are missing.

In the case of organizations, their growth and development also leads to the equivalent of secondary gain. Ways of organizing that are no longer functional with respect to the environment can be very functional for the members of various subgroups within the organization. Thus, even organizational pathologies such as distributing resources across too many projects or destructive internal competition among units may not create levels of discomfort sufficient to make members pay serious attention to the danger signals coming from the environment. Also, like any biological organism, a strong culture will protect its integrity through an "immune system" that rejects employees or leaders who do not fit the culture or who want to change some of its genes.

THE COMMERCIAL GENE, OR MONEY GENE

In the case of economic organizations in a capitalist society, their primary task and basic function is to provide a reasonable return to investors in the production of goods and services needed by the society and, in that process, to provide employment and technical and social innovations that help the larger society to adapt to changing environmental circumstances. For an organization to survive under these conditions it must have a gene that is concerned with making money, with economic growth and survival. The organization may have been founded on product, process, or service concepts that made it easy to make money initially, but sooner or later money per se becomes an issue as competition and technological evolution make the original idea economically less and less viable. The ultimate survival of the organization will then depend on the degree to which the commercial gene, or money gene, creates processes of innovation and adaptation that are geared to economic survival, even if that means abandonment of some of the original ideas, products, and services on which the organization was founded.

If we take this analogy into the DEC story, we will see that most of the genes in the DEC DNA were the technical and family values embedded strongly in an American individualistic tradition. DEC became a viable business because the basic individualistic, technical, and family values that Ken Olsen felt so strongly about created a management system that attracted extraordinary technical talent and produced a series of highly successful products that virtually sold themselves. In a sense, Olsen's vision put DEC in the right place at the right time to "catch a major wave." Ken Olsen anticipated a major societal value shift that henceforth would ascribe greater value to the person and would firmly place the individual instead of the monolithic mainframe computer in the center of the computing universe.

What was missing in this cultural DNA, however, was a set of genes for creating and sustaining a viable business, a commercial gene, a money gene, a set of shared values that would override the engineering and family values if those founding values became dysfunctional. This is not to say that DEC managers, including Ken Olsen, were indifferent to the values of making a profit, of giving a return to their shareholders, or of growing and stabilizing a business for the long haul. Ken Olsen cared deeply about profits and was proud to have produced profits in his very first year in business and every year thereafter until the late 1980s. At an espoused level, commercial values and the desire to run an effective profitable business were highly visible, and

DEC's management was continually reorganizing and developing new processes to improve "the business," to increase the value of the stock, to enhance the company's own economic well-being, and to protect the business for their stockholders and especially their employees. Over the years many professional managers were brought in to the organization who clearly had the commercial, or money, gene. But as we will see, the evidence that the money gene was missing in the basic cultural DNA was the unwillingness to honor those business values *above* the technical and family values. That would have required trade-offs that were never made.

For example, the presence of the money gene would have required earlier layoffs, pruning out some deadwood, setting clear priorities among development projects, killing some of their own obsolete products to free up resources for new development, designing products for new kinds of customers that were not seen to be glamorous, and giving more prestige to both marketing and finance as essential business functions.

Culture deals with all aspects of how an organization manages its relationship to the external environment and how it integrates its internal activities. We will therefore be dealing with all aspects of DEC's culture, especially some of its tacit assumptions about technology; strategy; and how to design, manufacture, market, and sell its products. A common mistake in cultural analysis is to limit the discussion to issues of how the human relations are handled in the organization. These issues are important, but equally important, or maybe even more so, are the tacit assumptions about strategy, markets, products, and finances, the functions that determine how an economic entity relates to its external environment.

SUMMARY

Throughout this book we will be referring back to the three streams: technology, organization, and culture. Of necessity, we will be selective in which specific historical details we focus on. DEC became a complex multinational corporation in a remarkably short period of time.

To lay out all of the events that occurred in all of the parts of DEC to make this happen is beyond our scope. But because DEC developed a very strong culture very quickly, it is possible to identify themes that ran throughout the company. It is also easy to identify variations—subcultures that grew up, sometimes by design and sometimes fortuitously because of the strong personalities of some managers. Some of these subcultures were to some degree countercultural with respect to the main values and assumptions fostered by DEC headquarters, yet they functioned effectively for a time within the larger cultural mosaic that was DEC in its prime. Indeed, as we will see, it was the interaction of these subcultures that was crucial in eventually creating some of the problems that DEC was not able to solve.

The DEC story occurred at a particular time in history and cannot be taken out of context. The information revolution was beginning to happen, and DEC played a major role in moving it forward. We will, therefore, also discuss the technical context within which DEC was created, how DEC changed the computing environment, how that environment in turn changed further, and how those changes created survival problems for DEC because it lacked the money gene in its cultural DNA. DEC's role in the evolution of computing is immense, but, as so often happens, the creators of change became victims of some of the very changes that they helped to create.

part one

The Creation of a Culture of Innovation

THE TECHNOLOGY, ORGANIZATION, AND CULTURE STREAMS ARE ONE AND THE SAME

The chapters in part I show how Ken Olsen's vision created both a technology and a certain kind of management structure and process based on strongly held personal beliefs, values, and principles. For purposes of exposition we present the several sides of Olsen's vision in separate chapters, knowing, of course, that these are highly interrelated. On the technical side Olsen had strong beliefs and values regarding science and electrical engineering, which will be examined in chapter 3. These technical beliefs and values were tightly intertwined with strong convictions and values about how people should be managed (chapter 4). Olsen the entrepreneurial businessman also had strong convictions about customers and how salespeople should relate to them (chapter 5). Taken together, these values and practices were highly successful in the marketplace and in creating an organization that employees loved and in which they thrived. The combination of external success and internal integration created the strong culture that is described and analyzed in detail in chapter 6.

The important lesson to be learned from this history is that the creation of a strong culture requires not only a clearly articulated set of values and practices on the part of a leader but also actual success in achieving organizational goals in the external environment and high morale, motivation, and commitment from everyone inside the organization. It is in this sense that in the early DEC the technology, organization, and culture were highly integrated.

The impact of that culture on leadership development is illustrated in chapter 7, and its impact on the evolution of organization development is described in chapter 8.

three

Ken Olsen,
the Scientist-Engineer

My ambition is to be remembered as someone
who challenged them, who influenced them to
be creative and enjoy work and have fun for
a long time.

Ken Olsen,
MIT graduation address, 1987
referring to DEC employees

To fully understand Ken Olsen's powerful impact on the evolution and
management of DEC, it is essential to understand the 1950s technological, cultural, and sociopolitical context within which he operated.
In this chapter we will also look at different facets of his personality,
character, and talents. Ken Olsen is a complex man of many facets, and
it is this complexity and his own evolution as a person that determined
DEC's fate to a considerable degree.

Ken Olsen was born in Bridgeport, Connecticut, in 1926. His father,
Oswald Olsen, was the son of Norwegian immigrants and a self-taught
engineer, machine tool designer, and inventor who believed strongly
in Puritan ethics applied both at work and at home. Ken and his two
younger brothers, Stanley and David, all became engineers. After
high school Ken joined the Navy, where he learned to be an electronics technician, a good preparation for his later MIT education in electrical engineering. He received both a bachelor's and a master's degree
at MIT and took a job in 1950 working for MIT's Lincoln Labs in the
newly formed Digital Computer Laboratory. There he was exposed to

Jay Forrester, Robert Everett, and Norman Taylor, who were working on the Whirlwind computer, a machine that was being used in support of the Semi-Automatic Ground Environment (SAGE) air defense system.

Post–World War II social trends were moving toward more individualism and liberalism, but the cold war was posing a continuing threat to U.S. security. The computer revolution and the development of interactive computing goes back to the 1940s, when World War II and subsequent cold war needs for defense stimulated the building of computers that could process data in real time. The Navy funded the development of the Whirlwind computer at MIT in 1944 to create an electronic flight simulator, "a machine for which there was never an 'answer,' just a constantly changing sequence of pilot actions and simulated aircraft responses. . . . Team leader Jay Forrester and his colleagues quickly realized that the computer they built to control the simulator would have to be interactive from the ground up and capable of responding to events as fast as they occurred. That is, it would have to be the world's first real time computer" (Waldrop 2002).

Jay Forrester had invented core memory, and Olsen's first real task at Lincoln Labs was to build the Memory Test Computer for this new invention, a job he was given because "he got things done." IBM had won the lucrative Air Force contract to build the main computer for the SAGE air defense system, and Olsen was sent in 1953 to be the liaison between Lincoln Labs, the primary designers, and the IBM engineers who would ultimately build the system. He spent thirteen months with IBM, which, he says, taught him a lot about what he perceived to be the bureaucracy and relatively unsophisticated engineering at IBM. These negative perceptions of how the corporate world worked—in combination with his intense involvement with Forrester, Taylor, and Everett in the academic environment of Lincoln Labs—gave him confidence that "he could beat IBM at their own game" (quoted in Rifkin and Harrar 1988, p. 24).

Many of Olsen's attitudes derived from the climate that existed around Whirlwind. Science and engineering were not only fascinating subjects in their own right but were also seen as crucial to the welfare of the nation. DEC was created in an environment of science and engineering that emphasized not only the development of knowledge for its own sake but even more important the demonstration of how this knowledge could become useful to a wider community. In an interview in 1999, Olsen reminisced about some of the factors that motivated him at the time of the founding of DEC:

1. To defend the country. The emphasis on computing at MIT was partially motivated by the needs of the DOD [Department of Defense] to have computing capability for a variety of projects.

2. To explore and discover the potential and the characteristics of interactive computing as a new way of thinking and of processing information.

3. To put ideas into practical form and explain what computing was all about in a world in which most people had *no* idea what you were talking about; to be an active part of a technological revolution.

4. To educate for posterity; to make a new tool available to everyone for further exploration (Ken Olsen, interview by author, March 12, 1999).

Implicit in the decision to start a company was, of course, the desire to make computing practical and to create a business that would make enough of a profit to survive and prosper. As we will see later, however, if there was a conflict between, on the one hand, making a profit and surviving as a business and, on the other hand, upholding basic values, those values won out. One of those central values was the engineer's love of a new technology. In reviewing DEC's origins Olsen describes some of his guiding values:

Whirlwind introduced the idea of networking as we know it today. It was a computer started toward the end of World War II to do the real time managing of a wind tunnel. This made it quite different from other computers, most of which were generating pages of numbers.

The few big computers of that time often had 64-bits or 128-bit word length because they were printing tables. Whirlwind, because it was working with real things that could not be measured with precision, chose 16 binary bits. This set Whirlwind apart from most other computers because it could measure things better than they could be measured physically. Also, because of its simplicity, it could go very fast.

Because it could go very fast and because it could measure physical phenomena with more precision than normally was needed, it was an ideal real-time computer to manage and record things in a computer that is running physical things like a wind tunnel or a machine.

There were three features of Whirlwind. First of all, the shortness of its word length. This made possible the second feature which was speed which made possible the third feature which was its usefulness to control real-time things where you really need speed and no great precision.

In the late 40's, it became clear that the US was completely vulnerable to bombing attacks from Russia flying over the North Pole. It also became very clear that the Whirlwind computer was the only computer that could develop the speed necessary for the job and had more than enough precision to guide aircraft. Out of this came the partnership with IBM that built the massive air defense system which I believe had twenty-three locations each with two computers containing over 128 thousand vacuum tubes. . . . The location of aircraft cannot or does not have to be measured with great precision, but the location changes fast and so Whirlwind was ideal because of its great speed.

Whirlwind was a classified project but it was possible for students and staff to use the machine off-hours. After we built the memory test computer [this was Olsen's first project and first experience in building a computer] it too became available to people. Because of the speed and short word length, much of this work was real-time on applications. The MTC computer was primarily built to test the CORE memory. It was very simple and very fast. Later, it was given to MIT for the students to use. Digital gave its first semiconductor machine called the PDP-1 to the same laboratory with the commitment that it be used twenty-four hours a day by any student for anything at any time. (Ken Olsen, memo, personal communication, 1999)

In the summer of 1957 Olsen and Harlan Anderson, an engineering colleague at Lincoln Labs, went to American Research and Development (AR&D), one of the first venture capital firms in the United States, with a proposal to found a business. The head of AR&D was

General Georges Doriot, who not only agreed to give them $70,000 in return for a 70 percent ownership of the new company but also became a mentor to Ken Olsen (a role Doriot maintained until his death in 1987). The choice of the name *DIGITAL* and the first products reflected some skepticism on the part of AR&D's board about the concept of *computing* and led to the decision that the first products should be modules (computer components) and test equipment, with computers coming later.

Ken Olsen, his brother Stan, and Harlan Anderson launched their business in an old unused woolen mill in Maynard, Massachusetts, a decision that proved wise in that it provided very flexible and easily expandable yet very economical space. Stan Olsen had been a technician at Lincoln Labs and became DEC's first employee. Within a year DEC shipped its first logic modules for memory testing to organizations such as Bell Labs and Cal Tech, and the company was making a profit. Ben Gurley, a talented design engineer and former colleague on the SAGE project, was hired in 1959 and designed DEC's first computer, the Programmable Data Processor (PDP-1), with the name still reflecting caution about getting into computers. The PDP-1 was revolutionary for its small size (refrigerator size) and price ($120,000) and was sold initially to the engineering consulting firm Bolt, Beranek and Newman, to the typesetting firm ITEK, and to the Lawrence Livermore National Laboratory. In 1962 the company's first commercial sale came through with a sale of fifteen PDP-1s to ITT. Connections to MIT remained very close and resulted in the hiring of Gordon Bell in 1960, a decision that many regard as crucial to DEC's ultimate success—Bell was considered a computing genius and the perfect intellectual partner for Ken Olsen.

Early in its history DEC contributed a computer to MIT to demonstrate its commitment to education and to further student opportunities to interact with computers. As Olsen recalls, "Digital Equipment Corporation set out to make high speed 18-bit computers in the tradition of Whirlwind, but with little floor space, relatively little cost. It was designed to be a delight for students or staff to play games, have fun, and do very disciplined, very useful real-time work that could exploit the speed of the computer and not be limited by the 18-bit word length" (Ken Olsen, memo, personal communication, January 27, 2001).

Several themes in these comments are worth underlining because they are crucial to an understanding of how DEC evolved. First, the design of the new computers with their interactive capabilities was strongly influenced by defense needs. What consumers want today is completely different from what the country wanted and needed in the 1950s and 1960s. The emphasis then was on real-time machine control and on solving problems that required the ability to interact with the computer.

Second, Olsen wanted computers to be available to students round the clock. He had a deep commitment to the idea that computers should be useful to scientists and engineers, who, it must be remembered, were the consumers who were most interested in what computers could do for them. The many uses to which computers are put today were inconceivable in the 1950s. However, in bringing into DEC young engineers with similar interests and commitments to the scientific and laboratory use of computers, Olsen created a marketing bias that was never overcome.

Third, Olsen wanted computing to be fun, exciting, involving, and stimulating. What was most evident in the young DEC that I encountered in the mid-1960s was a sense of excitement and fun. Whatever "parental" concern he may have had for students and employees was more than offset by his own "adolescent" excitement at founding a company and seeing it produce computers that the scientific and engineering community welcomed with open arms.

It is in this context that Olsen's famous quote in a 1977 *Time* article must be understood. Olsen was quoted as saying that "there is no reason for any individual to have a computer in their home," which was allegedly an explanation of DEC's later failure to capitalize on the rapidly growing personal computer market and the company's failure in the 1980s to develop any products that could compete with IBM's PC. Olsen reviewed what he said and why he said it in a conversation I had with him on January 3, 2000. His explanation is instructive of how he saw computing:

This [the quoted comment in *Time* magazine] is, of course, ridiculous because the business we were in was making PCs, and almost from the start I had them at home and my wife played Scrabble with time-sharing machines, and my sixth-grade son was networking the MIT computers and the DEC computers together, hopefully without doing mischief, using the computers I had at home. Home computers were a natural continuum of the "personal computers" that people had at work, in the laboratory, in the military.

I did make a number of statements and still make statements that people don't understand about computers, or delight in misquoting. A long time ago when the common knowledge was that PCs would run our lives in every detail, I said that if you stole something from the refrigerator at night you didn't want to enter this into the computer so that it would . . . mess up the computer plans for coming meals. Today, I still say that free access to almost infinite information is not the same thing as thinking and creating and inventing, and computers might be harming creativity for many people.

What Olsen focuses on retrospectively is that in the 1950s and 1960s there existed the notion that the computer not only could but would control all aspects of our lives. Images of the fully computerized home that automatically turned lights on and off and that prepared meals and controlled daily diets were popular. And the fear that computers might, as in the movie *2001: A Space Odyssey,* even try to take charge altogether was widely experienced. MIT had a major research project to investigate how the use of computers would limit and distort thinking processes. Computers were not seen as being as benign or helpful as they are today.

As Olsen explained to me at length and attempted to make clear, he thought it would be unacceptable to have the computer in the home *controlling* everything. Why would anyone want that? He did not object to the concept of a PC at all, but he had a particular way of thinking about it that colored the kind of product development that dominated DEC. In a memo he wrote to me, he elaborated on his own concept of the PC:

I think an important part of history would be to develop the idea of personal computers with the history of Digital. Of course, this is dependent on your definition of personal computers. Some people think a $1,000 or a $2,000 computer is a personal computer. Others think that a computer you can work on alone and interact with is a personal computer. Others think a personal computer is a machine that is so exciting, so much fun, that it overwhelms your conscious life. My definition of a personal computer is one where a person interacts with the computer directly, where every move the person makes the computer reacts, and every move the computer makes the person reacts, which often leads to an intense, often exciting, relationship.

Whirlwind, before I got there, introduced most of the concepts that make personal computing. It was fast and it interacted directly with the operator, and it was fun and it was exciting and overwhelmed people with the promise of what could be done as a "personal computer," even though it was much too big to have that name. The development of the computer for ordinary people to have access to, with more and more speed and more and more modes of interaction, was the story of Digital. The first PDP-1 we gave to MIT for student use. It had all the characteristics people think of in a personal computer. In a sense the computer was in the home of the students. It overwhelmed their lives with enthusiasm, excitement and fun, and allowed them to work with the computer and use the computer to work with their colleagues, it allowed them to create, to make games and to be creative.

I would suggest that the definition of a personal computer is not price, not size or weight, or even Bill Gates' software, but that the early MIT and DEC computers were personal computers and were the early steps in the development of hardware and software. (Ken Olsen, memo, personal communication, January 3, 2000)

Note again the themes of interactivity, of fun or excitement, and of the positive view of being "overwhelmed." For Olsen the concept and vision had to do with the activity of personal computing rather than with a concept of a personal computer as a commercial product. The early visions took it for granted that if one developed good products that the market wanted, profits would take care of themselves and a viable business would result. But the emphasis in DEC was on inventing a new technology, not on building a business. This emphasis on creating a new technology based on a technical vision is reflective of an *occupational culture* that characterizes many scientists and engineers.

THE ROLE OF ENGINEERING AS AN OCCUPATIONAL CULTURE IN THE FORMATION OF DEC

Culture as a set of shared tacit assumptions about the nature of the world and how to operate in it arises not only in organizations and work groups but also in occupations. Such assumptions in occupations come to be *shared* as a result of common education and work experience, and they come to be *tacit* as a result of repeated success in using them to govern daily life (Van Maanen and Barley 1984; Kunda 1992; Schein 1996). The shared assumptions of such *occupational cultures* become a source of *organizational culture* when those organizations are created by people of similar occupational background. DEC can only be understood by noting that its founders were all engineers, most of them electrical engineers. Many of the beliefs and attitudes that I observed in Ken Olsen and his early colleagues are characteristic of the occupational culture of engineering, particularly electrical engineering:

1. Electrical engineers are pragmatic tinkerers. One can try different kinds of circuits and see what works. If things work on a small scale, they can be scaled up and will still work, something that chemical or civil engineers cannot afford to assume. What may work in the chemistry lab may not work in the pilot plant. Electrical engineers, however, can try all kinds of experiments and build models. If the experiments work on a small scale, they can become full-scale products. As will be seen later, Ken Olsen tinkered with organizational and management processes in the same way that he tinkered with technical matters.

2. An important tacit assumption of the engineering culture is that elegance of solution is always preferable to mere practicality. If one has an elegant product that really works, it is assumed that this product will sell itself. Furthermore, it is assumed that the designers can judge the elegance of the product because they are designing for people just like themselves. I frequently encountered this attitude among the DEC engineers—their own judgment was final on whether a product should be built or not.

When Olsen and other managers talked about their products, they always emphasized quality and elegance. In fact, customers were talked about in a rather disparaging way, especially those who might not be technically sophisticated enough to appreciate the elegance of the product design. Interactive computing was the new glamour technology, so customers who wanted to be interactive, to influence the final product, to help debug it were the heroes. "Good" products would sell themselves, and profits would come as a natural result. And there were enough enthusiastic customers early in the game to provide a constant stream of positive feedback to DEC that it was doing great things and designing wonderful products. What was often not noticed was that these customers were also engineers who appreciated the quality of the DEC products and were willing to put up with whatever inconveniences were involved in using them.

3. An important implicit goal of this occupational culture was to advance computing technology. The tacit assumption was made that it is the engineer-designer who can best understand the technological issues and therefore be the best judge of which products would move the technology forward and be worth developing. The relevant audience is fellow engineers, wherever they might be. This assumption was of course reinforced because many of the people who were hired early in DEC's history were technically sophisticated engineers. DEC was one of the few companies that successfully implemented a "dual ladder" that permitted engineers who had gone into management to return to engineering without any kind of career penalty. Senior consulting engineers were a much-respected group that had status comparable to senior vice presidents. As we will see, destructive conflicts between engineering groups in the 1980s were largely about technology advancement, not about business issues per se.

4. A key characteristic of the engineering culture is that the individual engineer's commitment is to technical challenge rather than to a given company. There is no intrinsic loyalty to an employer as such. An employer is good only for providing the

sandbox in which to play. If there is no challenge or if resources fail to be provided, the engineer will seek employment elsewhere. In the engineering culture, people, organization, and bureaucracy are constraints to be overcome. In the ideal organization everything is automated so that people cannot screw it up. There is a joke that says it all. A plant is being managed by one man and one dog. It is the job of the man to feed the dog, and it is the job of the dog to keep the man from touching the equipment. Or, as two Boeing engineers were overheard to say during a landing at Seattle, "What a waste it is to have those people in the cockpit when the plane could land itself perfectly well."

Just as there is no loyalty to an employer, there is no loyalty to the customer. As we will see later, if trade-offs had to be made between building the next generation of "fun" computers and meeting the needs of "dumb" customers who wanted turnkey products, the engineers at DEC always opted for technological advancement and paid attention only to those customers who provided a technical challenge.

5. Engineering culture disdains management. Authority is acceptable only when it is based on superior knowledge, technical skill, or technical experience. In most technical organizations (such as R&D [research and development] divisions or in technical companies such as Bell Labs used to be), managers are second-class citizens relative to technical staff and are often called "administration" rather than "management." When Ken Olsen issued a company-wide memo, the address of the sending department was always "Administration." In a 1985 memo Olsen clearly differentiated "military management" based on permanent formal rank from "project management" based on technical leadership and a sharing of authority with the team: "In project management, there are no leaders because they have rights, because they have seniority, or because they are protected. They are only there to do their part in getting the project done" (Ken Olsen, memo to Strategy Committee, February 1, 1985).

6. Engineering culture disdains marketing. It is assumed that good products sell themselves, and what is "good" is defined by objective technical criteria. Olsen emphasized absolute integrity in designing, manufacturing, and selling. He viewed the company as highly ethical and strongly emphasized the work values associated with the Protestant ethic—honesty, hard work, high standards of personal morality, professionalism, personal responsibility, and integrity. Especially important were the values of honesty and truthfulness in employees' relations with one other and with customers. Marketing was viewed with some skepticism because it might involve "lying" to customers. Lying to one other about the product, the schedule, or the budget was similarly unacceptable. As DEC grew and matured, it put many of these values into formal statements and taught them to new employees. DEC managers and employees viewed their culture as a great asset and felt that its precepts had to be taught to all new employees (Kunda 1992).

It was DEC's commitment to technical innovation that attracted talented engineers to the organization early in its history. Notable among these was Gordon Bell, who was recruited out of academia in 1960, became a central figure in the early designs of DEC computers, and, after a sabbatical at Carnegie Mellon University, returned to DEC and became the primary architect of the VAX computer line. Many observers credited DEC's success to the combination of Ken Olsen's commitment to engineering innovation and Gordon Bell's talents in developing computer architectures. Throughout its history, DEC sought out the best and brightest technical talent.

This absolute respect for engineers is tellingly illustrated in Gordon Bell's account of the career of Dave Cutler. Cutler wrote the VMS software for DEC's VAX line, was later involved in helping to introduce the RISC architecture, and left DEC when his project was undermined and eventually canceled. He ended up at Microsoft, where he wrote the basic software for the Windows NT program. In my 1998 interview with him, Gordon Bell expressed his admiration for Cutler:

Dave is, above everybody, the ultimate engineer. I mean Dave is just out of sight. I mean there is no software engineer in the world like him. . . . I viewed Dave as an unparalleled resource . . . because he had done VMS, he had then done a compiler because he wanted to do that. And he said, I'm tired of all this BS, I want to do something else. I said, "Look Dave, take anyone you want, go anywhere you want, do anything you want. Just tell me what you want to do." And so he took his little team. They looked at a bunch of places, and they ended up in Seattle, and they said, okay we want to build a really smaller system, we want to build a real-time system, and it will be VMS compatible. It will run VMS applications. And that's what they did. And after that they pioneered a bunch of things. . . . I regard him as totally unique because of what he was able to do with VAX in terms of compatibility.

Olsen came from the engineering culture and hired people who fit in. What is often called DEC's "arrogance" was a natural attitude in a group of people with a particular point of view toward the world and a particular set of goals to revolutionize the nature of computing. The genes for advancing technology were present in the DEC culture, but the genes for building a business were not. In spite of this lack of the money gene, DEC was for several decades a very successful business.

In 1962, then five years old, DEC had sales of $6.5 million and showed a profit of $807,000. New faces that would be critical to future development were now on board—Jack Smith, Ted Johnson, Nick Mazzarese, Win Hindle, and Jack Shields. The world's first minicomputer, the PDP-5, was introduced in 1963; the first 36-bit computer, the PDP-6, was introduced in 1964; and the PDP-8, considered the first mass-produced minicomputer, was introduced in 1965. In 1966 DEC went public, and by 1967 sales were up to $38 million (Pearson 1992). DEC began to expand internationally in 1963–64, with offices in Canada, Europe, and Australia. By 1968 there were fifty sales and service offices located in eleven countries and a production facility in Puerto Rico. European and Japanese headquarters were opened in 1968–69.

At its fifteenth anniversary in 1972, sales reached $188 million and DEC employed 7,800 people. In the next three chapters we will review what lay behind this growth. What were the values and management principles on which DEC was founded, and how did these values and principles create the kind of culture of innovation that DEC embodied? To explain that we will look at other facets of Ken Olsen's personality, character, and talent.

four

Ken Olsen,
the Leader and Manager

There is a story that Ken Olsen tells on himself, that he learned the basics of management as a young adult in his pre-DEC days when his church put him in charge of the Sunday school. He says that he went to the library and read all the management books that he could find and developed from that a concept of how to manage. Whether or not he found Alfred P. Sloan and Douglas McGregor at that time I do not know, but in subsequent interviews he often attributed his own managerial theory to those two people. From Sloan he says he learned how powerful it is to "divisionalize" and give autonomous units profit and loss responsibility; from McGregor he says he learned how important it is to believe in and trust people.

He had observed, of course, the style of his mentors in the MIT Lincoln Labs, especially Jay Forrester, and was especially impressed by the freedom they gave everyone in the lab. Giving freedom to subordinates became the most basic aspect of Olsen's philosophy, but, as we will see, he made some implicit assumptions about how people would use freedom that often proved wrong. The central managerial issue of how to empower people and give them freedom while retaining some kind of managerial discipline and control becomes the basic dilemma around which DEC's culture evolved.

To understand how DEC grew and, in the end, failed, one needs to understand the complexity of Olsen's managerial philosophy and style. Most management theories tend to look for simple ways to categorize what managers do. My experience of observing Olsen over a thirty-year period is that his behavior was anything but simple. Olsen was a complex man whose values were often in conflict with one another. Some of his managerial practices changed over the decades as his company changed, yet he retained many of his basic values to an extraordinary degree. If we are to learn from an organizational saga such as this one, we have to deal with this complexity up front.

I will break down the various elements of how DEC operated by a combination of stories. The stories illustrate themes that reflect the beliefs and values that Olsen brought with him from his background and that he learned in his early years as a successful entrepreneur. And though one can identify separate themes, together they combined into a cultural pattern of a kind that was more integrated than in most organizations and that made DEC a unique experience.

ENCOUNTERING DEC AS A CONSULTANT

My direct involvement with DEC resulted from a call in early 1966 from Win Hindle, Olsen's administrative assistant, asking if I would be willing to do some consulting for DEC's senior management. I was at the time a professor in the Sloan School of Management at MIT specializing in social psychology and group dynamics. Hindle had been recruited to DEC from MIT's Industrial Liaison Office to be Olsen's assistant in 1962. I was interested because this was my first real opportunity to function as a consultant on my own. I had attended many workshops on group dynamics, communication, and leadership and felt that there was a good match between what Hindle described as the communications problems in the group and my skills. I agreed to meet Olsen to check whether our personal chemistry matched enough for him to be comfortable in giving me access to the workings of the

Operations Committee, at that time DEC's senior executive structure. My first visit to see Olsen was my first culture shock.

To gain entry into DEC's main building, an old woolen mill in Maynard, Massachusetts, I had to sign in with a guard who sat behind a counter where there were several people who were chatting, moving in and out, checking the badges of employees coming into the building, accepting mail, and answering phone calls. They were friendly and informal, casually dressed, and clearly on a first-name basis with one another and with the visitors. Once I had been given a temporary badge, I waited in a small, casually furnished lobby until Olsen's secretary came out personally to pick me up and escort me to Olsen's office.

What I recall most vividly from my first encounter inside "the Mill" was the ubiquitous open office architecture, the extreme informality of dress and manners, a very dynamic environment in the sense of rapid pace, and a high rate of interaction among employees, implying enthusiasm, intensity, energy, and impatience. As we passed cubicles or conference rooms, I got the impression of openness. There were very few doors, and I learned later that this was by design because Olsen believed that engineers should be easily accessible to one another at all times.

The company cafeteria spread out into a big open area where people sat at large tables, hopped from one table to another, and obviously were intensely involved in their work, even at lunch. (The cafeteria always seemed to have lots of people in it at all hours of the day.) I also observed that there were many cubicles with coffee machines and refrigerators in them and that food seemed to be part of most meetings. I later learned that having coffee machines and refrigerators placed near every group was a conscious design. If meetings were held early in the morning, someone always brought a big box of doughnuts for everyone.

The physical layout and patterns of interaction made it very difficult to decipher who had what rank, and I was told that there were no status perquisites such as private dining rooms, special parking places, or offices with special views. The furniture in the lobbies and offices was very inexpensive and functional. The informal clothing worn by most managers and employees reinforced this sense of egalitarianism.

Olsen's office was spacious, rustic, and housed many computer artifacts as well as a large stuffed beaver symbolic of Olsen's MIT connection and his interest in the outdoors. He was informally dressed, cordial, soft-spoken, and very interested in my view of groups and organizations. What struck me most is that he said almost nothing about what he expected from me. He suggested that I attend the regular Friday staff meetings of the Operations Committee to see if I could "help improve communication and decision making." I experienced immediately what many others talked about—Olsen's style engendered a sense of freedom and responsibility in the people around him. It was going to be up to me to figure out how best to help. The committee consisted of Ken Olsen; his brother Stan Olsen and Nick Mazzarese, both of whom functioned as product line managers; Ted Johnson, head of sales; Peter Kaufmann, head of manufacturing; Harry Mann, head of finance; and Win Hindle, Olsen's assistant.

As I began to attend these staff meetings, I was struck by the high level of interpersonal confrontation, argumentativeness, and conflict. Group members became highly emotional at the drop of a hat and seemed to get angry at one another, though it was also noticeable that such anger did not carry over outside the meeting. One of the most emotional members was Ken Olsen himself. He would spend long periods of time just listening and then suddenly erupt in response to some point that he considered wrong or poorly considered. If I made a point that he did not agree with, he would often say very bluntly, "Ed you don't understand *at all*," and then go into a lengthy version of his own understanding of the matter.

With the exception of Ken Olsen, there were few people who had visible status in terms of how people deferred to them. Stan Olsen did not enjoy any special status by virtue of being Ken's brother. Ken was obviously the boss, but his behavior implied that he did not take his position of power all that seriously. Group members argued as much with him as with one another and even interrupted him from time to time. His status did show up, however, in the occasional "lectures" he delivered to the group when he felt that members were not under-standing something or were wrong about something. At such times he could become very emotional in a way that other members of the group never did. He could also be openly critical of group members in front of the whole group. This often came across as "paternal" at one level but also signaled that Olsen expected the target person to ac-cept the criticism in an adult manner as legitimate logical analysis rather than as personal criticism.

I was made quite nervous by the level of confrontation I observed and had a sense of not knowing what this was all about. I learned from further observation that this style of running meetings was typical and that meetings were very common, to the point where people would complain about all the time spent in committees. At the same time, they would argue that without these committees they could not get their work done properly.

The company was organized primarily by several product lines and by several centralized functions such as sales, service, finance, and man-ufacturing, but there was a sense of perpetual reorganization and a constant search for a structure that would "work better." The central functions were services to be "bought" by the product lines, and engi-neering was in perpetual flux. This created what many have called one of the first versions of a *matrix,* but this term was rejected and struc-ture was viewed as something to tinker with perpetually until one got it right.

DEC was one of the few companies at that time that had a clearly defined dual career ladder. The ladder was supported by strong state-ments from Olsen that it was all right to try out to be a manager and, even more important, all right to return to the technical ladder if the management job did not work out. The strong engineering bias made the technical ladder work successfully in the sense that people valued remaining on, or returning to, the technical ladder. Engineers could rise to the high rank of consulting engineer and be well compensated in that rank.

There were many levels in the technical and managerial hierarchy, but I got the sense that the hierarchy was just a convenience, not something that was taken very seriously. Olsen felt completely comfortable going around supervisors and talking directly to the troops, asking them how things were going and getting very personal with them. Most managers accepted this and could see the great value in everyone knowing Olsen and in Olsen knowing everyone. To most people in the company, he became known as "Ken."

Open communication as a central means of coordination and cooperation was taken seriously throughout all levels of the company. There were many committees already in existence with new ones constantly being formed, the company had an extensive electronic mail network that functioned worldwide, and engineers and managers traveled frequently and were in constant telephone communication with one another. Olsen would get upset if he observed any evidence of under- or miscommunication. As the company grew and became dispersed geographically around New England, it built an "air force" of helicopters to shuttle people from one site to another. Underlying all of this was the frequent pronouncement from Olsen that there should be complete freedom of information across the company. As we discussed in the last chapter, freedom, truth, and open communication were central values of the engineering culture.

ESPOUSED BELIEFS, VALUES, AND SHARED TACIT ASSUMPTIONS

What does all of this mean? In deciphering a culture it is very important to recognize that some of the most salient features are also the hardest to understand, for example, the high level of conflict in the group meetings. What were the beliefs, values, and assumptions that Olsen held that made him organize DEC the way he did, that could explain his day-to-day behavior and that of his subordinates? What was in the cultural DNA, and what was not there? I knew what my emotional reactions were, but I did not really understand why these things were happening and what significance they had for members of the company.

As I talked to people about my observations, especially those things that puzzled and scared me, I began to elicit some of the *espoused be-*

liefs and values by which DEC ran. Many of these were embodied in slogans or in parables that Olsen wrote from time to time and circulated throughout the company. Almost all of them ultimately reflected Olsen's conscious and unconscious beliefs, values, and assumptions. What was especially striking to me was the degree of congruence between the espoused values and the managerial practices that I observed. In this chapter I want to highlight these beliefs, values, and practices, reserving for chapter 6 a deeper analysis of the DEC culture in terms of shared tacit assumptions.

1. Belief in Rational Problem Solving

Olsen was above all the scientist-engineer committed to rationality and an orderly search for truth. One made decisions in terms of information, as was well illustrated in how the "Woods Meetings," which became a major part of the management process, came to be invented at a Friday afternoon staff meeting of the Operations Committee in 1967.

We were sitting around Olsen's kidney-shaped conference table at four o'clock. Above the table there was a mobile that consisted of five hanging hands with the index fingers pointed randomly around the room as the breezes moved the mobile. I could not help wondering about the symbolism of the roving pointing index fingers, but I never did learn why Olsen had chosen this mobile.

The agenda comprised a long list of items, so we started down the list, going slowly because each item was debated in a spirited fashion. Olsen did not run the meeting. He was mostly silent, often looked distracted, and clearly sent the signal that he expected the rest of the group to decide what to do. I realized that I would have my work cut out for me, since people were shouting one another down, interrupting one another, and holding on to their own points of view rather than seeking consensus. I remained puzzled and silent because even if I had wanted to say something it would have been difficult to break into the intense debate.

By the end of two hours, the group was frustrated because time had run out and most of the agenda items had not been addressed.

Curious how the agenda had been constructed in the first place, I asked, "Where did our agenda come from, and how was it constructed?" Everyone looked puzzled. Olsen said that his secretary had prepared it. He called her in and inquired how she had constructed it. She said that people phoned in agenda items and she typed them up in the order received. The members of the group were astonished that they had been working in such an inefficient manner, that the items they were working on had not been prioritized but had been arranged in a completely arbitrary manner based on when people called in. Out of this insight came two major modifications of how DEC was to be run for the next three decades.

First, the group decided on the spot to rearrange the agenda at each meeting in terms of priorities. Olsen's secretary would still collect the data chronologically, but the group would decide at the beginning of the meeting the order in which to address the items. Second, the group recognized that some items constituted "fire fighting" and needed to be dealt with immediately and efficiently but that other items were strategic and would need more time. One member suggested that the group take up the two kinds of items on alternate Fridays, which prompted me to point out that the strategic items would require longer, more thoughtful meetings. This was met with approval and a proposal was made to have alternate Fridays be longer meetings.

My prior experience with off-site meetings had been positive, so I decided to make a bold suggestion: to have these longer meetings away from the office. Both Olsen and his brother Stan were outdoorsy types and had cabins in the New Hampshire and Maine woods. The idea of an off-site meeting completely separated from the Friday staff meeting concept was accepted, and the "Woods Meeting" was invented. Woods Meetings lasting one, two, or three days were held approximately once a month for just the Operations Committee, but in later years these evolved into two- or three-day major strategy meetings to which the top forty or fifty senior executives would be invited.

In retrospect, one of the most striking things about my attendance at meetings was that I was not asked to make any presentations or to do anything except sit in and figure out for myself when and how I could be helpful. My question about the agenda led to some gathering of information by the group, but once the group had the information they solved the problem quickly by themselves. I did not realize it until years later, but this attitude of giving people jobs and then letting them have the freedom to figure out how best to do those jobs was one of the most significant elements of Olsen's managerial style and eventually became one of the central elements of the DEC culture, as we will see.

Another experience that provided me with insight on how fact-oriented this group was occurred around my efforts to show people the dysfunctionality of constantly interrupting each other. When I did this, the members of the group always thanked me, said they agreed, and would try to do better, but they never changed their behavior. They assured me I was being helpful, but I could tell that I was not having much impact. After many meetings of this sort, I essentially gave up, sat back, and decided to just listen to the group. I became aware of how many ideas were lost in the hectic arguments, so I decided one day to go to a flip chart that was sitting in the corner and write down ideas as they were presented. I then found that if someone had been interrupted I could ask that person to finish his thoughts. The results were dramatic: the group focused on the points on the flip chart, permitting me to steer the group to maximize communication. Members said in a much more heartfelt manner that "now I was really being helpful." Instead of punishing the group for its "bad" behavior, I had learned how to facilitate their intense and hectic communication process.

It was repeated experiences of this sort that led me to the realization that being "helpful" to the group required an understanding of what the group was trying to do in the first place. The Operations Committee members were not in the business of being nice or polite to one another but were battling out which of the many ideas that were proposed were good enough to be acted on. My interventions had to be geared to their agenda and values; I had to decipher enough of their culture to get into their "cultural process." And it was repeated experiences of this sort that led me to the formulation of process consultation as a way of helping individuals and groups (Schein 1967, 1987, 1999b).

2. Belief in Active Problem Solving

DEC people were always ready to look at management situations as problems to be solved, reflecting their engineering and academic orientation. Once a problem had been identified, it took no time at all to figure out a good solution and to accept help from an outsider in improving on that solution. It was also notable that though the group had been using a very inefficient process of building and managing their agenda, no one seemed to care how this had come to be, and no blame was sought. The focus was on moving forward, not on diagnosing the reasons for the past events. This forward orientation produced immediate positive results but did not allow for much reflection on why the group had not learned earlier in its life to manage their agenda and problem-solving process better. As we will see, lack of reflection later allowed many inefficient processes to survive and prevented some crucial learning. The point is that this cultural characteristic was already evident in 1966.

3. Belief That Giving People Freedom Will Make Them Responsible

Olsen placed a very high value on personal responsibility. He assumed that if one is given freedom, one must be responsible in exercising it. Two slogans heard frequently around DEC captured both the freedom and the responsibility side of this issue: "He who proposes does" and "Do the right thing." If you made a proposal to do something and it was approved, you had a clear obligation to do it or, if it was not possible to do, to come back and renegotiate. Olsen always talked about taking responsibility as a moral issue. Being irresponsible or making proposals in areas where you had never had any responsibility, was virtually immoral.

"Do the right thing" as the key slogan was an invitation to think for yourself and not to accept dictates from above that did not make sense. If your boss asked for something that did not make sense, your obligation (responsibility) was to "push back," and if the boss persisted, to decide for yourself what was right. If it worked out, you were a hero; if it did not work out, you would get your wrist slapped and, depending on how serious the error, maybe be put into the "penalty box" for a while. In the extreme, you could lose your assignment but not your job.

In practice there was not a lot of "insubordination," because if one pushed back the boss typically listened and the issue would be reopened for further debate. Here again the commitment to rational problem solving surfaced, and it was made clear to everyone that arbitrary authority did not count for anything. On the other hand, being on top of your job and having all the relevant data pertaining to it was crucial.

4. Belief That Responsibility Means Being on Top of One's Job

The centrality of this principle became very clear in a 1967 meeting of the Operations Committee. As part of the normal business of the meeting, Chief Financial Officer Harry Mann reviewed a variety of data on several product lines and pointed out that one of these lines that reported to Nick Mazzarese was in financial difficulty because of falling sales, excessive inventories, and rising manufacturing costs. Olsen asked Mazzarese about this, and Mazzarese reported that he had not seen the figures before and could not, therefore, give any explanation. He was surprised and embarrassed to have Mann point this out in front of the whole group and indicated that it might have been nice if Mann had let him know this earlier and outside the group.

Olsen got very upset at this point and lost his temper. I thought he would point out to Mann the inappropriateness of revealing new negative data about one manager in front of the whole group. Instead, and to my complete surprise, Olsen became very angry at Mazzarese for not being totally on top of his job, for not knowing everything about his situation, for allowing himself to be put into a position where he could be embarrassed.

Mann, the CFO, was not off the hook, however. After Olsen made it clear to Mazzarese what he expected of his line managers, he lectured Mann on what he wanted from his CFO, something that was very difficult to achieve—to be both a teacher and a cop. Just being a cop was not doing the job. Olsen made it very clear at the time and in subsequent lectures to the group that Mann and other corporate staff managers should educate Mazzarese and other product managers to be on top of their numbers, not expose them in front of the group.

This incident also revealed how much Olsen favored his line managers, especially the ones with engineering backgrounds, and how difficult it was for staff managers, especially the ones in finance and marketing, to function effectively. The demand to be both an educator and a cop in finance and accounting was impossible in an organization in which engineers were king and staff managers were second-class citizens in support roles. It was no accident that in its thirty-year history, DEC had five different CFOs, and all of them struggled in their efforts to be effective.

For Olsen it was a *moral* principle that if you took responsibility for something it was your absolute duty to be on top of it. As I observed other meetings over the years, nothing seemed to upset Olsen more than managers or vice presidents who did not take full responsibility for their area of work. That also meant knowing what your job was and being highly articulate about it. The implicit message was that each employee and manager should be intellectually and emotionally sufficiently committed to be very clear about what he or she was doing and why. Referring to a job description was not acceptable. One needed a clear articulable concept of what one was doing and how it fitted into the larger scheme of things in the company. The other side of this principle was the freedom that once you had a broad area of responsibility it was up to you to define the dimensions of the job. There were no clear job descriptions or clear limits to the authority of a given job. A person who kept asking what his or her job was would be forcefully told that it was up to him or her to figure that out, and once figured out, to get on top of it. Olsen would go around asking people what their jobs were, and if someone did not have a clear and articulate answer, Olsen would get irritated.

Asking the boss what was expected was considered a sign of weakness. If your own job definition was out of line with what the boss or the department required, you would hear about it soon enough, as the example of the Operations Committee illustrated. The role of the boss was to set broad targets, but subordinates were expected to take initiative in figuring out how best to achieve them. This value required a lot of discussion and negotiation, which often led to complaints about time wasting. Still, everyone defended the value of doing things this way.

To illustrate how strong this principle was, a young Frenchman who had the job of human resource manager in the French subsidiary said to me that to learn how to function in the company he "had to give up his Frenchness," meaning his reliance on formal protocol, authority, and hierarchy. He added that once he learned how to work in DEC and learned to enjoy the freedom that this provided, he could never again work for a French company.

The lesson was clear: line managers were to understand their jobs and be fully responsible, and staff managers were to educate them, even as they were policing them. Of course the incident reported above, and many others like it, led each product line and geographic region manager to build his or her own finance and accounting organization to ensure that they would be fully informed in the future. Huge "just in case someone asks" files began to accumulate until in the 1970s Olsen realized that there was enormous duplication and waste. This realization, along with a variety of other factors, eventually led (in 1982) to a reorganization into a more complex organization, a highly controversial version of the matrix organization in which the staff functions regained some of the accountability that they had lost in the product line organization.

5. Belief That You Must Own Your Own Problems

Taking responsibility was illustrated in another way by the principle that you ought to own your own problems and should not propose things for others to do that you could do yourself. In particular, Olsen did not like having people who had never had any responsibility of their own, and therefore had not accomplished anything specific, making decisions that would tell others what to do or what was correct. From his MIT background Olsen brought with him the mentality and skills to tinker, to get involved with projects physically, to try to solve problems and not to pass them on. If he could not solve a problem directly, he involved others in the problem and encouraged them to solve it, although never in an authoritarian fashion.

Mike Sonduck tells the story of how the principle of taking responsibility became embedded in his own psyche. When he first encountered the manufacturing organization, he observed some problem areas and told his boss and mentor Bill Hanson about the situation. Hanson said, "Well, Mike, what are you going to do about it?" Sonduck replied, "I don't know." Hanson responded, "Well, you've got three choices: (1) You can do nothing and brush it under the rug; if you do that I will fire you. (2) You can try to sell the problem to someone else; if someone else is foolish enough to take it on, you are off the hook and good luck. Or (3) you can figure out what to do yourself and get to work on it." It was perfectly clear to Sonduck that in the DEC culture only the third alternative was acceptable.

The clear message to think for yourself and to take responsibility for your own decisions created strong employees and managers. Thinking for yourself, being empowered to act on your own judgment, and being licensed to push back also created a very thorough and careful decision process, but one that made it very difficult to be efficient and quick. As in academic circles, reaching a carefully thought-out truth was respected more than quick but possibly sloppy decision making. What was not anticipated at that time was that eventually the organization would be in an environment that required faster action. It was virtually impossible, as we will see later, to convert to a more disciplined, efficient decision process because deep inside themselves DEC managers and employees did not believe in it.

6. Belief in "Truth through Conflict" and Getting "Buy-In"

I once asked Olsen why he did not make decisions when the group seemed hung up on an issue such as which development project to support or which product to build. His answer came in two parts: (1) "I'm not that smart . . . but when I get a group together and hear it debate the issue, I get smart very fast. (2) But even if I know what we should do, I learned the hard way once when I did make a decision; I was marching down the road and looked back over my shoulder, only to discover that there was nobody there. On the other hand, if I let the group thrash it out and everyone sees what the correct direction to go is, then everyone will go there."

The assumption that truth could be found only through a process of debating issues to a logical conclusion is, of course, the essence of the academic process that Olsen learned during his days at MIT. One might ask, isn't the academic process to rely on research and facts? Yes, if the facts are available. But how do you arrive at something that you can believe to be true if you are dealing with a new technology where exploration and intuition are needed because facts are not available? To create an organization that will advance truth in such a new technology, one must have not only bright, articulate individuals but also a decision process that forces them to get "buy-in," from each other.

It was an explicit rule that one should not do things without getting buy-in from others who had to implement the decision, who would be influenced by it, or who had resources that the decision maker needed. To reach a decision and get buy-in, you had to convince others of the validity of your idea and be able to defend it against every conceivable argument. This caused the high levels of confrontation and fighting that I observed in the meetings; but once an idea had stood up to this level of debate and survived, it could then be moved forward and implemented because everyone was now convinced that it was the right thing to do. This process took longer to achieve, but once achieved, led to more consistent and rapid action. One had to be individualistic and, at the same time, willing to be a team player, which meant both to speak up and push back if one did not agree, and to listen to arguments carefully and to support decisions on which consensus had been reached after the debate. Hence, the simultaneous feeling that committees were a big drain on time but that the organization could not do without them.

I also found out that people could fight bitterly in group meetings yet be very good friends. There was a feeling of being a tight-knit group and an acceptance of the norm that fighting did not mean that people disliked or disrespected one another. This norm seemed to extend even to bad-mouthing one another, where someone would call another person "stupid" behind that person's back or say that someone was a real "turkey" or "jerk" yet would respect the other person in work situations. Olsen often criticized people in public, which embarrassed them, but it was explained to me that this meant only that the person should work on improving his area of operations, not that he was really in disfavor. Even if someone fell into disfavor, he or she was viewed merely as being "in the penalty box," and stories were told of managers or engineers who had been in this kind of disfavor for long periods of time and then rebounded to become heroes in another context.

This decision process reveals one of the crucial interactions between technology and the organization. Group debate and consensus was necessary because the group was inventing a new technology; no one knew the answer, and no individual was smart enough to figure it out. Debate was the only way to reach "truth" to a sufficient degree that everyone could commit to it.

7. Belief in Internal Competition and "Let the Market Decide"

Olsen believed that the best decision maker was the market itself. If there were multiple strong proposals that had merit, Olsen believed that instead of setting priorities at the top of the organization, one could and should support a number of projects to see which ones would survive in the marketplace. I saw how this principle operated in a 1967 Woods Meeting at a hotel on Cape Cod. The Operations Committee decided to review all projects that were under way in the various parts of DEC. The presenter was Ted Johnson, who stood at the blackboard and wrote down what he knew and what others contributed. I watched with interest and awe at the number and variety of fascinating projects that were mentioned and discussed.

The list reached some thirty projects, and my curiosity began to be aroused as to how the group would now set priorities and make decisions about where to allocate resources and effort. Olsen, as usual, was very quiet and seemingly uninvolved. The group took a long look at the list of the thirty projects, nodded approval, and then went on to the next item on the agenda! Olsen said nothing, thereby tacitly approving all of the projects. The implication was clear: each project should go forward until it either reached a technological roadblock or the market showed lack of interest. The market at that point was engineers and scientists like the DEC developers, so, in the short run, most projects found ready customers.

A year or so later I was in another Woods Meeting in New Hampshire. We had come up on Friday and were to go home on Sunday. Having a number of meals together and having two overnights was seen as desirable to get to know one another's styles and to get deeper into issues. The Operations Committee had a number of agenda items, among which was the decision of whether to support a certain project. Win Hindle had the job of chairing the meeting, a role that the group rotated on a monthly basis among all the members except Olsen.

The ambience of the meeting was extremely informal. There were some couches, a few chairs, and pillows for sitting on the floor. Olsen sat in a corner of the room listening intently but also distancing himself from the discussion by busying himself with building a tower out of Coke cans. Gordon Bell, the VP of engineering, was reading his mail. Pete Kaufmann, the VP of manufacturing, looked like he was asleep part of the time, and may have been. Win Hindle tried to keep the discussion focused, but it wandered all over the map. At times, the proceedings became very emotional. Some comment would trigger Olsen, causing him to get up and deliver some strong messages of his own, but he did not take a position on the proposed project. The meeting was more like an emotional free-for-all than a rational business meeting trying to reach a decision.

After several hours no decision had been reached. Everyone was frustrated and exhausted. Hindle as chair could not make the decision, and Olsen let the meeting end without resolution. After the meeting Olsen wanted to walk in the neighboring woods with me and told me that the issues were much clearer now, that it did not matter that no formal decision was reached, and that in fact it had been a very good meeting. He felt he now understood the issues better as a result of the debate and that such understanding was at times a sufficient end product for several hours of group meeting time. The fact that others might have been frustrated or disappointed was not as important as the fact that the issues were getting clarified in Olsen's mind.

Olsen clearly believed that competition among projects was a good motivator and that the market would ultimately decide which decisions were the correct ones. His faith in people, his belief in giving freedom, was a tremendous stimulus to creativity in all areas of company performance. At the same time, the early success and rapid growth of the company created enough cash flow to support a wide range of projects; there was no need to set priorities.

I also observed over many meetings that Olsen had a genuine reluctance to say no. He preferred the group or the responsible manager to make the decision, especially if the decision was negative. Senior managers reflecting back over the years pointed out that Olsen was scrupulously neutral, always playing devil's advocate whenever any group member strongly advocated a particular position.

8. Belief That Work Should Be Fun and Enjoyable

There were no slogans embodying the idea that work should be enjoyable and fun, but it was obvious as one entered the DEC environment that this young group of entrepreneurial engineers was having a blast. The emotional climate was totally upbeat, people loved coming to work, and if you did not share this sense of enjoyment, the implication was that there was something wrong with you. It must be remembered that the DEC of the 1960s was actually very young in chronological age. DEC was inventing the future; how could this not be fun?

In talking to alumni of DEC in the late 1990s, I found remarkably that almost every person views his or her days at DEC as a wonderful, peak experience, as a time of learning and great fun, and as something to reproduce in his or her current organization.

9. Belief in Management by Passion

One of Olsen's most salient characteristics was his trait of letting his emotions flow freely in his interactions with people. He often lost his temper at meetings and became very punishing to individuals and groups. As I observed this behavior, I tried to figure out what triggered it and concluded that the most salient cause was anxiety. Whether he was aware of it or not, Olsen blew up when he was anxious about something that was not going right, and usually that something was a failure on the part of a manager to be on top of his job in some way, as Olsen perceived it.

Giving Olsen feedback on the potential negative impact of his outbursts was not effective because he was passionate about his perceptions and his values. However, the members of the Operations Committee learned that the way to avoid being punished in this way was to reduce Olsen's anxiety. One of my most important interventions in the early years was to help the group to understand this psychodynamic, that when Olsen got angry he was *anxious* about something. The way to deal with the situation was then to figure out what he was anxious about and provide him data that would reassure him. This almost always worked.

10. Belief in Benign Manipulation or Controlled Chaos

Many have raised the question of whether Olsen's practice matched his philosophy. Did he really give as much freedom as the above points imply, or was he subtly manipulating the situation during these early years to guide the company where he wanted it to go? It needs to be said at the outset that manipulation is not necessarily bad. It depends on whether the aims and goals are ones that the persons being manipulated would have chosen for themselves anyway. In a recent interview Olsen told me that he was not surprised to discover that some of the senior managers who left DEC after it was acquired by Compaq failed in their various CEO jobs. The reason, he argued, is that they were not aware how much their success within DEC was the result of the teamwork that he (Olsen) subtly engendered. Olsen believed that the product line structure that required getting buy-in from other units forced teamwork. By forcing decisions into a group process, he enabled people to discover ideas for themselves rather than being given them. What then is the reality? Were DEC managers all through the years manipulated like puppets, or was the kind of freedom that he encouraged real?

My own observation over the years suggests that it was a bit of both and that it changed over the course of DEC's history. In the 1960s and 1970s as DEC was flourishing, I saw Olsen genuinely stimulating and tolerating innovation and creativity in all aspects of how DEC functioned. On the other hand, if what someone wanted to do ran afoul of one of Olsen's strongly held values, he would vocally and articulately attack what was proposed and would, of course, eventually get his way.

Where the manipulation came in is in the way Olsen created and mandated management processes that forced people to learn things and do things that they might otherwise not have learned or done. The best example is how Olsen dealt with proposals that were brought to him. He told me that sometimes he would ask the person to present the proposal to the board of directors in order to get him or her to think through the project more thoroughly. Another example was Olsen's publicly embarrassing a group of his managers at a large meeting by asking them to assemble onstage the set of components that made up one of their computing systems, something he knew they could not do because they were too removed from the details of their projects. These and other examples were usually viewed by the "victims" as clever and benign, and they taught important lessons.

Olsen's scrupulous neutrality and the unpredictability of something triggering an emotional outburst led to a climate that some labeled "controlled chaos." Things always seemed to be chaotic and out of control, but, at the same time, the notion persisted that the master puppeteer was in control all the time.

11. Belief in Perpetual Learning

Olsen felt that it was important to be open to learning from your experience. "The person with whom you would like to walk in the woods for an hour, or two, or four, or eight is not one who is so smart they did not have to learn anything for the last twenty, thirty or forty years. The enjoyable walking partner is one who for all their life has been in-quisitive, enthusiastic, and life is exciting and fun because they are always ready to explore, consider, try new ideas and new experiences, and learn about anything that comes up regardless of how mundane" (Ken Olsen, memo, personal communication, July 22, 1993).

Just as Olsen believed that competition, debate, and ultimately market forces would resolve all conflicts, so he believed that humans could and should learn from their own experience. He often railed at his managers for "not learning," and he often represented himself as always being open to learning. However, where strong values were involved, Olsen had difficulty learning, most notably in the area of human behavior. He did not see how politics and power dynamics inevitably would creep into any organization or how to fix what he viewed to be human failings. In particular, he came to believe that many of the problems that DEC had in its later years resulted from intergroup fighting based on jealousy. He could not, however, see either how such jealousy was inevitable in the kind of competitive free market he had created in DEC, nor how to deal with it once it was identified.

12. Belief in Loyalty and Lifetime Employment

Olsen believed in hiring the best and the brightest and employing them for life so long as they did not behave immorally. Failure in a job meant that the person and the job were mismatched and one had to find a better match. Once hired, the person was assumed to be competent. Olsen expected the person to be loyal to the company and the company to be loyal to the employee. When cost pressures in later years required layoffs, Olsen was extremely resistant, preferring to find ways to grow enough to absorb the surplus of people. In 1994, Olsen expressed his feelings about loyalty:

> It is common knowledge, today, and in all the literature that loyalty has disappeared from American companies . . . where [once] employees were loyal to the company and often stayed for their full working life,

and companies were loyal to employees to the point where the relationship was solid often from generation to generation.

People lament this change and feel the nation has lost a lot. Indeed,
this is true [because] the company which shows loyalty and earns
loyalty and develops the efficiency and the enthusiasm and the creativity
and even love of the company has an enormous competitive advantage
over all the others. . . .

We did suffer from the loss of people who continuously were offered
more money to go to other companies, but when there was a surplus of
technical people [in the economy] and indeed, to some degree, a surplus
of technical people within Digital, we showed loyalty to employees
which meant after the economy recovered the employees had a sincere
and deep loyalty to Digital which made them very effective employees.

Digital, also, had a policy of showing loyalty to the customers. Often
companies with commission sales plans had no place, no time, no
energy for those customers who did not have the capability for buying
more products because of the economy, or because of the situation
the company was in at the time. Digital insisted that the sales people
continue to service the customers, even though they could not buy
enough equipment to justify this service.

The result, as one might expect, [was] that after the economy recovered, or when the government slackened the policy not to buy foreign
built equipment, or when they recovered their business position, Digital
was held in very high regard by the customer.

Digital enjoyed loyalty from its employees and loyalty from its customers like very few other companies did. Any cost involved in that loyalty was small compared to the return that came from this loyalty. (Ken
Olsen, memo, personal communication, June 2, 1994)

THE PARADOX OF EMPOWERMENT

Ken Olsen the entrepreneur, manager, and leader was a large, powerful, articulate, emotionally intense man. His track record of early success combined with his strong visionary stances in conversation made
him an imposing figure to deal with. In his presence you knew immediately that you were dealing with a brilliant and powerful person.

This power was often misused in public situations, as when Olsen would lash out at one of his subordinates to denigrate some of his or her decisions or strategies. Some people could not tolerate this kind of threat and left, but most people stayed and paradoxically not only tolerated public criticism from Olsen but came to recognize that those he criticized were usually the people he respected the most. Of course, much of this was rationalization, but it never ceased to amaze me how much respect people had for Olsen, even when he was brutal to them.

How can a man so powerful and often so brutal to others around him command such great respect and admiration? The answer lies in a simple psychological truth: if a very powerful person empowers you, trusts you, and gives you freedom and responsibility, that strengthens your own ego immensely. Being empowered by someone powerful gives you confidence in yourself, which helps you realize that criticism implies that you should do better, and that, in turn, implies that you are capable of doing better.

CONCLUSIONS

The beliefs and values discussed in this chapter were interconnected and created a managerial climate that was, in my experience, unique. Olsen's neutrality and willingness to go along with whatever a proponent could sell to his or her colleagues ("Doing the right thing," "Getting buy-in," and "Pushing back") were among the most powerful forces for innovation that I have ever seen. It was pointed out over and over again in interviews that many of DEC's innovations were not Olsen's ideas but that Olsen created a climate of support for new ideas so that subordinates felt empowered to try new and different things. People learned that Olsen would argue against a position or a proposal but that he expected the final decision to come from the proposer. It was the proposer who would have to implement the proposal, so he or she should have the responsibility ("He who proposes does").

This managerial climate created in Olsen's subordinates a level of self-confidence, maybe even arrogance, that made it hard to reach efficient decisions in later years. Supporting everything and letting the market decide was a slow and often erratic process, but it became so much a way of working during the successful years that it was virtually impossible to convert to a more efficient hierarchical process when more management discipline and speed were needed.

five

Ken Olsen,
the Salesman-Marketer

Ken Olsen's approach to product development, marketing, and sales merits a separate chapter because, on the one hand, it was paradoxical and self-contradictory yet, on the other hand, it was innovative and exciting. DEC's approach to sales was one of its contributions to the field of management, as we will see. Olsen's beliefs about sales and marketing were derived from his engineering background and his general managerial philosophy, as described in the previous chapters. His sales philosophy was based on three interlocking beliefs:

1. Customers' needs were the primary basis for how one designs, markets, and sells products, and customers had to be dealt with honestly at all times.

2. Customers did not always know what they wanted, and it was the job of sales to educate them by working with them to solve their problems.

3. It was the job of engineering visionaries to educate salespeople on what they should be advocating and selling to solve the customer's problems. Even though the market is the ultimate decision maker in terms of what products will succeed, one

should not ask marketers what products to develop but should trust one's own technical vision.

As we have seen, when DEC was founded, computing was just coming into its own and was of greatest utility to scientists and engineers. The postwar needs for sophisticated capabilities in defense created a technical bias in what computers would be used for. The customers who were delighted with DEC products were the scientists, engineers, and laboratory directors at organizations such as the Jet Propulsion Laboratory, Lawrence Livermore Laboratory, ITT, and the Center for European Nuclear Research for whom interactive computing was the perfect solution, even though all had different needs.

Ted Johnson, a graduate of the California Institute of Technology (Cal Tech), was hired in 1958 when DEC was still a seven-person start-up trying to sell modules. Johnson created DEC's sales force and was the VP of sales until 1982. In line with Olsen's philosophy, Johnson described himself in a 1992 retrospective as follows:

> I built up good relationships with people. I learned that people were buying faith and trust, and respect. And that's the way I sold. They were buying that as much as they were buying the product. . . . Some engineers were prepared to use computers in new ways, wiring them directly into their systems, or to use them for unmediated data collection and manipulation. But finding smart customers was a challenge. Few customers knew how to use computers, let alone program and maintain them. So from the very early days, sales, service, and customer training were interrelated. . . . You'd take their problem and show them how to solve it. It was a lot of fun. The customer could order the modules, wire them together the way you had it on the blackboard, plug them in, and that was it. You had a new customer. . . . Sales engineers focused on educating and working with customers, impressing them with on-the-spot solutions to logic problems. The success of this approach during the formative years helped determine the character of Digital's later marketing and selling styles. (quoted in Pearson 1992, p. 142)

Selling a new technology required locating customers willing to learn. This technical reality fitted well with Olsen's notion of how to define the sales job and how to compensate salespeople. One of DEC's unique features was that Olsen strongly resisted commissions as an incentive for selling, as he explained:

Digital Equipment Corporation started off with a number of assumptions. One of them was that we would not have commission sales people. The results were great. For many years, we grew 30, 40, sometimes 50 percent a year, and had the highest yield of sales per sales person [of] anyone in the industry. It is interesting to observe that the press, financial analysts, Board members and those who came to stockholder meetings assumed, without looking at the data, that the yield for direct sales people was low because we had no commissions. The data showed otherwise. They were convinced that if we commissioned sales people we would grow even faster. I remember patiently listening to young reporters lecturing me on commission sales because they felt I had never heard of them.

One first has to decide the sales philosophy. One philosophy is to sell anything that makes money today regardless of whether it is what the customer needs or not. It is believed the ultimate measure of the success of a sales person or a marketer is in selling something to a customer that the customer does not want and does not need.

The other extreme philosophy is to only sell to the customer those things they need. This takes skill and knowledge of the products, knowledge of the customer, knowledge of their business and knowledge of their needs because they often do not know what they need. It also means not accepting orders for products that the customer does not need or which would not be good for their business. The motivation for the sales people then is not only to sell products for the company for which they work, but they are also motivated to make the customer successful. . . .

It is also a very satisfying job for the sales person to not only sell, but to be interested in the customer. With the commission plan it is impossible to have the philosophy that in bad times when the customer cannot buy enough to justify the support they are receiving, the sales person can maintain that support without losing out financially.

It is hard to collect data to compare the results of two different philosophies, but it has been the experience at Digital that when one is truly interested in the customer, and the resulting pressure is to have excellent products and services for the customer, and when one is patient when the customer does not buy, the yield per sales person ends up being significantly better than competitors whose sales forces are strictly interested in their own immediate financial return. (Ken Olsen, memo, personal communication, September 10, 1993)

This philosophy worked well in building up a strong and loyal group of customers. The customers were eventually organized into DECUS (the Digital Equipment Corporation Users Society), a group that met regularly to exchange insights, learn about new applications, and provide feedback to the company on how things were going. With hindsight it is also evident that such a strong, loyal, and positive group of customers allowed Olsen and many other senior engineers to overlook the huge growth of another set of customers—individuals who wanted what PCs ultimately became. Ed Kramer, who was to play a key role in developing DEC's marketing philosophy and practice, comments on the role of DECUS:

> I always referred to DECUS as DEC's secret weapon. It helped build wonderful customer loyalty and gave engineering a chance to "show its stuff." I was responsible for the US DECUS for about 10 years starting in the mid 70s. There were European and Asia/Pacific counterparts. In the very early days, 1960–1975, customers exchanged software tools they wrote to supplement what DEC provided. DECUS provided a media library to supply this "freeware." The organization had a paid professional staff (DEC employees) but was managed by a Board of Directors comprised of and elected by customers/users. The DEC representative was a non-voting member. DECUS derived revenue from attendance fees and at the end of my tenure, had a surplus of several million dollars. DEC paid for the small DECUS staff, but the rest of the DECUS activities were self-sustaining. The events were annual major technical conferences (typically several thousand attendees at the US events), also held in almost every country with a DEC office.
>
> The seminar part of the meetings had multiple parallel tracks organized by product, application, branch of science or technology, etc. and the meetings were usually 4–5 days in duration. Over time, users were more interested in trying to influence DEC's product direction than they were in listening to how someone automated the data gathering

of the mating habits of barnacles (an actual paper that was given). DEC provided more and better tools, and there was less need for the DECUS library. Eventually, every DEC development group had workshops where they directly interacted with users and discussed and prioritized features of future software releases as well as new hardware products. The engineers who worked on the products were encouraged to come to these meetings and talk to the actual users of their products. This was a convention of nerds! Salesmen and all other marketing types were strongly discouraged from attending as per the DECUS Board (with my blessings). Olsen rarely participated, although he was always personally invited. (Ed Kramer, letter, personal communication, August 25, 2002)

When Olsen and others would later be confronted with the accusation that they did not pay attention to customers, they often felt unjustly maligned because they saw themselves as intensely involved with their customers. They did not realize, or maybe did not care, that those customers were percentagewise a smaller and smaller proportion of the total customer base for computers.

Of course, at a deeper cultural level there was the tacit shared assumption that the problems of these new "dumb" customers were not challenging or interesting. The cultural DNA was more concerned with technical challenge and innovation than with building a commercially successful business, and this showed up in the company being intensely customer oriented, but mostly with customers who had interesting technical problems to solve. One of Olsen's memos on marketing, sales, and service points this up clearly.

MARKETING

It is commonly believed that the truly competent marketer is one who can sell a product the customer does not need and does not want. We see this all the time on television when trying to find something worth looking at. However, marketing of a complex product has to be quite different. Selling a product that the customer does not need, selling a product that will not satisfy this need, selling a product that will become quickly obsolete, or that will cause trouble and make them non-competitive is not good business. In fact, it is not even good business to sell a product to a customer, even though the product might be specified by the customer, when you know it will not do the job they need to have done.

Our society admires a great marketer who creates an image, and sells a poor product. However, marketing for a complex product should be first understanding the customer's needs, second understanding the solution to their needs, and then getting the customer to understand that combination. Sometimes, flash and flair help, but they are not a substitute for understanding.

SELLING

All the activities of all the parts of the company have to work together as a team. In a very clear sense, they all work together to satisfy the sales person who in turn satisfies the customer.

SERVICE

For most complex systems, service is exceedingly important. Some customers understand this so well they will not buy from a company whose service department does not make a reasonable profit. They want the insurance that that service department will stay there and continue to do a good job. The success of that customer is the motivation of the service department. (Ken Olsen, memo, personal communication, October 10, 1993)

The commitment to joint problem solving with customers in combination with the high degree of freedom that Ted Johnson and Jack Shields (the latter was head of the service function) enjoyed led to significant innovations in how computers were sold and serviced. In 1964 Olsen had organized the growing company into four product lines that had profit and loss (P&L) responsibility, but kept sales and service (as well as engineering, manufacturing, and finance) as central services to be shared. This organization allowed Johnson and Shields to develop new corporate approaches, especially in the service area, as described by Shields: "Quietly and without a lot of fanfare, Digital changed the way companies view service. We took an activity that companies have always thought of as a nuisance and a problem, a necessary evil, and we made it into a profitable business. We started showing a profit way back in the early 1960's, and over the years we were able not only to provide high-quality service, but also to develop new techniques which allowed us to become more productive and cost-effective and pass those savings on to customers. We created a new way of approaching service that today the rest of the computer industry is trying to emulate" (quoted in Pearson 1992, p. 149).

One of the key elements of this approach was an extensive customer training program, reflecting once again the close connection that DEC sales and service people felt to their customers. Not noticed, however, was that DEC's close connection to one customer segment was dangerous in that it allowed DEC to continue to believe that it was intensely customer oriented and that as long as it satisfied that segment nothing could go wrong.

In response to our general inquiries to DEC alumni, we received one letter (see below) that captures well the feelings that DEC's sales philosophy engendered in some of its salespeople. (We quote it in its entirety to provide details on the what might be a typical experience of those in sales.)

As we will see, with growth and geographical dispersion the sales philosophy that was so clearly articulated in DEC's early days evolved toward a more traditional format and ultimately ran into difficulty as the market shifted. But it is important to recognize how consistent DEC was in its early days around "Doing the right thing" for customers, and how Ken Olsen's values permeated to some degree all of the business functions.

A CASE EXAMPLE OF A SALESMAN

A little bit about my background before joining DEC. I graduated from Stanford with a BSEE in '59 and spent five years in design engineering at North American Aviation. During this time, I received an MSEE from USC in '64. In '65 I went to work for a Stanford classmate at Lear Sieglar Corp. in Anaheim, CA. He was in charge of several military contracts for data acquisition systems and was using a PDP-7 and had several, newly introduced, PDP-8's on order. This was my first introduction to DEC.

I became responsible for a data acquisition and test system to be placed aboard a submarine. I was able to get DEC's Special Systems Group to package a PDP-8 into three separate metal containers to get down a 19" submarine hatch and then be cabled together.

It was after performing some sales support functions in presenting our department's engineering capabilities to potential customers that I decided to pursue a technical sales career. I liked presenting and dealing with people more than designing and programming.

I approached our head of the sales organization, and his reaction was, "You're an engineer. Leave the selling to real salesmen." Those were the days of true peddlers who focused on entertaining the customers to get sales.

So I contacted the local sales manager for DEC. At that time there was one office in Southern California, located in Anaheim. It turned out this division of Lear Siegler was DEC's largest customer at the time. The DEC manager had a philosophy that he wouldn't hire from his customer base. So I waited awhile and the management changed at the DEC office (I learned later on how dynamic DEC was), and the new manager didn't have that problem and was interested in hiring me, even though I had no sales experience.

After the initial interview, I was sent to Ken Larsen, the Western Regional Sales Manager, in Santa Clara. We had a good interview, and he wanted me to meet with Ted Johnson, the National Sales Manager, who was stopping by the office on his way to Australia. I came back up in a week and met with Ted. I will never forget the interview. Larsen introduced me to Ted, and Ted said a few words and just looked over my resume. He mumbled, "Hmmm, a BSEE, good; an MSEE, very good. But you have no sales experience?" I thought to myself oh-oh, I'm going to get rejected again because I don't have any actual sales experience. So I replied, "No I don't, but I know your products. I have worked with designing interfaces to them and programming them. And I know I can sell them." And Ted responded, "Good, just what we are looking for!"

I became one of six sales people in Southern California, joining DEC in Nov. '66 with badge # 2816. I remember the company's sales, ending the prior June, were around $37M. DEC did not have any formal sales or product training at that time. I was out in the field for three months before I signed up for a PDP-9 Assembly Language customer course, just to have an excuse go back to the Maynard Mill to see what it was all about.

Immediately out in the field, I found myself talking to other engineers and scientists who were making the buying decisions for minicomputers. We didn't talk to many DP [data processing] managers in those days; they didn't know who we were and what we were about. Our focus was on the engineering and scientific markets. In fact I remember running into an IBM salesman who was calling on the corporate DP manager of one of my accounts. And when I introduced myself as a DEC salesman, he said, "Oh, you're the guys that take out the logic diagrams of the computer and walk the customer through them." That was an interesting, but somewhat incorrect, perception of our sales techniques.

Ken Olsen had the right strategy in forming a technically educated, salaried sales force to drive sales in a highly ethical manner in what was to become the age of the minicomputer. Those early days for me were very exciting and fun. I loved the independence but being still able to get help and support from a bunch of dedicated people three thousand miles away. It truly was like being a member of a very special family.

It was during this last activity (joining Digital) that I had what I regard as a seminal life experience. I had been invited to the Leicester office for my final (out of 6!) interview and I was left to extract a cup of what was alleged to be coffee out of the vending machine. Whilst waiting I glanced at the small wooden plaque on the wall that bore a plate declaring "Ken Olsen's 10 rules of doing business." You know, Ken, for the life of me, I cannot recall numbers 1 through 9, but number 10 stood out like a beacon. It simply read:

10. When in doubt, do what's right by the customer.

So simple and clean! Why had no one ever told me that before? Right there and then I resolved that would be my watchword in my customer relationships for Digital. And it worked. I never laundered the company's dirty linen in public, I just solved problems and then took any flak internally. And usually, there wasn't any. Even at times of real challenge and stress I could go back to that very simple precept and see a way through the fog of confusion. (R. Carmichael, letter, personal communication, October 26, 2000)

six

DEC's Cultural Paradigm

To fully understand a culture one must look at the pattern of interrelationships among the shared tacit assumptions that drive day-to-day behavior. These assumptions are often consistent with an organization's espoused beliefs and values, but not necessarily so. Many organizations espouse teamwork yet have completely individualized management systems, or they espouse an open-door policy but employees learn that their ideas are not really welcome. So we must examine in DEC's case the relationship of the espoused beliefs and values as reviewed in the last several chapters to the deeper tacit assumptions that evolved and increasingly governed DEC's daily behavior.

These deeper assumptions derived originally from (1) the broader culture in which Ken Olsen and his founding group grew up and (2) the environment that was created by that broader culture, namely, U.S. technical entrepreneurial capitalism (Roberts 1991). However, it must be reiterated that Olsen's personal beliefs and values came to be shared tacit assumptions only because the behavior based on them produced success, both in the external and internal environments. A culture evolves as a result of continuing success, and what were originally just the beliefs and values of the founders gradually come to be a *shared* set of beliefs and values, and with continued success these dropped out of awareness and become *shared tacit assumptions*.

The assumptions listed below will strike readers as repetitious of the beliefs and values discussed in the previous chapters. What distinguishes them is that they now represent a deeper level and that they have now come to be shared and embedded. In previous chapters we reviewed Ken's own beliefs and values. We now describe a pattern of widely shared assumptions that governed the behavior of DEC's managers and employees throughout the company's history. We are now talking about a culture that was not only accepted but that was also eventually made explicit and taught to newcomers.

The essence of the DEC culture, its DNA, can be viewed as two sets of interlocking cultural genes as shown in figures 6.1 and 6.2. What made DEC "magical" in the description of so many of its past employees was the degree to which the assumptions shown in figure 6.1 worked together to create a climate of empowerment and creativity. These genetic elements held together and formed a pattern that made culture evolution so difficult later. What made DEC so successful in the first thirty years of its life was the addition of several other cultural genes that are shown in figure 6.2. In the absence of a commercial or money gene these same assumptions further undermined DEC's ability to cope with changing environmental circumstances.

1. Innovation: We can and will revolutionize computing.

2. Rugged individualism: The individual is ultimately the source of original ideas.

3. Truth through conflict: No one individual is smart enough to evaluate his or her own ideas; therefore, to arrive at validity or truth, one must debate ideas to see which ones can survive critical debate or empirical test where that is possible ("Push back," "Get buy-in").

4. Personal responsibility: Individuals are not only capable of taking responsibility and doing the right thing but must do so at all times ("He who proposes does," "Do the right thing").

5. Family paternalism: Once in the family, one cannot be ejected; failure is the result of a mismatch between person and job and

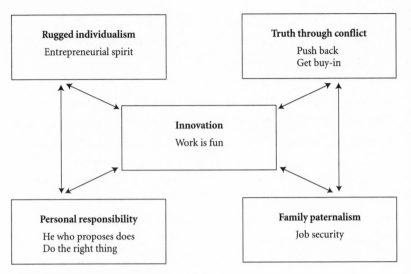

FIGURE 6.1. DEC's Cultural Paradigm: Part 1

is not the fault of the person; hence, every member of the "family" can feel secure in his or her membership.

Figure 6.2 shows five additional assumptions that derive directly from the core group shown in figure 6.1 but that deal more directly with the external task of surviving in a dynamic environment.

6. Engineering arrogance: A good product will sell itself, and the initial judgment of what is a good product can be made by the designer himself or herself.

7. Moral commitment to customers: The ultimate role of business is to identify and solve the customer's problem and to deal with customers in a completely open and honest way.

8. The market as arbiter: The best way to determine priorities is to let products compete with one another internally and let the market decide which products and services should survive.

9. Organizational idealism: Individuals of goodwill can and will work together to successfully coordinate their activities in the interests of the company.

10. Central control: No matter how much freedom employees and managers had, Ken Olsen always kept some degree of

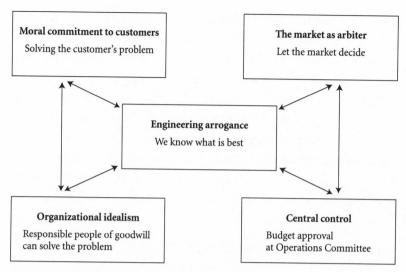

FIGURE 6.2. DEC's Cultural Paradigm: Part 2

central control, and the organization always maintained some respect for the founder–father figure, which gave Olsen a degree of power and influence even when things were going out of control.

What made DEC so remarkable was that overt behavior, espoused values, and tacit assumptions were so consistent with one another. Ken Olsen's principles and values were not only attractive to the people who joined DEC, in that it gave them so much freedom and personal security, but the resulting behavior was also immediately and consistently successful in creating the innovative products that produced a viable business.

Taking all of these assumptions together and seeing how they interrelated, one can understand how the intense and often acrimonious debate at the highest management levels produced not only good ideas and important innovations but also a friendly familial environment in which people got along well and worked well together. The innovative ideas did not necessarily come from the Operations Committee or Ken Olsen. Rather, the climate of freedom to think and debate made it possible for people in all parts of DEC to feel confident that if they tried out some new way of doing things it would be supported. The belief in internal competition and "letting the market decide" justified all kinds of innovations locally that might never have been approved if they had gone through a centralized screening process. DEC created within itself the possibility of many skunk works, and some of these continued on even after senior management withdrew support from them. What comes through in all of the alumni stories is the incredible sense of empowerment that DEC employees and managers felt. In a sense they were truly treated as adults who were expected to make their own decisions and be responsible for their own behavior.

THE ACADEMIC BIAS IN THE ENGINEERING CULTURE

One way of understanding the uniqueness of this combination of assumptions is to note that it reflected (1) the American culture with its emphasis on individualism and entrepreneurship, (2) Western values of individual moral responsibility and humanism, (3) the engineering culture described in chapter 3, and (4) the academic culture of MIT. The art of the possible, the need to solve "big problems," and the heroic need to change the way the world worked were all strongly felt by DEC employees in the 1950s. From an academic point of view, trying things out that were on the edge technologically was normal because the consequences of failure were minimal.

THE PATERNALISTIC BIAS IN THE CULTURE

What made the individual empowerment so effective was the morally based paternalism and idealism that accompanied it. The assumption that failure in your job was the result of a mismatch rather than of personal incompetence was crucial in giving people the feeling that no matter what "they would be taken care of." This feeling was especially strong in the community of Maynard, where DEC was the major employer for forty years. In a recent interview with an alumnus who was employed primarily as a temp in what was called the Temporary Assistance Group (TAG), the ex-employee recounted how his mother had worked there in the "board shop" for several years and his father had worked for a contractor that did most of its business with DEC, as well as working there full-time for a period. Even during the period when there was a hiring freeze in the late 1980s, this person was able to get a TAG job and still felt the strong sense of personal worth and pride that DEC engendered.

The alumnus's commitment to DEC was based on two strong feelings: (1) the sense of personal worth that was communicated ultimately from Ken Olsen and the climate he created, and (2) the sense of security that was engendered by the social contract of "we will take care of you, no matter what." In the interview there were frequent references to "Mother DEC" and "Father Ken." Implicit in this social contract was also the assumption of lifetime employment: "get a job in DEC and you are set for life." To the employees in the trenches Ken Olsen was a kind of mythical figure: "with Ken at the helm we would all be taken care of." These aspects of the culture were captured well in the feeling expressed by this ex-employee: "Only put into a company as much as it puts into you, and DEC put a lot into you. We were proud of how the company treated us and how we treated each other." Ken was also a source of strong moral stands; for example, there would be no drinking at company functions and liquor could not be listed on expense accounts.

The workplace spawned informal activities of all kinds—sports teams, clubs, support groups of various sorts, bulletin boards and chat rooms on the internal network—creating a strong community feeling within the company. The women's support group, for example, has been frequently mentioned as critical to the morale of a number of female senior engineers and managers who had to function in the 1960s and 1970s in the male-dominated technical environment that characterized DEC in those decades. Olsen encouraged a strong diversity program and made consistent efforts to ensure that Equal Employment Opportunity (EEO) and affirmative action programs would be successful. He gave away turkeys to all employees every year at Thanksgiving in a paternalistic gesture but, at the same time, kept the company aloof from direct involvement with the community because of the feeling that not only individuals but also communities should be responsible for themselves. Little information was shared with employees about the technology or the economic situation of the company, and the extreme degree of geographic decentralization often left employees outside of Maynard feeling out of touch yet trusting that all would be well.

WERE THERE MISSING GENES IN THE CULTURAL DNA?

If one examines the shared tacit assumptions from the point of view of building a viable business that would survive in the long run, one notices one critical assumption or goal that is missing. Economic growth and survival was neither a shared, taken-for-granted assumption nor a primary goal. It is this missing assumption that I label as the missing money gene in the cultural DNA of DEC. It is true that Ken Olsen promised profitability to General Doriot in his first year and very proudly achieved that goal. It is equally true that the debate around budgets, costs, and investments appeared to be about building a business, but I saw the group depending almost completely on the assumption that if they just produced good enough products the profits would take care of themselves. Growth would always be sufficient to cover the costs of experimentation and inefficient processes.

DEC's immediate success in turning a profit in its first year strongly supported the assumption that it was their innovative products that were the reason, and their continued success made it unnecessary to examine closely whether they were evolving into a well-run, efficient commercial entity. Furthermore, the excellent products were perceived to be the result of the innovative climate and culture that I have described above. What DEC learned in its growth phase is that a climate of innovation will guarantee success. This early success so strongly reinforced the DEC cultural paradigm, and continued positive feedback from established customers was so steady, that one could see already in the late 1960s and early 1970s that DEC managers and employees were hooked. This was clearly the way to run a company.

How general was this paradigm in DEC in its first decade? That is,

if one studied workers in the plants, salespeople in geographically remote units, engineers in technical enclaves, and so on, would one have
found the same assumptions operating? One of the interesting aspects
of DEC is that, at least for its first twenty-five years or so, this basic
paradigm would have been observed in operation across all of its rank
levels, functions, and geographies. The surveys that I conducted
confirm this (see chapter 8).

However, in those functions that required a more disciplined approach to coordination, the paradigm was overlaid by a more tightly
managed hierarchy. Such a disciplined hierarchy was especially evident
in the customer service unit created and managed initially by Jack
Shields and in manufacturing under Pete Kaufmann. These variations
reflected another American value that was highly evident—pragma-
tism as a basis for doing what is right.

A second, less critical but nevertheless important, assumption that
was missing was the assumption that learning requires reflection. The
truth-through-conflict model was so strong that it tended to override
efforts to reflect, contemplate, and consider alternatives carefully.
The absence of reflection is a fairly common characteristic of the managerial occupation, but it was especially noticeable in DEC. Everyone,
especially Ken Olsen, was always very sure of himself or herself when
entering the debate. Reflective dialogue would have required the collaboration of the whole Operations Committee, something that I
never saw them achieve.

SOME ALUMNI ASSESSMENTS OF THE CULTURE

Some retrospective reactions from former employees provide an insight into how this culture was perceived:

> Certainly, the timing of macro economic and technological factors
> played an important part in DEC's success. However, it is much deeper.
> It was the employee culture that Ken created. It was an environment
> where people could grow, learn and make mistakes. It all sounds too
> trite for these days, but it was about making a difference, doing some-
> thing significant and having responsibility to be creative and entrepre-

neurial. Simply, Ken created an environment where everyone believed they mattered and made a difference. He unleashed thousands of people to care about the customer and the company. So the success was about people; people who were empowered to care and to act. (Tom Colatosti, letter, personal communication, 2000)

What made Digital great? The single most important aspect that allowed Digital to grow into a Fortune 100 company was the pursuit of the original vision of the founder, Ken Olsen. At a time when computers were reserved for the biggest corporate jobs, and locked up in limited access clean rooms, Ken envisioned a higher utilization by downsizing the machine and giving more people access.

The instant impact was to allow greater computer utilization for more applications. This not only created a new dimension of computer user, but stimulated the creation of perhaps thousands of related products, both ancillary hardware as well as utility software applications.

Digital itself formed into an entrepreneurial structure both allowing and encouraging new business opportunities. It was a management concept perhaps unprecedented in large companies. Digital was able to identify a market need and quickly move to develop product to meet the requirements.

The other key Digital principle was product compatibility, which allowed users to always expand rather than having to first retrench. This one aspect alone set Digital apart from all others. Through the late 70s and early 80s Digital was unique in its customer-centric principles that focused on the user needs and minimized customer investment. Rapid growth in multiple markets always ensured that there was sufficient revenue to support corporate profitability as well as internal sources for expansion funding. (Russ Monbleau, letter, personal communication, 2000)

What Ken Olsen created in 1957 is historic in industrial management. He brought the research environment of an academic institution into a commercial enterprise. With the organizational insight from General Georges Doriot and the participation of his initial management team, he established a unique organization, which we will describe as dynamic (i.e., the "D-Form"). This is not to diminish his technical contribution to the industry; but, rather, to define and position Digital Equipment

Corporation with the managerial leadership which leverages intellectual capital as a strategic resource in global enterprise management.

Since its inception, the Corporation has been an enigma organizationally. In some cases, experts refer to "the DIGITAL mystique." Others define it in simplistic terms as organized chaos . . . or the chaotic organization. In fact, it is neither. It is a networked, "knowledge-leverage" form of learning organization positioned for 21st century sustained profitable growth. Perhaps Digital would be better thought of as a "knowledge-utility" or a "global innovation system." It has a managerial foundation that preceded appropriate labels, language, defined concepts and principles simply because its origins were so ahead of its time. Now they are more defined. (Debra Rogers Amidon, memo, 1991)

In this last memo we see what many alumni and observers of the DEC culture regarded as an organization ahead of its time, a way of organizing that takes account of knowledge workers coordinating their many activities through creative use of network technology by committing to a set of norms about truth, buy-in, and doing the right thing. As we will see, the staying power of this culture turned out to be stronger than the economic necessities that overcame DEC, and this model of an organization is being reinvented over and over as the world's organizations become more and more knowledge-worker based. It is for this reason that we must understand this culture in some detail, especially to assess where its strengths and its potential weaknesses lie.

seven

DEC's "Other" Legacy

THE DEVELOPMENT OF LEADERS

Tracy C. Gibbons

Digital Equipment Corporation's technical legacy is well known and widely respected. Its innovation in minicomputers and networking was the basis for the evolution of new ways of computing and the democratization of technology. But DEC also made other significant contributions, technical and otherwise, to the larger community. Among the contributions was an approach to employee and leadership development that produced leaders at all levels of the organization. During their time at DEC, the talents and abilities of many employees were discovered, nurtured, developed, and honed, and these employees helped Digital become the technical and organizational powerhouse and much-sought-after employer-of-choice that it was until the early 1990s. Many employees were profoundly influenced by their experiences at DEC in ways that have had lasting impact. As these people left the company, first through normal turnover and attrition and later by less voluntary means and in greater numbers, they went on to other companies and enterprises where many held positions of considerable influence, and they continued to make significant contributions. This is DEC's "other" legacy.

During its lifespan, DEC employed more than 130,000 people.

Most went on to other work situations—in other established corporations, as entrepreneurs and consultants in private practice, as partners in start-ups, and to positions in education and community service—and with them they brought what they had learned. Their styles
of leading, managing, and influencing; their approaches to work and
innovation; and their beliefs about organizations and what is possible
were all shaped by the DEC culture and their experiences as DEC employees. As it turned out, DEC's unique culture had provided an optimal environment for the development of leadership ability and entrepreneurial behavior.

This chapter explores those aspects of the DEC culture that created
this crucible or laboratory for leadership development, how it shaped
both personal and professional development, and the lasting impact
of these experiences. The stories of several former DEC employees illustrate the connection between the developmental effects of their
years at Digital, their subsequent career choices, and the contributions
they have made to other companies and the community at large. The
material for this chapter is drawn from several sources: research that
I conducted in 1986 about the developmental attributes and processes
of transformational leaders, formal interviews with former employees,
and anecdotal data from continued contact with former colleagues
and clients.

SOME THOUGHTS ON LEADERSHIP
AND LEADERSHIP DEVELOPMENT

Several key constructs are the basis for understanding what it was
about DEC that contributed to the leadership development of so
many of its employees and how that worked. The subject of leadership—what it is and isn't, the related processes and dynamics, the results and outcomes—has been debated for centuries. In the late 1970s
and early 1980s, some new formulations and definitions emerged,
largely the work of James MacGregor Burns (1978), Bernard Bass and
his colleagues at SUNY Binghamton (1985), Warren Bennis and Burt
Nanus (1985), and Warren Bennis (1989). Their contributions are im-

portant because they differentiated management and leadership and described the attributes and effects of each; the work has been both enduring and relevant through the intervening years. As a result of their work, and for the purposes of this discussion, the terms *transformational leader* and *leader*, and *transactional leader* and *manager*, respectively, are synonymous and are used interchangeably.

The fundamental differences between managers and leaders are well summarized by Bennis and Nanus (1985):

> There is a profound difference between management and leadership, and both are important. To manage means to bring about, to accomplish, to have charge of or responsibility for, to conduct. Leading is influencing, guiding in direction, course, action, opinion. The distinction is crucial. *Managers are people who do things right and leaders are people who do the right thing.* The difference may be summarized as activities of vision and judgment—*effectiveness* versus activities of mastering routines—*efficiency.* (p. 21, original emphasis)

The literature has also been clear and consistent about the attributes, roles, and contributions of leaders. In this formulation, relevant business and technical background and expertise are necessary but not sufficient—the price of admission, so to speak. It is leadership ability that is the differentiator of who will make significant, lasting, and transformational contributions to enterprises and communities. While this does not mean that managers don't make important contributions, the sort of leadership that we're talking about is more an orientation and a way of being than it is a set of skills or techniques. The key differences are summarized in table 7.1.

Although there have been thousands of studies about the content, processes, and effects of leadership on both followers and organizations, much less is known about how leaders acquire the attributes associated with the transformational orientation, the effects of individual differences on leadership outcomes, and leaders' on-going development processes. There are three key points to be made: First, development is assumed to refer to a process that occurs gradually and incrementally over time, across the entire life span of the individual.

TABLE 7.1. Attributes of Transformational Leaders and Managers

Transformational Leaders	Managers (Transaction Leaders)
Are visionary and mission oriented	Are goal and strategy oriented
Use inspiration, charisma, and inherent excitement of the vision to enroll and motivate others	Bargain or contract for the exchange of effort/output for rewards as primary way to motivate others
Are individually and developmentally oriented	Stress and value rationality, limiting options and choices, problem solving
Look at old problems in new ways	
Stress and value intellectual ability, problem exploration, experimentation	Are day-to-day and operationally oriented
Are future and change oriented	Generally accent established norms, values, culture, and beliefs
Question existing culture, norms, values, and beliefs	Are risk controllers
Are risk takers	

Therefore, it is important to look at critical events and influences that have taken place throughout a leader's life when seeking to understand the process of leadership development.

Second, we know that one of the key functions of transformational leadership is the development of followers, so leaders are themselves agents of others' development; however, a leader cannot facilitate the development of another beyond the developmental level that he or she has achieved. While leadership can therefore occur at all levels, the developmental level of the leader poses a constraint, and the continuous development of leaders is essential to ongoing and continuous transformation of both people and organizations.

Third, a review of both the leadership and human development literature reveals seven factors that explain the origin, acquisition, and development of transformational leadership:

- Family factors: Early experiences, especially those with parents, that are the basis for opportunities and events that contribute to the development of a personality structure that favors leadership ability.

- Once-born, twice-born: This theory was formulated by Zaleznik (1977) and encompasses aspects of both the family factors and conflict and disappointment factors. According to Zaleznik, people who are once-born made adjustments to life that were reasonably straightforward, and their lives are mainly peaceful and harmonious with little discrepancy between expectations and reality. For those who are twice-born, life has been more of a struggle resulting in a sense of isolation, being special, wariness, and greater involvement in their inner world. Greater self-reliance, increased expectations of performance and achievement, and sometimes a desire to do great works are developed. *Leaders* are those who are twice-born and developed by mastery, and *managers* are those who are once-born and developed by socialization.

- Conflict and disappointment: This theme refers to the extent to which individuals have effective ways of dealing with conflict and disappointment in their lives. Those who deal effectively with conflict, face disappointments and resolve them, and engage in self-examination are more effective leaders.

- Developmental tendencies: Leaders tend to move toward higher levels of development during their lives and appear to have engaged in both intra- and interpersonal development activities to a greater extent than non-leaders.

- Previous leadership experiences: Previous opportunities for leadership, often early in life, and the transferability of learnings from those experiences are factors in the development of leaders.

- Influence of mentors: This theme pertains to the developmental effects of a strong interpersonal and professional coaching relationship between an older or more experienced individual and a more junior person in whom the mentor has taken a strong personal interest.

- Workshops and events: This theme pertains to workshops, training events, and other formal or structured learning activities that purport to teach leadership skills or behaviors.

These interrelated factors include events and influences of family and childhood and resulting developmental tendencies or predispositions as well as other more conscious or deliberate choices in service of developmental outcomes that occurred during the individual's life to date, for example, leadership experiences, developmental events, and the influence of mentors. (For a more thorough discussion of these factors, see Gibbons [1986] and Avolio and Gibbons [1988].)

WHAT WAS SO SPECIAL ABOUT DEC?

Given this background on leadership development, we can now explore the unique combination of conditions, cultural attributes, operating principles, values, and management practices that prevailed at Digital and that resulted in an environment in which leadership development flourished.

A culture that was empowering. There is a list of rules of the road for how to succeed at DEC that are synonymous with the company. Anybody who ever worked there knows them, most still subscribe to them, and many wish that the workplaces of today were more like this. It is easy to make the list: they are a part of me, and the people whom I interviewed all routinely mentioned all or most of them when describing their experiences at DEC and those factors that impacted their career and leadership development (note that these characteristics mirror closely the ones identified in chapter 6 as some of the core elements of DEC's culture).

- See what needs to be done and do it; develop a vision for what you want to accomplish
- He/she who proposes does
- Do the right thing; don't wait to be told what to do or how to do it

- Make it happen
- Push back if you don't agree or think the wrong thing is happening
- Invest in and build trusting relationships
- Truth will be discovered through conflict and debate
- Keep/deliver on your commitments
- Get buy-in before moving forward, even in the face of conflict and competition; influence is the way to do this

The result was a place that, on the one hand, actively and explicitly valued diversity in many ways that were ahead of the times: encouraging experimentation, risk taking, and creativity; expecting and stimulating push back, debate, and questions about what didn't make sense or seem right; hiring and promoting women and people of color; and formally supporting the exploration and understanding of differences of all kinds. On the other hand, DEC had a culture that was widely understood and well embraced and a set of norms that were practiced in relatively consistent ways. This paradox contributed to an ideal environment in which leadership ability could be recognized— by oneself and others—and grown: the "rules" were about the importance and necessity of freedom and innovation, exercising influence, taking responsibility, debating the relevant issues on their merit, respecting and trusting others, and getting buy-in before moving forward. The meaning, origins, and evolution of each of these principles were elaborated in the preceding chapters.

From a leadership development perspective, it would be hard to live in such a culture and work this way over an extended period of time and not develop at least some leadership ability. For if we compare these "rules" to the list of attributes of transformational leaders found in table 7.1, we see that there is a great deal of similarity and congruence between them. So it's not a surprise that Digital was a laboratory for leadership development and that those who were successful at Digital also embodied and practiced those attributes.

Fast growth. From the mid-1970s to the mid-1980s, Digital enjoyed a period of extraordinary growth that provided unparalleled opportunity technically, professionally, and managerially. Employees changed jobs frequently, the result of both promotions and "growmotions"— taking on added responsibility or getting increased opportunities for innovation without a formal change in title, job level, or pay. Employees were encouraged to identify problems and needs and propose solutions, so there was a continuous supply of intellectual stimulation and an endless outlet for creativity—more than enough to go around—which in turn continuously fueled the growth and provided challenging opportunities for the taking. Many new jobs were created during this time, which resulted in large numbers of new hires. With this influx of newcomers came the recognition that the culture and mores of DEC had to be formally transmitted, and many programs were created to do this. The importance of preserving the culture was on the minds of many, if not most, and current employees saw it as their responsibility to orient and integrate (and sometimes initiate) new people. Digital became the largest private employer in Massachusetts and New Hampshire and was seen as one of the most desirable places to work, for both technical and nontechnical people alike, since the opportunities to innovate were not limited only to those who were designing minicomputers.

From a leadership development perspective, there were also plenty of opportunities for people to be in leadership situations and roles and to learn and grow in this arena. The system rewarded taking initiative in this way by providing many opportunities (both formal and informal), offering fast career growth, and delivering generous monetary rewards.

Recruiting, attracting, and hiring the best people—very carefully. During Digital's fast-growth cycles, the recruiting and attracting of new employees pretty much took care of themselves. DEC was seen as *the* place to work, and those who wanted a job there worked very hard to make contacts and get themselves hired. Again, there was considerable awareness that the fit between a prospective employee and the company's culture was very important, and despite the need to fill jobs quickly, the screening and hiring processes were quite rigorous. A parody of the standard DEC print employment ad that circulated in the

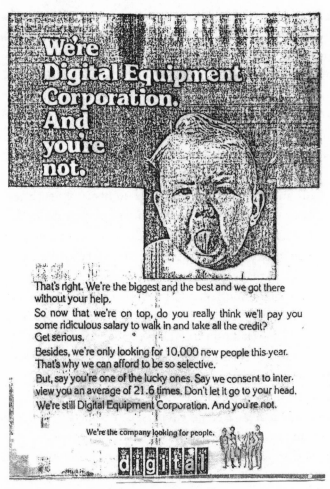

FIGURE 7.1. Parody of a DEC Employment Ad

late 1970s portrays both the heady arrogance and the rigor of the times (see figure 7.1)

In fact, there was a willingness to hire people who were a good fit, even if they turned out not to be a good match for the opening for which they were being interviewed, and these candidates were quickly referred for other openings. Sometimes they were hired without a specific job and either encouraged to create a job for themselves or considered part of a talent pool and given the right job when it came along. DEC was clear that it needed technically and professionally talented and creative people who could make a contribution and that it was inviting membership in a family that could last for a very long time. Layoffs were unheard of, and the average age of the employee population was twenty-eight. The prevailing belief was that if things weren't working out in a particular job, once you were in the family there would be a place for you to make that valuable contribution and you would be encouraged to find or create it.

This resulted in an employee population that was both self-selected and carefully screened before it was hired. Because DEC's culture and reputation as an employer were well known in the local area and beyond, prospective employees could assess whether it was a place they wanted to work, and not everyone did want to. The research on the development of transformational leaders shows that there is a predisposition toward this orientation that has its origins early in life and that is subsequently reinforced by oneself and others. Therefore, if an organization were to design a process for leadership development, it would make sense to seek participants who had this predisposition and motivation to engage in personal development. Given the overlap between the attributes of transformational leadership and the tenets of DEC's culture, it would seem that DEC was, however inadvertently, screening and hiring such people.

Coming of age—personally and professionally—while at DEC. Many theories of human development subscribe to a model that says that certain developmental tasks are related to and typically occur during phases or stages of life and that there is a predictable sequence of developmental challenges through which we progress. The mastery of one task or level is a prerequisite for, and launches us into, the next level. The tasks associated with people in their twenties and thirties are focused primarily on becoming differentiated from the family of origin, establishing an identity as an adult and creating a life and possibly a family of one's own, developing mastery of work and career, "making it," shifting the locus of evaluation and control from external to internal, and establishing a sense of personal and professional competence.

During the 1970s and 1980s, a very high proportion of the employee population at DEC ranged in age from mid-twenties through thirties, and during this time the population more than doubled. The employment tenure was long by today's standards—often ten years or more. This large cohort then moved together through both an exciting time in DEC's history and through the same age- and stage-related developmental tasks. The impact and effect of this convergence of events on future career choices, preferences for particular ways of working, values about what it means to make a contribution, and definitions of what constitutes personal and professional competence and integrity cannot be overstated.

A high level of cultural attunement and alignment to DEC's values and mores characterized the work environment. Because DEC was the largest employer, there was also a sense of community that extended beyond the workplace. Family members; parents of children's friends; neighbors; members of community, religious, and social groups; and other clients of local service providers were often DEC employees. It was not unusual for all or most of one's friends also to be Digital employees. Digital treated its employees with high regard, recognizing that people are different. Flexibility, adaptiveness, and responsiveness to individual needs did much to bind people to the company, and most employees felt tremendously loyal in return. Overall, employees loved their jobs, the work they got to do, and the sense that they were making a valuable contribution to an emerging and exciting industry. They were willing to go the extra mile, spending considerable time and energy in the service of Digital and their work there. Several of those whom I interviewed who left DEC voluntarily said, "Leaving DEC was the hardest decision I've ever made." Today we might say that DECies had "no life." But then, for many, life seemed well balanced and integrated, and they didn't experience themselves as being exploited or disposable once they had been used up. It is no wonder, then, that the relationships and connections made by many during their time at DEC are still important to them, even years later. As one alumnus said, "No one should misunderstand how important the DEC alumni connection is: once DEC, always DEC. It made a big impression on people's lives."

This was a system that was extraordinarily self-reinforcing. And it was in this milieu that people experienced the developmental activities, conscious and intentional or otherwise, that formed indelible and lasting values, beliefs, and behaviors that continue to define who they are and how they approach work and career. In the words of one, echoed by others, "I came of age at Digital."

High value on individual development. Beyond the generally developmental culture and environment at DEC, there was specifically a high value placed on individual development—personal, technical, and professional. From a leadership development perspective this is noteworthy for two reasons. First, it ensured that employees received the formal training that is essential to becoming and keeping current in one's field—be it technical or professional—and that is a necessary but not sufficient requirement for leaders. Second, it enabled considerable interpersonal, intrapersonal, and management development. Competence in these arenas is also essential to leadership development.

Digital expended considerable resources in this arena. It had an extensive internal employee and organization development capability that was well utilized and valued. A wide range of custom-designed programs was created, augmented by a menu of courses and programs purchased from external vendors in support of development initiatives and individual needs. It also had a very generous tuition reimbursement plan that made it possible for many to receive academic degrees in their chosen fields so long as the proposed program could be related to their current work or the needs of the company. The health care plan provided access to therapy for those who wanted it, without the limitations that are typically imposed by the corporations, employee assistance plans (EAPs), or heath plans of today. Many used this as a vehicle for personal development work, which can be an important aspect of the development of transformational leaders. Digital was also a big customer of suppliers of personal development programs such as NTL Institute and the Center for Creative Leadership. Employees were encouraged to attend these programs, which made it easy for those who were so inclined to take advantage of numerous opportunities for development that would contribute to their leadership abilities.

There was at DEC a convergence of values, resources, and rewards that created an environment in which leadership development could and did occur.

WHAT WAS LEARNED AND HOW WAS IT USED?

The biographies feature the people whom I interviewed for this exploration of leadership development at DEC. They give a sense of people's careers at DEC, their significant sources of impact and learnings, what they've done post-DEC, and the contributions they've made to their companies, professions, communities, clients, and customers. These people's accomplishments are noteworthy and illustrative, but there were other criteria by which they were selected. Their entry into DEC, their career progression, the opportunities that came their way, and their experiences of the significance of their time at, and relationship with, the company were quite typical. Most of them came to DEC when they were in their twenties and early thirties, starting out in entry or midlevel individual contributor or managerial positions. In this small sample, an effort was made to represent the variety of corporate functions as well as differences in gender, ethnicity, and nationality that characterized DEC. In keeping with the value that was placed on all forms of diversity, each of these people is a unique individual whose personality and life experiences shaped his or her development and practice of leadership while at DEC.

What these people have in common is a particular mix of individual predisposition and motivation that combined with the opportunities and environment afforded by the DEC culture to produce extraordinary leadership development and significant contributions, both at DEC and beyond. And what they also have in common is their love of DEC and their recognition of, and appreciation for, the part it played in their lives and careers.

Three themes emerged from these interviews that describe the most lasting and impactful aspects and significant learnings from the years at DEC:

- Respectful and trusting relationships: Building and sustaining respectful and trusting relationships as the basis for working successfully with others, for transacting business, and for collaborating to achieve goals; supporting and growing other people.

- Freedom and opportunity: The empowering effect of being given freedom and opportunity; the invitation and expectation that you will see what needs to be done based on what is "right" for the company; following through, taking responsibility, engaging others, and being accountable for the results of your vision or proposal.

- Freedom to question assumptions: Questioning assumptions and pushing back; debating ideas, proposals, and products on their merit, despite inherent conflict; the belief that truth and the best path will emerge from this process; focusing on the content and not attacking or diminishing individuals.

This, in the end, is the lasting legacy and contribution of the Digital Equipment Corporation: thousands of people, shaped and impacted by these values and ways of working let loose on the world to influence others and make lasting contributions to technology, the practice of leadership and management, global enterprise, and the community at large.

WHERE ARE THEY NOW?

Gordon Bell

Gordon Bell worked at DEC from 1960 to 1966, leaving to teach at Carnegie Mellon University. He returned to DEC in 1972 as VP of engineering and was there until 1983. During his time at Digital, he was responsible for helping to develop the PDP family of minicomputers and was the architect of DEC's VAX series, a set of products that transformed both the company and the computer industry. Indeed, it would be difficult to overstate Bell's contributions to both Digital and the industry.

Bell joined DEC at the beginning—three years after its founding—

so he was more a shaper of the culture than one influenced by it. "I don't think I ever thought about team creation or leadership. It evolved from the MIT environment; [it was] an engineering-scientific culture: question everything in an open environment. . . . We looked at multiple alternatives, worked to resolve conflict quickly, learned how not to personalize failure, and built on that." He had learned the importance of finding the balance between being firm about something and destroying a personal relationship while working in his father's electrical supply company as a boy.

It was hard to get buy-in for the VAX strategy, and it put him at odds with Ken Olsen. "I led from an understanding of the technology and what should be done from a technical strength point of view, and I was looking at it issue by issue. Ken and I disagreed. He was into options and playing them. . . . I made it happen, just kept on until the machines changed and the roles of the product lines changed." But the stress took a toll; Bell had a heart attack and soon after left the company.

His years and experience at DEC enabled Bell to develop a heuristic, rule-based model for building products, an approach that says that the most appropriate next step or solution to a problem will emerge as a result of learning or experience in the preceding steps: "The product decides the rules, not people. People have to organize to enable the product to work and be built."

Since leaving DEC, Bell has continued to make innumerable contributions to the industry. He did work at the National Science Foundation that pulled together all the computing research and also led the cross-agency group that created the strategy by which the Internet was put in place. "I foresaw the idea of the network and saw what the structure might mean but not what it might turn into. Three hundred people missed what it could enable!"

He has been involved with sixty-five start-ups as an angel investor. In 1988 he established the Gordon Bell Award to recognize significant achievements in high-performance computing. He has published several books and was involved in the establishment of the Computer History Museum at Moffett Field in Mountain View, California.

Since 1991, first as an advisor and now as an employee, he has worked with Microsoft on future development efforts, continuing his presence at the forefront of computer technology.

Crawford Beveridge

A native of Edinburgh, Crawford Beveridge came to Digital in 1977 following ten years at Hewlett Packard in Europe and the United States. While at DEC, he oversaw the establishment of European manufacturing sites and then became personnel manager for Europe.

"At HP, I learned about management, and at DEC I learned about leadership." The assumption at DEC was that everyone should and would do what's right, not wait to be told what to do or how to do it. At HP and other places he's worked, there were manuals and policies, and he recognized the importance of developing trusting relationships and a trust-based culture that enabled people to make mistakes without the fear of being fired for them. "DEC was a humane place that looked after people's concerns. . . . It was a commonwealth, not an empire. No one insisted on anything. It was the goodwill of individuals that made entities work. . . . It loosened me up: I realized that it wasn't about policy manuals, it was about vision, enabling, clearing barriers, and supporting talent. It rebuilt my head about how to apply what I knew. . . . [There were more] degrees of freedom and fewer constraints."

In 1982, Beveridge was recruited by Analog Devices. "Nothing about DEC made me leave. . . . I concluded that I wanted to run my own shop, and this was a VP-level position in a smaller company. . . . DEC was a coming-of-age for me."

Beveridge has done two tours at Sun Microsystems. From 1985 to 1991, he was VP of corporate resources, which included responsibility for human resources (HR), management information systems (MIS), real estate, purchasing and logistics, security, and corporate affairs. During his tenure, company sales grew from $100 million to $3 billion, while the employee population increased from eight hundred to over twelve thousand. He returned in 2000 as VP and chief human resource officer. "If I'd come [straight] from HP to Sun, I wouldn't have made it."

In the intervening nine years, Crawford went home to Scotland, where he was CEO of Scottish Enterprise, the economic development organization for Scotland. At this 1,700-employee, $800-million organization he was responsible for business development, infrastructure development, skill building, and venture capital. "I realized that I could be a chief executive. I marshaled all my skills and learnings, especially leadership skills from DEC, to loosen up a government organization."

Beveridge is a member of several boards of directors, including those of Autodesk, Memec, Scottish Equity Partners, and Young Enterprise Scotland.

Peter DeLisi

Peter DeLisi left IBM to come to Digital in 1977 and stayed for sixteen years. Among the positions he held were product line manager for the Distributed Data Processing Group, sales training manager, and several others in the field services organization.

After leaving DEC, he started his own consulting company, Organizational Synergies, specializing in strategy development. DeLisi credits his success with his company to what he learned at DEC about being an entrepreneur and running a business.

Coming to DEC after years in parochial schools, a Jesuit college, the military, and IBM, DeLisi said, was "a culture shock—no one telling you what to do. . . . I'd never been anywhere where I hadn't been told what to do." At DEC, he learned the importance of team, family, collaboration, and buy-in. He came to appreciate the power and value in seeing what needed to be done—not in what was assigned—proposing it and doing it, and in so doing leveraging talent and a unique vantage point. "When you get a group working together this way, you can have tremendous impact and results. . . . It broadened my vision of what's possible."

Having learned that "He who proposes does," DeLisi was emboldened by this imperative, and he has made many proposals since leaving DEC that have benefited his company and his clients. One of these proposals led to a part-time position at Santa Clara University, where he is now academic dean of the Information Technology Leadership Program.

Barry James Folsom

Barry James Folsom worked at DEC in the early 1980s as manager of the Rainbow (PC) Development Group. Of his time at Digital he says, "Professionally, this was the best time in my life. . . . It was the foundation for me and my career."

Major learnings included the importance of having a vision with passion and energy, of never giving up despite naysayers, of improvising and changing the rules, of being flexible, and of creating the foundation for sustainability. "Part of leadership is getting people to go there, and also sustaining it. There are lots of houses of cards lately. [I learned that] you have to build a foundation that can sustain growth and then decide where you can and can't take short cuts. . . . I also learned about risk management and always had a contingency plan, and I got it agreed to by those involved in it ahead of time."

Folsom left DEC for Sun Microsystems, where he was a member of the corporate management team during its growth from $100 million to $1.7 billion in sales. He is currently chairman of the board at PlaceWare, a Web conferencing company whose bookings have grown from $3 million to $50 million since he arrived as CEO in 1997. Prior to taking his current position, he did several start-ups and turn-arounds, including previous positions as president at Spectrum Holobyte, where revenues grew from $13 million to $70 million in a year, and CEO of Radius, where he also turned it around in one year, growing revenues by 50 percent.

Kevin Melia

A native of Ireland and an accountant by training, Kevin Melia joined Digital at the company's manufacturing plant in Galway in 1972 and moved to the United States in 1976. DEC was one of the first companies to locate a plant in Ireland, and for Melia it was "like a university, a window to the world," offering opportunities for which he is still grateful to Ken Olsen. He held a variety of positions in finance, logistics, purchasing, and materials. His last position at Digital was VP of materials, in which he transformed the company's approach to supply chain management (SCM, before it was called that).

Though he believes that by the late 1980s DEC was twenty years ahead in SCM (and he still uses what he learned and experimented with at DEC), it was frustration with his inability to make additional changes that he felt were essential to DEC's survival that led to his departure after being recruited by Sun Microsystems in 1989. There, as VP of worldwide operations, he saw an opportunity to do many of the things he couldn't do at DEC, and he encountered less resistance to creating a globalized "lean" manufacturing operation that relied on outsourcing. During his time at Sun, he also became CFO and president of Sun Microsystems Computer Corporation.

In 1994, back in Boston, Melia cofounded (with Bob Graham, also a Digital alumnus) Manufacturers Services Limited (MSL), a global, full-service electronics manufacturing service provider for OEMs. By acquiring the OEMs' own manufacturing plants and producing their products more efficiently, he grew the company from zero to $1.5 billion in revenues in six years, making it one of the largest firms in that business.

Asked how his experience at DEC helped prepare him for MSL, Melia said, "DEC was a very entrepreneurial company which grew very fast. It gave me a taste for taking on responsibility." In 2000, MSL opened a facility in Galway.

Dorothy Terrell

Dorothy Terrell came to DEC in 1977 from the not-for-profit sector, starting as training manager in the Westminster final assembly and test manufacturing facility. She quickly moved up through a succession of plant and group personnel positions and in 1984 became the plant manager for the Boston manufacturing facility. "Even at DEC, it was an unusual opportunity to go from personnel to a high-level line management job." And even at DEC, it was a more unusual opportunity for an African American woman. In 1988, in what was another "unusual opportunity, a chance of a lifetime," she relocated to Silicon Valley to start up the Cupertino plant, where the VAX 9000 would be manufactured.

Asked about the most impactful aspects of her career at DEC, Terrell said, "I joined DEC at the best possible time and place—the late seventies in Westminster and in final assembly and test. DEC was growing again, and it was exciting. All the pieces [of the company] came together [in Westminster]." Echoing a familiar theme, she also recalled that people were given opportunities to do different things that went beyond what a position or job might suggest. "People saw more in me at that time, things I didn't see in myself. They looked for talent and gave you as much as you could stand." Manufacturing, even more than in other parts of DEC, paid attention to differences of all kinds (not just the obvious ones) and their impact on individual and organizational capability and productivity. In addition to her own learnings from the many innovative programs in this arena that were developed at DEC, Terrell also influenced, led, and contributed significantly to others' understanding of issues of race and gender.

By 1991 Terrell and her staff had succeeded against difficult odds in bringing the VAX 9000 to market, but the product wasn't selling, and the first non-voluntary downsizing in the history of Digital occurred in Cupertino. Although she recognized that downsizing was "the right thing to do" for the company, Terrell described this experience as one of the most wrenching things she has ever done. At that moment, she realized that DEC would never be the same.

Later that year, she left to become the president of Sun Express at Sun Microsystems, where she started Sun's worldwide aftermarket and on-line services business unit, joining several other former DECies on the executive staff. In six years, she grew Sun Express to $300 million in revenues, expanding into eleven countries. "DEC was preparation for Sun, Cupertino, [because it was in Silicon Valley] even more so. I couldn't have hit the ground running at Sun without Cupertino," and it helped to have other DEC people to call on. She had also learned at

DEC that the people whom you hire are the key ingredient and that surrounding yourself with talented people who also understand the importance of relationships and trust is essential to success.

In 1997, Terrell moved to NMS Communications, a telecom infrastructure and services provider. There she was senior VP of both corporate operations and worldwide sales and president of platforms and services. About her diverse range of responsibilities she said, "I did so many different things at DEC—big different things. That was part of the opportunity, I was empowered to do them." During her tenure at NMS she drove a 100 percent increase in year-over-year revenue. In 2001, Terrell was recognized as one of Technology's Most Remarkable Women by *Upside* magazine and one of the 50 Most Important African Americans in Technology by the editors of blackmoney.com.

Recently retired, Terrell is a member of many community and corporate boards, including those of General Mills, Sears, Herman Miller, the Commonwealth Institute, Massachusetts General Hospital, and the Massachusetts Software Council.

Fred Traversi

Fred Traversi came to DEC in 1979 following five years at General Electric (during which he took a year off to obtain an M.B.A. from Harvard). Since leaving DEC in 1994, he has held senior positions at Taco Bell and Lexmark and is now president and CEO of AdvizeX Technologies. "And [of all of these] DEC was the most influential in shaping my management and leadership philosophy and approach."

Key learnings that Traversi took with him to subsequent positions include the benefits of decentralized decision making and local option; the applications of business process discipline (*business process discipline* is determining a standard, repeatable way of performing a particular activity or process that gets a consistent result); the importance of solid, trusting relationships to getting things done; the usefulness of constructive tension and conflict; and the effectiveness of giving people the freedom to see what needs to be done and the opportunity to do it without a complicated approval process.

While VP of operations at Taco Bell, he introduced the structure and processes for decentralized decision making that enabled regions to operate in ways that better matched their local markets. He also opened restaurants in each region to test new concepts and products, enabling faster new-product introductions.

Traversi summarized the impact of his tenure at DEC: "My most significant personal and professional relationships are from the DEC years. None from other companies are still important."

Tracy Gibbons

After a first career as a program director and branch executive for the YMCA, Tracy came to DEC in 1977. Starting as an employee and organization development specialist in the Westminster final assembly and test facility, she held a variety of positions as organization development consultant and manager. In 1989 and 1990, as member of the Corporate Organization Consulting Group, she worked with the plant manager and staff in Cupertino, California, to start up the manufacturing facility for the VAX 9000.

While at Digital, Gibbons earned a Ph.D. in human and organization systems at the Fielding Graduate Institute. Her research investigated and modeled the developmental origins and processes of transformational leaders. "It was my experience at DEC that piqued my curiosity about both organization transformation and leadership, and it provided both the opportunity and an amazing laboratory in which to study both."

In 1991, Gibbons joined Advanced Micro Devices as senior organization development consultant; there she worked with DEC alumnus Bob Krueger to create a team-based engineering and marketing organization. It was also there that she began to discover and appreciate that the work that she and her HR and OD colleagues had done at DEC was—and continues to be—state-of-the-art. "We had enormous freedom and encouragement to innovate. The work I did and what I learned while I was at DEC is still the foundation for my practice, especially the stuff about complex, interdependent, matrixed organizations. What DEC was doing twenty or more years ago is still new to some of my clients."

In 1997 Gibbons realized a longtime career goal of being in private practice as a consultant. She is now president of CoastWise Consulting, a bicoastal firm that focuses on creating competitive advantage by leveraging the power of organization design, strategic alignment, and collaboration.

eight

DEC's Impact on the Evolution of Organization Development

Some of the unique aspects of DEC's culture surfaced in my own efforts to be a helpful consultant to Ken Olsen, to the Operations Committee, and eventually to many other individuals and groups throughout the organization. I have already described how some of my early efforts to improve communication in the Operations Committee forced me to learn that "expert consulting" would not be helpful but that if I got into the flow of the group and figured out what they were trying to do, I could help them to do it better. This was the essential lesson that led to the whole philosophy of *process consultation* (Schein 1967, 1999b).

In my further work with various parts of the organization I learned many more lessons, both about the DEC culture and about the role of organization development (OD) in such a culture. In that process I learned some important principles that apply to the practice of OD in all organizations. In addition to sitting in on Operations Committee meetings, I became involved with the whole human resource function, management development and training, and employee surveying. Working within and across groups made it very clear how difficult it is to distinguish *contact clients* who recruit you, *primary clients* who ultimately want help and pay for the services, and *ultimate clients* who will be impacted by all the interventions you make. In all of the work I did at DEC over a twenty-five year period, one overarching lesson had to be learned over and over again, a lesson that Kurt Lewin taught us sixty years ago but that we still don't get: when you are dealing with a complex human system, if you want to influence people you have to involve them and you have to be willing to be influenced yourself.

MANAGEMENT DEVELOPMENT AND TRAINING

Ken Olsen and Win Hindle recognized in the late 1960s that some form of management development and training would be necessary to manage growth. To stimulate development and "professionalize" the HR function, DEC hired Dennis Burke in 1969 to manage HR and, in particular, to focus on employee and management development. Prior to his involvement, Win Hindle and I had launched a "management development program" that reflected completely the DEC culture. Instead of specifying what managers should be learning, we asked the members of the Operations Committee what they would like to learn. The topics they chose for their monthly seminars were surprising. The top choice was accounting and finance! We put the topics in a priority order and planned monthly meetings with outside resource people for each topic. The main effect was that the meetings were well attended and exciting, primarily because we were working on what the group itself had chosen.

The development model that then evolved required each member of the Operations Committee to meet with his immediate subordinates and ask them what topics they would choose for their seminars. The principle was that unless people pick their own learning topics based on their own needs, the program will not succeed. We saw that a common thread of what managers wanted, and what we felt they needed, was interpersonal communication and supervisory skills.

With the help of the HR people in each of the major groups, especially engineering, we designed two- and three-day workshops that involved "action learning," hands-on exercises, role-plays, and other interactive learning methods. Whenever possible the topics for analysis were real DEC issues, an essential component of action learning. For example, on the topic of group problem solving, we had each of three groups of managers use the problem-solving model on one of these topics: (1) How do you adjust to growth and complexity and help others to recognize the problems? (2) How do you manage cross-product complexity and fractionalization? And (3) should the Operations Committee be involved in lower-level salary decisions?

These workshops became a regular part of the educational program and were attended by all senior managers except Ken Olsen. We recognized the need for Olsen to be educated as well, so we invented the two-day "Corporate Seminar," with the topics chosen aimed at Olsen because he would attend these events. The open climate and lack of authoritarian bureaucracy were amusingly revealed around one of these Corporate Seminars. We had carefully planned to educate senior management, especially Olsen, on matters of strategy and organization. Working with me on the planning was Sue Lotz, who had an administrative position in the CEO's office. A week or so before the seminar, Olsen indicated that he was not going to be there because of a conflict. Sue Lotz marched into his office and said that he "had to be there because the topics had been chosen to educate him!" He changed his other commitment and attended the seminar.

As DEC grew, it launched in 1967 a regular supervisory training program for first-line supervisors that focused on how to motivate, give feedback, improve morale, impose discipline, give orders, delegate, set examples, handle the problem employee, follow company policies, give performance appraisals and set goals, modify group behavior, improve intergroup relations, and so on. Dennis Burke also organized workshops on various interpersonal and managerial skills for senior managers, and John Cronkite, the internal OD consultant for engineering, and I organized workshops for engineering managers focused on "role set analysis" to help them understand the complexities of functioning effectively in a "matrixed network organization."

In addition to the workshops and Corporate Seminars, DEC had an effective tuition reimbursement program that encouraged employees at any level to take courses at various local colleges. At the management level, Olsen encouraged senior managers to take time off to attend executive education programs at MIT, Harvard, Northeastern, and schools farther afield. Each manager was encouraged to do something for personal development, but what it was was left to his or her discretion. By 1977 the outside educational opportunities for DEC employees and managers were described in a booklet that listed twenty-five U.S. and European university programs for which DEC would pay tuition. In the mid-1970s DEC had a deal with Boston University to teach various courses for employees at DEC's facilities; the university administrators admired DEC's willingness to bring faculty out to the company.

One thing that was lacking, however, was a systematic rotation program that would help managers to become generalists. There was relatively little movement from one function to another because the incentives to become a generalist were not very strong. There were no divisions planned, and the product-line structure taught managers only how to market and manage their finances. They got little training in sales, manufacturing, product development, or service. As the need for general managers grew, more were brought in from other companies, but the strong technically based culture never really accepted or understood what *general management* meant, and people were, to some degree, suspicious of it. This suspicion showed up most clearly in derogatory remarks made by Olsen and others about M.B.A.s and their relatively small contribution to corporate performance.

My role in all of this cut across the various activities. Management development was one of my research areas, so I was, in a sense, trying to look at the whole picture companywide and "educate" senior management on the issues of development. Work on communication and interpersonal relationships continued through my direct interventions at the Woods Meetings and through occasional advice to Ken about policy statements he was considering. He would show me a memo he was proposing to send out and ask what I thought its impact might be. We would then "debate" the issue, often leading to new wording in the memo.

Sometimes the need for intervention caught me by surprise and required improvisation. For example, at one 1967 Woods Meeting, Ken decided that all of the members of the Operations Committee should give one another feedback on how they were doing in the eyes of their peers. Each person would be discussed by the whole group. Ken turned to me and said, "Ed, you know about this stuff, give us a way to do this." The dilemma, of course, was to do it in a way that would save face for the person being discussed and allow the group to be frank in front of that person and Ken. I knew that retrospective critique would be dangerous, so I proposed that we do it in a planning mode. We would take each person's role one at a time, and the rest of us would discuss what we would like to see more of or less of in that role in the future. This made it possible to give negative feedback in a safe manner and also made it possible for the group to talk to Ken in a constructive way.

In the mid-1970s Sue Lotz functioned as manager of human resource planning and evolved a variety of tools and processes that enabled senior managers to plan for the evolution of the jobs under them and to make succession plans that would ensure both filling those jobs and providing the right kind of developmental opportunities for their subordinates. A corporate group of the top 250 managers was identified with the intention of monitoring their career progress closely. One three-day Woods Meeting in 1977 was devoted entirely to human resource planning, reflecting DEC's continuing concern in this area. This same concern was reflected in the 1980s when DEC hired Eli Ginzberg as a consultant to examine the company's HR policies worldwide.

The job of HR director outgrew what Dennis Burke was good at, which led to his departure around 1975. In 1978 Sheldon Davis was hired to create a centralized HR and organization development function.

EMPLOYEE ATTITUDES AND ATTITUDE SURVEYING

The impact of DEC's culture and Olsen's management style is dramatically illustrated by the way in which attitude surveying first evolved in the engineering organization. Today, surveying is taken for granted, but in the mid-1960s the methodology and philosophy behind surveys were not all that well worked out. As it turns out, the way in which Ken wanted surveys done created a whole different concept in my own mind that became central to my subsequent thinking about how to consult effectively on survey and feedback projects. I had already learned the hard way that the only way to influence the workings of the Operations Committee was to get into their flow and occasionally provide process help around whatever they were trying to do. I learned this same lesson around surveying, as the account below will show. Though Ken might not have been aware of it, one of his most powerful influences was on the practice of organization development.

Morale was a concern of Ken's from the beginning. As I began to attend meetings of the Operations Committee, the question arose of how people down in the organization were feeling, as the company was growing by leaps and bounds. Ken and the Operations Committee knew that they were highly dependent on the creativity of their engineering organization. As the company grew in numbers of people, the distance between the working engineers and senior management grew. How then to assess how things were going down in the trenches? To deal with these issues, Ken asked me to go into the engineering, product line, and manufacturing organizations to interview people and identify problems that needed to be worked on.

Surveys of this sort were not new in industry (Bennis, Benne, and Chin 1961). However, Ken's approach was, from the beginning, different from what I had experienced or read about. I asked Ken when and in what form he wanted to see the results and, to my surprise, he indicated that he did not want to see the results! What he wanted was for the problems to be identified and fixed by whoever had the knowledge and tools to fix them. I was quite skeptical about this at first, but as we will see, Ken's attitude about fixing problems at the level where they occur led to a whole different way of conducting surveys and providing feedback by "cascading upward."

The first survey was to be conducted in the engineering group. Over a period of several months I interviewed all of the key engineers with an open-ended approach, asking "How is it going?" "What is working?" and "What is not working?" I then brought together each project group or team, usually about ten to fifteen people, and shared with them my findings from that team. Bringing the team together was a direct intervention toward building a problem-solving process rather than just gathering data. We allocated two hours to the meeting, with the following agenda:

1. Are the data accurate? Did I hear or interpret correctly what you have said? (These questions provided opportunities for correction, elaboration, and determination of the relative importance of the issues identified.)

2. Which of the problems that were identified could be addressed and fixed by your group? (The group members were reminded at this point that they were the first to see their own data and should take responsibility for fixing at their level whatever could be fixed.)

3. Which data, about both what was working and what needed fixing, should be fed upward to the immediate boss? (This provided opportunities to tell higher levels only those things that required the intervention of those higher levels rather than dumping all the data on senior management.)

Each project group went through this exercise, providing us the opportunity to test and collate the data from that organization into a more coherent analysis of what was working and what was not in the total organization. But that was not the most important result. In almost every group, I got the reaction that the sorting of problems into what we can fix and what we need to tell higher management was a welcome task that gave the group a real sense of ownership. One group put it this way: "Finally we are getting a task that provides the group a real opportunity to influence how the place is managed." This comment and others like it showed early on that even though Ken gave a great deal of freedom and responsibility to his immediate subordinates, some of those subordinates often acted quite autocratically, resulting in high variability of morale lower down in the organization.

In spite of this variability, Ken's philosophy of "Do the right thing" prevailed in that managers who could not justify their particular style would either lose people or fail to get results from their people.

ENGINEERING SURVEY RESULTS

What were the actual results in terms of morale? How were engineers, the critical resource group, feeling in this young, innovative organization? Not surprisingly, the four factors they named as "good things" about their jobs were (1) interesting and exciting work, (2) opportunities to learn things, (3) freedom, and (4) variety of work.

On the negative side the three "bad things" they most often mentioned were (1) too much fluctuation in work load; (2) poorly defined channels for getting things done, underorganization; and (3) poor physical facilities (lack of air-conditioning, limited cafeteria hours).

The most frequent comments of engineers about relations with their managers were (1) sets target, then leaves you alone; (2) helps you if you need it; (3) is very sharp; (4) will stand behind you; and (5) is too busy. Working conditions, salary, and benefits were all seen as satisfactory. Some engineers felt they got adequate feedback on their work, but others thought that it was hard to get negative feedback and that it was often too roundabout.

Looking at these results, it is clear that Ken's style of giving freedom and expecting high levels of personal responsibility was working effectively in the engineering organization. The taking of personal responsibility was also illustrated in how the groups dealt with upward feedback. In all surveys of this sort, it is inevitable that much will be said about the immediate boss in the form of both commendations and complaints. These comments are typically passed on to the boss by the consultant, with often disastrous results in that the boss is not ready for this kind of feedback. Yet if the consultant sanitizes the data, the boss cannot learn how to improve his or her relationship with the subordinates.

In the group meetings I typically gave the group members all the data that they had provided in unedited form, with the task of the group being to decide what to tell the boss, how to tell it, and who should tell it. What I observed in these meetings was striking: the group members would first have a kind of catharsis sharing all the bad things about their boss; they would then gradually recognize that telling the boss all of this stuff would not really help matters. They typically displayed great insight and empathy in terms of why the boss acted as he or she did and then made considered decisions on which matters should be brought up to the boss and by whom. The group members became aware that it was not just a matter of dumping data onto the boss but that the data could be used to build a better relationship.

OTHER SURVEY RESULTS

A similar survey conducted in the product line organizations revealed similar results: (1) the work itself was challenging, interesting, and taxing, and it used talents and energy to the hilt; (2) relationships with management were good, being characterized by openness of communication, trust, and high respect for managers' technical abilities; (3) relationships among the product lines and with the service groups were good, being characterized by free communication among the engineers, use of one another's talents, and willingness to help one another to solve problems.

Problems that were identified could be predicted from the high growth rate combined with Olsen's style of frugality. Services such as drafting and model shops were of high quality but of insufficient quantity, forcing all kinds of political games to get one's job done. Job definitions were vague, which was considered both an asset and a liability. Performance feedback was scarce; hence, many people did not know where they stood. Communication with sales and engineering needed to be improved at two levels: sales should stop selling products before they were designed, and field service should give better feedback to engineering on problems discovered in the field.

Of greatest interest in these surveys were the findings on how employees perceived Ken Olsen. Everyone respected Ken's overall ability, business judgment, and general leadership. He was seen as absolutely indispensable to the company, and most people respected his technical ability, but there were differences of opinion about which areas Ken really understood and which areas he didn't understand as well as some engineers.

Almost everyone welcomed Ken's help on technical problems, provided the help was helpful, that is, well timed and sensitive to feedback. If it was not well timed or sensitive to feedback, a variety of responses occurred. Some people ignored the help; some people pushed back; and some people just accepted what Ken wanted even though they disagreed or saw no advantage to what he was offering. The worst problems arose around half-finished projects that were redirected by Ken, causing not only loss of time but also resentment that he did not respect his employees more.

Ken's emotional outbursts and criticisms of his subordinates in front of others created some resentment, but most people felt that he was an excellent judge of people's abilities and built his organization around what certain people could or could not do. It was recognized that he was exceedingly ethical, moral, and concerned about his people, and was always trying to do his best for them, often to the point of doing too much.

Surveys of this sort were also conducted in the manufacturing organization, with similar results. Although they were called "surveys," they were in fact direct interventions into the organization to help employees identify and solve their own problems, and this is exactly what Ken Olsen intended. By treating them as interventions, not just as gathering data, Ken communicated once again that he expected people to be smart, to figure out what was going on, to identify problems as they arose, and, most important, to fix their own problems as they recognized them.

This interventionist attitude on Ken's part not only influenced how DEC worked but also influenced my own understanding of how the technology of surveying employees could and should work. Because any kind of surveying of employee feelings and attitudes influences those feelings and attitudes in unknown ways, it is important to design the feedback process in such a way that the organization benefits. I learned that such benefits do not come from giving top management the data first but from involving the employees immediately in the processing of their own data and then cascading only relevant data upward into the higher management levels.

IMPLICATIONS AND LESSONS

Several things can be said about the DEC of 1966–67 based on these surveys.

1. It was already clear in 1966 that a model that was ideal for growth could run into difficulty with continued growth. In particular, as the organization became more differentiated and as individual managers learned how to manage their own units, the need for a centralizing vision or strategy became greater and greater yet remained largely implicit, invisible, or perpetually changing. It was also evident that the implicit assumptions around the role of engineering, marketing, and sales were becoming more ambiguous, and there were no good mechanisms in place to define these roles and communicate the definitions to the troops. "Do the right thing" and "Define your own job" continued to be a license for each group to do what it thought was best, and of course that meant best not only for DEC but also for that group itself. "Taking responsibility" began to mean being responsible for one's own employees as well.

2. Because Ken Olsen remained true to his original mandate of wanting the problems that were identified to be fixed locally rather than getting himself involved with the data on what the problems were, he trained his subordinates to become self-reliant. Olsen's attitude was, in my experience, quite remarkable, since most CEOs who launch surveys are anxious to see the data, even though most of those data will neither concern them nor pertain to issues that they can do anything about. By not getting involved with the data, Ken signaled clearly to people in the organization that it was their responsibility to identify problems and fix things. Ken remained aloof from the

whole process and only occasionally would involve himself deeply, usually in a problem that he himself had identified. He wanted others to identify problems and fix them even at the level of his own immediate subordinates. He did not want to see lists of what those problems were and did not particularly solicit feedback on his own style. His style could best be characterized as "helicopter hovering," with occasional landings and then deep involvement.

3. Paradoxically, DEC in the first decade or so was an organization driven more by a "management philosophy" vision than by a technical or strategic vision. Olsen had a very clear idea of how he wanted his organization to work and allowed great freedom to the technical organization to develop products that made sense to them so long as those products fitted his own broader vision of interactive computing. Of course the kinds of engineers that were hired and the success of the early minicomputers and interactive computing reinforced the implicit technical vision of interconnected minicomputers as the long-range strategic answer for the company. But almost more striking was the degree of innovation that occurred in manufacturing, in sales, in service, in human resource programs, and in community relations. Everyone in DEC, at all levels, felt empowered to try new things if they made sense.

part two

The Streams Diverge, Causing an Organizational Midlife Crisis

Part I focused on the creation of a certain kind of culture. In part II, we focus on the impact of that culture as DEC the organization grew and evolved and as the technological context and markets evolved. In its first decade or so the technological context, the organizational structure and process, and the culture were synchronized, creating a powerful engine for innovation. On the technological side Gordon Bell and the engineering organization he created kept inventing and developing new products that the science and engineering market gobbled up eagerly. DEC had created what came to be called the "minicomputer revolution." The term *mini* is attributed by many to John Leng, one of DEC's product line managers who was working in London at the time when the miniskirt came into vogue. DEC had not only created a computer revolution but it also continued to spawn incredible products: the VAX family of computers, DECnet, local-area networking through Ethernet, DECmate, DECtalk, AltaVista, Aquarius (the VAX 9000), the Alpha chip, and countless other products, many of which won prizes.

Organizationally, Ken Olsen had evolved a complex mix of functional and product line organization that worked well all the way into the 1980s. And, as the previous chapters showed, Olsen's personal style and management philosophy created a culture of innovation that empowered people throughout DEC to think for themselves and "Do the right thing." This culture created striking innovations in management and community relations: the Springfield, Roxbury, and Enfield plants that led the way in affirmative action and new production systems; customer support centers and other innovative sales techniques; enterprise integration services that offered complete systems consultation to large customers; and the early use of matrix management and the effort to make that work on a large scale with the New Management System and other new approaches to how corporations could conduct themselves vis-à-vis customers, stakeholders, and the community. Many of the managerial innovations were ahead of their time in that they foreshadowed how knowledge-based learning organizations would ultimately have to organize themselves. Numerous DEC alumni successfully took such innovations into their post-DEC jobs and became leaders in their new organizations.

By any criterion that one might choose, DEC in its first thirty years was successful as an organization. The company went public in 1966 and by 1972 had sales of $188 million, with 7,800 employees scattered throughout the world. Through the 1980s DEC continued to grow. As we will see in the next several chapters, this growth was not without turmoil, but by 1987 DEC had reached the position of the number two computer company in the world with over $10 billion in sales and a stock price that peaked at 199 in 1987. Ken Olsen had been named by *Fortune* as Entrepreneur of the Century in 1986, and DEC had been named the Eighth Most Successful U.S. Company by *Business Week* in 1987. The basis of this success was synergy between the technological, organizational, and cultural streams.

DEC's economic bubble burst in the 1988–92 period with two years of losses, product failures, growing organizational turmoil, and, in 1992, Ken Olsen's resignation. The board promoted Robert Palmer to take over and bring DEC back to profitability. Palmer attempted to do this by selling off many of DEC's units and imposing a new and more disciplined business model, one that was experienced by most DEC managers and employees as a big "change in the culture." DEC was brought back to profitability, but from most points of view, only to make it attractive as an acquisition, resulting in the purchase of DEC by the Compaq Corporation in 1998.

This midlife crisis and its ultimate result will be examined in the next several chapters from different points of view, in particular from the point of view of the three developmental streams—technology, organization, and culture. As we will see, DEC's growth, peak achievement, and ultimate demise can be explained in part by the divergence of these streams during the 1980s. In particular, we need to understand:

1. How technological and market changes required new organizational and managerial responses

2. How organizational success produced growth, and how both growth and aging created some visible and some invisible consequences that required new managerial responses

3. How the culture that resulted from earlier successes became more and more stable

4. How elements of that culture became dysfunctional as the organization's technological and economic environment changed

We begin in chapter 9 with an analysis of the evolution of the technology stream by Paul Kampas. Chapter 10 analyzes the organizational impact of success, rapid growth, and aging. In chapter 11 we refocus on the culture and show how some elements of that culture became so rigid that it became difficult for DEC to learn and adapt to the technology changes that were occurring. In other words, what Kampas shows us very clearly is *what* happened, and in chapters 10, 11, 12, and 13 we endeavor to explain *why* it happened, what the underlying causes of DEC's inability to adapt to the changing technological and market environment were, and how DEC came to its end as an economic entity.

nine

The Impact
of Changing Technology

Paul Kampas

During DEC's forty-year history the technology of information processing and computing changed dramatically. Some of these changes were the direct result of DEC's own innovative products, some of them were the result of competition that DEC stimulated, and some of them were simply a product of the times. As a result, DEC in its midlife was operating not only in a different technological environment and market but at the same time the organization was growing and the products themselves were becoming more complex.

THE TECHNOLOGY STREAM AND ITS DYNAMICS

The computer revolution is the technology wave that transformed processing power from scarcity to abundance. Because processing is the "engine" of an information system, it was a very important advancement and one to which DEC made a great contribution.

Perhaps the first notable automated information processing device was Herman Hollerith's tabulating machine, invented in 1890 expressly for the purpose of processing the information gathered in the U.S. census of that year. Though this electromechanical machine did no computing, it stored and sorted records using eighty-column per-forated cards. Based on this technology, Hollerith formed the Tabu-lating Machine Company in 1896. Thomas Watson, who had been a salesman for the National Cash Register Company, became president of this company in 1914 and changed its name to International Business Machines in 1924.

The initial stored-program computers developed in the early 1940s were unreliable behemoths, made first from relays and later from vacuum tubes. They had very limited storage capacity and were extremely difficult to program. The first actual computer company was formed in 1946 by the designers of the University of Pennsyl-vania's ENIAC, J. Presper Eckert and John Mauchly. The company, called the Electronic Control Company, set out to build the Universal Automatic Computer, or UNIVAC. The UNIVAC I shipped in 1951 and was installed (as was Hollerith's first machine) at the U.S. Census Bureau. This event initiates the emergence of the commercial com-puter revolution.

Products designed to meet a specific need often develop through a series of paradigms, where a newer, improved approach and model augments or replaces an older approach. For example, in recorded audio, early grooved cylinders were replaced by vinyl records, which were in turn replaced by optical disks. In television, analog black and white TVs were replaced by analog color TVs, which will soon be re-placed by digital, high-definition color TVs.

The computer revolution developed in three distinct styles, or paradigms, of computing (figure 9.1). These paradigms differ primar-ily in how the computer and user interact with each other. As hard-ware became smaller, cheaper, and more reliable, the computer and the user could become more closely connected. However, these styles or paradigms influenced not only who used the computers and how they used them but also how and by whom they were purchased, financed (bought or leased), managed, and serviced.

Paradigm 1. Batch computing: In the first paradigm, batch com-puting, the user was forced to adapt to the computer. Here, users

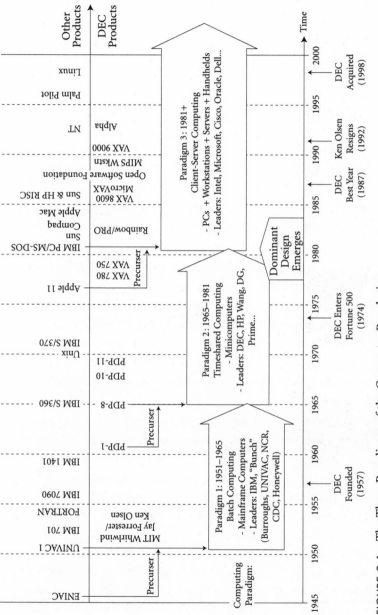

FIGURE 9.1. The Three Paradigms of the Computer Revolution

submitted jobs on punch cards or magnetic tape to an operator
and waited for their results to be returned hours or days later. If
mistakes were found upon evaluating the results, jobs were resub-
mitted with changes. Batch computers were typically large (that
is, mainframes), expensive, often leased rather than purchased at
the corporate or divisional level, and kept in climate-controlled,
secure "glass rooms" with raised floors for running cables underneath. Early computer rooms often had floor-to-ceiling glass
windows so they could be showcased to the public as a symbol
of the firm's advanced capabilities. Leading manufacturers of
batch computers were IBM and the "BUNCH" (Burroughs,
UNIVAC, NCR, Control Data, and Honeywell).

Paradigm 2. Time-shared computing: In the second paradigm,
users had direct connections to a shared computer via terminals.
Each user was allocated a slice of time every second. If the computer wasn't too heavily loaded, responses would be fast, and
users would have minimal wait-time between their actions.
Though some time-sharing was done on mainframes, it was
more common on minicomputers. Minicomputers were
medium-sized computers that were usually purchased and
managed at the divisional or departmental level. Many did
not need special facilities and could be installed and run in
the back room.

Paradigm 3. Client-server computing: In the third paradigm,
inexpensive client computers (personal computers [PCs] or
workstations) were networked with larger servers where shared
data and applications resided. Inexpensive and fast networking,
a key enabler of this paradigm, became available in the early to
mid-1980s. The dedicated client computers allowed users a rich
graphical user interface and speedy response time, while the
server allowed easy communication and collaboration. The introduction of the World Wide Web and Web browser in 1993 further
enhanced this approach. The PCs or workstations were located,
of course, on the user's desk, while the servers could be located
anywhere, from the back room to the data center. As PC hardware
and operating systems became faster and more sophisticated,
they were also used as servers.

DEC GROWS FROM A COMPUTER COMPANY TO
A FULL-SOLUTION VENDOR

Information technology systems and networks are composed of many hardware and software layers that all must work together in an effective manner for the whole system to function properly. Through both of the first and second computing paradigms (1951 to 1981 in total), large computer vendors such as IBM and DEC individually provided users a proprietary "department store" of interoperable hardware and software products. These product sets typically included computers, disks, tapes, terminals, printers, operating systems, programming languages, database management software, communications hardware and software, and some applications software.

When DEC created the interactive minicomputer wave in the early 1960s, very few peripheral devices suitable for systems of that size existed. And almost no software was available for interactively programming and debugging applications for such computers. So it became necessary for DEC to begin to develop such products. IBM and others had followed much the same path in the early 1950s when they embarked on building mainframe computers. But with mainframes selling typically for over $1 million and DEC's minis selling typically for under $100,000, a huge gap existed between the two.

In addition to the need for such products at that time, DEC's culture from the beginning was one of "we can do it better than others." By hiring the best and brightest from MIT and Lincoln Labs in an era when not a lot of off-the-shelf parts existed, DEC engineers were accustomed to inventing solutions to problems and were never timid about taking on such challenges. Starting with DECtape in 1962, a personal mass storage device that was the forerunner of the floppy disk, DEC started down the road of expanding into just about every significant peripheral device and layered software (software that sits above the operating system software) arena that existed (see figure 9.2). In some of these arenas, DEC became the industry leader:

Video Terminals. DEC's VT-100 became the industry-standard video terminal.

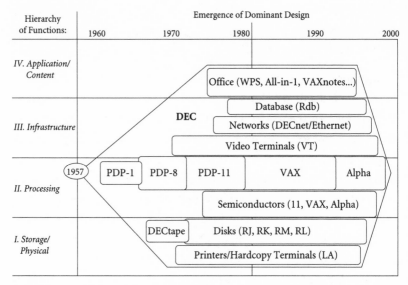

FIGURE 9.2.   The Development of DEC into a Full-Solution Company by the Mid-1970s

Hardcopy Terminals. DEC's LA-36 matrix printing terminal was extremely popular.

DECnet. DEC's peer-to-peer networking capabilities were the envy of the industry.

Office Software. DEC was the leader in departmental office automation, including All-in-1 electronic mail, WPS word processing, and VAXnotes.

By 1980, DEC offered a competitive department store of compatible VAX computers, peripherals, and layered software products. But the industry was already beginning to change.

THE ANATOMY OF A TECHNOLOGY WAVE

Technology waves have two distinct stages: the *creation stage* and the *commodification stage* (see figure 9.3). In analyzing the successes and failures of information technology (IT) producers, understanding the

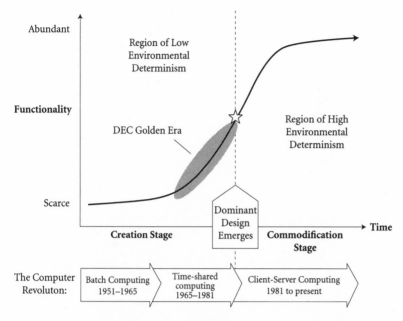

FIGURE 9.3. Anatomy of a Technology Wave

differences between these two stages is critical to understanding the shifts in competition and competencies and how success in the creation stage can breed failure in the commodification stage. The transition point between the stages is the emergence of a *dominant design*, which is a set of characteristics that win overwhelming approval in the marketplace (Utterback 1994).

The creation stage is a period of product scarcity, giving vendors the upper hand because the market is hungry for enhanced functionality and performance. Market success is primarily based on product innovation stemming from proprietary invention. Since the products are typically expensive, somewhat unreliable, and difficult to install and operate, the most active customers are often the sophisticated early adopters who are willing put up with these challenges in order to get leading-edge capabilities. As products become successful in the creation stage, human factors innovation gains importance to reduce "bleeding edge" hassles and expand the range of qualified users.

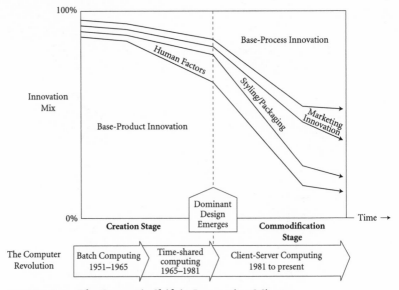

FIGURE 9.4. The Dramatic Shift in Innovation Mix as a
Technology Matures

Sooner or later, based on the rate of technology and design progress, a highly satisfactory approach emerges in the form of a dominant design. Once a dominant design has emerged, the importance of
product innovation begins to diminish. The market has found an approach it likes, and buyers don't want major changes made.

The second stage, or commodification stage, begins here. In this
stage, product functionality and performance become abundant, and
vendor differentiation diminishes. This gives the buyers the upper
hand. Here, process innovation becomes more important, helping to
increase reliability, enhance ease of use, improve quality, and reduce
cost. With these problems being addressed, the product begins to
move into the large mainstream market. To battle diminishing
product differentiation, vendors begin to use styling/packaging and
marketing innovation (for example, branding) to attempt to slow
commodification and loss of customer loyalty (see figure 9.4).

The degree to which the market drives the vendors versus the vendors driving the market is sometimes called the level of *environmental determinism.* Environmental determinism is typically low before

the dominant design emerges (vendors having the upper hand) and high afterward (buyers having the upper hand).

In the computer revolution, the emergence of industry-standard PCs networked in a client-server style of computing signified the emergence of the dominant computer design. This event had a huge impact on DEC, which had been highly successful in, and optimized for, the creation stage.

By the mid-1980s it was becoming clear that the DEC strategy, heavily shaped by its inwardly focused culture, was beginning to become disconnected from the evolving industry. Third-party software and semiconductors were beginning to surpass computer systems as the dominant strategic force, and DEC's disdain for both mass-market personal computers and nonproprietary or non-DEC standards (for example, UNIX) eventually became barriers and blocked the company from taking advantage of the next big wave and the growing commodity market for PCs.

THE EMERGENCE OF CATEGORY KILLERS

Multiple "disruptive technologies" were emerging by the mid- to late 1970s that began to usher in the new computing paradigm of client-server architecture and low-cost PCs and workstations (Utterback 1994; Christensen 1997). Spreadsheet programs such as VisiCalc increased the usefulness of the desktop PC, and DEC's advantage in networking was somewhat eroded by the competition from groupware such as Lotus Notes. The disruptive technologies included low-cost third-party microprocessors (from Intel and Motorola), high-performance RISC architecture desktop workstations (from Sun and HP), third-party operating systems (MS-DOS from Microsoft and UNIX from AT&T), and third-party networks (from 3Com, Cisco, and Novell).

As the market for computers grew rapidly in the 1960s and 1970s, and as technologies matured, a new breed of competitor began to emerge: the category killer. *Category killers* are vendors who specialize in one or a few very closely related product categories. They are

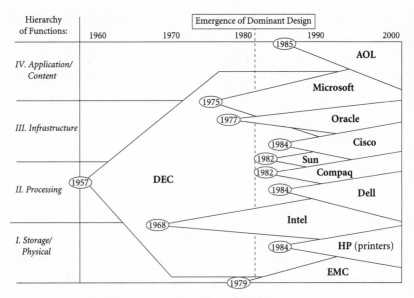

FIGURE 9.5. The Emergence of the Category Killers

highly focused on developing a culture, a set of competencies, and a business model that are optimized for a particular task (see figure 9.5). And since their products are typically based on standards (de jure or de facto) or are portable and run on different computer systems, customers can mix and match products from different vendors and no longer be beholden to a single, powerful department store computer vendor.

Many of the category killers came into power around the time of the dominant design in 1981. Some were founded earlier and catalyzed its emergence (that is, Intel and Microsoft), while others came into existence shortly after 1981 and fueled the era of client-server computing (the third computing paradigm).

THE IMPACT ON DEC

The emergence of the category killers created a huge competitive challenge to DEC. The two biggest competitive issues were cost and openness.

Cost. DEC was never a low-cost vendor, even during its prime. In that era, even when minicomputer competition heated up, the early adopters were willing to pay more for DEC because they got more. And DEC's phenomenal growth rate was hiding all kinds of financial sins. Once the dominant design emerged, however, IT began to commodify, mainstream adopters didn't care about sophisticated capabilities, and the category killers were leaner and meaner. DEC was in big trouble. To keep its hardware prices even barely competitive, it kept raising its prices for VMS and services. Loyal, captive VMS customers howled about the prices DEC was charging compared to UNIX.

Openness. DEC VMS ran only on DEC VAX computers. Microsoft's Windows operating system runs on any clone PC from Dell, Compaq, IBM, Gateway, and so forth. Microsoft's NT operating system, UNIX, and Linux are capable of running on any computer architecture. DEC's Rdb software ran only on VAX. Oracle's relational database software runs on many different computer systems. When customers bought from the DEC department store, they had to make a huge commitment to one vendor. Perhaps even more important, third-party software vendors were much more eager to write their applications for high-volume standard operating systems than for lower volume single-vendor operating systems. And where the applications go, the customers are soon to follow.

THE IMPACT OF PARADIGM SHIFTS

To better understand the broad scope of a paradigm's influence, it is useful to identify both a paradigm's key elements and the important shifts that occurred between paradigms in implementing these elements. In table 9.1 nine distinguishing elements are listed and characterized regarding how they were implemented for each of the three paradigms. (Please note that elements which changed significantly in a shift are denoted with asterisks.) Some very important implications for DEC's fate can be identified by analyzing these shifts.

The shift from the second to the third paradigms was massive. The

TABLE 9.1 Characteristics of the Three Paradigms and the Shifts between Them

Paradigm Elements	Paradigm 1: 1951–65 Batch (IBM, "Bunch")	Paradigm 2: 1965–81 Time-sharing (DEC, HP, DG . . .)	Paradigm 3: 1981–Today Client-Server (Intel, Sun, HP, IBM . . .)
A. *Systems and Storage*			
1. Processor	Proprietary, CISC	Proprietary, CISC	* Third-party, RISC
B. *Infrastructure*			
2. Operating System	Proprietary	Proprietary	* Third-party
3. User Interface	Punch cards, printout	* Terminal	* PC or workstation
4. Networking	Proprietary	Proprietary	* Third-party, open standards
C. *Applications*			
5. Office	Proprietary	Proprietary	* Third-party
6. Other Applications	Customer-written	Customer-written and some third-party	* Mostly third-party
D. *Other*			
7. User Influence	Low	* Medium	* High
8. Installation/ Service	Skilled technicians	Skilled technicians	* Self-service for PCs; skilled technicians for server
9. Price/Cost Structure	High	* Medium	* Low
Element shifts from previous paradigm	N/A	3 of 9	9 of 9

Note: Elements that changed significantly in a shift are denoted with an asterisk.

number of elements that changed *significantly* was much higher in the shift from the second paradigm to the third paradigm (nine out of nine) than in the shift from the first to the second paradigm (three out of nine). As it is always harder for leaders to cannibalize their own business than that of a follower in a paradigm shift, this created an enormous challenge for DEC to change when the third paradigm emerged. In addition, time-sharing augmented batch computing to a large degree in the first shift, whereas client-server computing was a direct substitution for time-sharing in the second. A lot of computing today is still batch, database-oriented computing, residing in back-office systems. On the other hand, personal computers and workstations have all but eradicated terminals and time-sharing.

Virtually all of DEC's product competitive advantages were undermined in this shift. In this table elements 1 through 5 were DEC competitive advantages. Each one of these advantages was very negatively impacted in the shift to the third paradigm:

- *Processor and operating system products* (elements 1 and 2): The advent of third-party microprocessors (for example, Motorola M68000, Intel 8086) and operating systems (for example, CP/M, MS-DOS, UNIX) greatly lowered the barriers to entry into the computer business, virtually destroying DEC's design advantage in these areas. And not only were these third-party offerings sold in high volume at a low price, they attracted thousands of application developers, who created tens of thousands of off-the-shelf application programs for them, which were very attractive to buyers.

- *Time-sharing, terminals, and command line user interface products* (element 3): Personal computers running a graphical user interface virtually eliminated the market for a time-sharing operating system, terminals, and command line interfaces (for example, DEC's VMS time-sharing capabilities, DEC's VT terminals, and DEC Command Language [DCL]), all being DEC advantages. Losing the desktop to Microsoft and Intel resulted in a huge reduction in competitive power. Microsoft has wielded the power of the desktop to great advantage, so great the U.S. courts have proclaimed them anticompetitive in recent antitrust actions.

- *Networking products* (element 4): DEC, which had excellent networking, was late in moving from an OSI (Open Systems Interconnect) standards strategy to a TCP/IP (Transmission Control Protocol/Internet Protocol) strategy, and was unwilling to spin off the network group so it could develop a new business model and platform independence that was necessary to compete with category killers such as 3Com and Cisco.

- *Office software products* (element 5): Client-server office software for networked personal computers (for example, Microsoft Office, Lotus 1-2-3, and Lotus Notes) virtually eliminated the market for DEC's proprietary terminal- and time-sharing-based office software (for example, WPS, All-in-1, VAXnotes). In addition, client application software needed to be user-installable, a capability that DEC software sorely lacked.

In summary, the latter part of the computer revolution dramatically changed the IT competitive landscape in the shift from time-sharing to client-server computing. This shift made computers small, cheap, easily interconnectable, and mass marketable. DEC was poorly situated to exploit this shift.

THE RESULT

By the end of the 1980s, DEC was losing tremendous amounts of business to Sun, Intel, Compaq, Dell, Microsoft, Oracle, and others. When Palmer took over DEC in 1992, he began systematically selling off DEC's noncore businesses, trying to stem the bleeding. He sold the disk business to Quantum, the video terminal business to Boundless, the database business to Oracle, the networking business to Cabletron, and the semiconductor fabrication business to Intel. And, of course, he finally sold off the computer business to Compaq in 1998.

Today, the category-killer model has flourished. Many of these category killers have grown into large and powerful players. As of

October 2001, AOL (now merged with Time-Warner) is an $8 billion (in annual sales) business, Microsoft is a $25 billion company, Oracle is a $9 billion company, Cisco is a $22 billion company, Sun is an $18 billion company, Compaq is a $30 billion company, Dell is a $32 billion company, Intel is a $34 billion company, HP (imaging only) is $22 billion business, and EMC is a $10 billion company. Collectively, these companies total $210 billion in annual revenues. Just for comparison, DEC was, at its peak, about a $14 billion company.

ten

The Impact of Success, Growth, and Age

DEC's growth, innovative capacity, and ultimately its economic difficulties all resulted from the interaction of the technology, the organization, and the culture. In chapter 9 Paul Kampas analyzed how the evolution of the technology stream created particular transition difficulties for the company. In this chapter I want to highlight how those difficulties were compounded, even created to some degree, by DEC's incredible success and subsequent rapid growth. Growth is generally regarded as a desirable condition. But as we will see in this chapter, an organization that lacks the money gene, an organization that is growing on the strength of its technical vision, in this case the minicomputer, develops particular difficulties as it grows and ages. Continued technical success and positive feedback from some segments of the customer population strengthen certain core elements of the culture, as we will see in chapter 11, but growth and age *inevitably* erode other core elements of the culture. I say *inevitably* because the phenomena that will be discussed in this chapter characterize all organizations. How DEC dealt with them is a unique product of its own culture, but the issues DEC had to face are general results of growth and age.

STAGE 1: DEC AS A YOUNG, SMALL, COHESIVE FAMILY

DEC was initially organized by business function, but in 1964 it migrated to product line managers who were "matrixed" with still-centralized functions of sales, service, manufacturing, and finance. The company began to expand internationally in 1963–64, with offices in Canada, Europe, and Australia. By 1968 there were fifty sales and service offices located in eleven countries. European and Japanese headquarters were opened in 1968–69. Harlan Anderson, DEC's cofounder, left in 1966, and Ken Olsen consolidated his founder-CEO position.

As DEC grew, it became obvious to Ken Olsen and the founding group that they would need more experienced managers than could be grown internally and that they would need managers who had worked in larger organizations. A number of such managers were hired, and all of them were destined to become key players in DEC's evolution.

- In the first significant hire of an outside manager, Peter Kaufmann was hired from Beckman Instruments in 1966 to manage manufacturing.
- Ed Kramer joined DEC in 1967 from Sylvania, bringing both technical and marketing skills.
- Jean-Claude Peterschmitt was hired in 1967 to head European operations and led that group until 1987.
- Pier Carlo Falotti was hired in 1969 and managed European operations from 1987 until 1992.
- Andy Knowles was hired from RCA in 1969 to bring in a large-company marketing perspective.
- Julius Marcus, Roger Cady, Irwin Jacobs, and others were hired from General Electric, Honeywell, and other older, larger, and more established companies.

Even with all this new blood, the feel of the organization in the 1960s and early 1970s was still that of a small family tied together by a strong father figure. In 1969 the senior management group, the

Operations Committee, consisted of Ken Olsen, three group vice presidents who managed the product line managers, and the vice presidents of sales, manufacturing, engineering, and finance. The service function under Jack Shields was part of the sales organization. Personnel and other corporate functions were not represented in this top group. The Operations Committee with Ken Olsen as its leader was clearly the main point of integration as the organization grew and became more differentiated.

But the way DEC worked was paradoxical. On the one hand, senior management required a great deal of detail in what was brought to the Operations Committee. On the other hand, both functional and product line managers had enormous freedom in running their own operations. Once a plan had been approved, the manager was expected to execute responsibly, and if schedules or budgets were not going to be met, to report this immediately to the Operations Committee so that remedial action could be taken and the plans renegotiated. To meet their business plans, the product line managers had to fight with one another for time and attention from the sales and manufacturing organizations that often thought they knew better where effort should be allocated (the matrix). The heavy emphasis on taking personal responsibility and "Doing the right thing" created the necessity to engage in negotiations with multiple parties on whom the product line managers were dependent. Central services such as drafting and the model shop were in short supply, so whoever needed them had to negotiate for time. Product line managers were in perpetual negotiation with sales to ensure that their products were getting the appropriate amount of sales attention, and product developers were in constant negotiation with software and manufacturing.

Perhaps most important at this stage was the commitment to open communications and problem solving rather than assigning blame, withholding information, or outright lying. Problems encountered were considered to be normal events, and problems denied or brushed under the rug or deliberately concealed were sins to be severely punished. Telling the truth was not merely a pragmatic issue but a moral issue. Since everybody knew everybody else, negotiations were intense and often full of conflict, but everyone accepted the system as the best way to resolve complex issues. The fact that budgets and schedules might not be met was considered normal and did not matter because the level of growth and the success of products remained high.

The role of the Operations Committee was evolving erratically. On the one hand, it clearly fulfilled the function of integrating the product line plans at the corporate level. On the other hand, the value of "Doing the right thing" led individual members to continue to compete as individuals and to be conflicted about the need, at the same time, to protect their own organizations. Ted Johnson in sales and Peter Kaufmann in manufacturing built walls around their organizations. The vice president of finance, Harry Mann, continued in the impossible role of being both a teacher and a policeman while sensing all along that his function was viewed as a necessary service, not integral to running the business (Mann died in 1974 and was replaced first by Brewster Kopp, then Al Bertocci, and finally Jim Osterhoff).

Many managers felt that coming to the Operations Committee to make proposals, get approvals, or have projects reviewed was a painful process because of the relatively undisciplined group process in the meetings. One might be asked anything, be shouted at by Olsen, or never get onto the agenda at all because some other topic had captured the group's attention. The committee did not demand clear, well designed presentations, which meant that basic facts were often difficult to determine. In fact, one of the most surprising things to me over the years was that overheads done in ordinary type size, filled with large numbers of figures, and often full of typos were tolerated well into the 1980s, even as everyone lamented how illegible they were and agreed that "we ought to learn how make better presentations." I saw this as another element of the engineering culture—presentation and interaction skills are not high-priority competencies to be an effective technical contributor or manager.

Ultimate approval or disapproval of the proposal might have little to do with the information presented and more to do with the outcome of the verbal debate that the proposal sparked. Verbal skills were very important in this environment and, as will be seen, in later years created increasing cynicism about the culture, as those skills came to be seen as more important than actual technical competence. On the other hand, the lack of formality and discipline in the meetings reinforced the climate of innovation and creativity that everyone loved. Results was what counted—good products loved by the customers—not living by arbitrary formal procedures. And Gordon Bell's presence in the meetings provided some technical leadership and integration if the debate did not resolve itself. His track record gave him credibility, even though during the debate he was often less articulate than others in the meeting.

The Critical Role of Functional Familiarity

What allowed all of this to succeed was the small size of the total organization and the high level of *functional familiarity* brought about by early success and the open culture previously described. In particular the open disdain for formal hierarchy and the commitment to open communications made it possible for all of these negotiations to be conducted in a helpful familial way. *Functional familiarity* meant that people knew one another well enough from past experience of working together to know how to work together, to know how to "calibrate" one another, and to be able to predict to some degree what others would do.

Functional familiarity does not necessarily mean that people like or trust one another. But it does mean that people understand one another and have enough shared experience together to know how to deal with one another. Trust implies that "the other" will not only not take advantage of me but will actively use his or her skills to my advantage. In a trusting relationship I can make myself vulnerable to the other person. And many of the relationships I observed at DEC were mutually trusting as well as high in functional familiarity. But in many other relationships it was enough to have functional familiarity, which meant that people knew whom to trust and how much, who could be counted on, who told you exactly what you wanted to know, who played politics, and so on. The point is, if you are functionally familiar with other people, you can compensate for their traits because you know what they mean and what they will do. If you are stuck on a project team with someone whom you don't trust, if you are functionally familiar with him or her, you know what additional things you have to do to ensure that your own needs will be met.

The importance of this concept became clear to me on one occasion when I observed a hardware engineer asking his software counterpart in another part of engineering whether the software would be ready in six months for a product that was to be launched at that time. The software engineer said, "Sure." As I was talking to the hardware engineer, I had occasion to ask him what was meant by "sure," and he told me that he figured the product would be three months late, because he knew exactly how his software colleague worked and what his words meant. I had occasion to observe a similar conversation ten years later when DEC had become a much larger differentiated company. I was told by the hardware engineer at that time that he didn't have a clue what a verbal assurance of "sure" meant, so he would have to follow up, get it in writing, and check with more senior software managers; in this case "sure" might have meant anything from on-time delivery to "it depends on what else comes in over the next couple of months" to "I'll do yours when everything else is done."

In a family that lives and works together, functional familiarity is pretty high. DEC was such a "family" in its first decade or so. The "children" might fight, get mad at one another, and be envious, but they were all part of one "family" that knew how to get along and get things done, because they knew they could depend on one another, could predict one another's behavior, and had a strong father figure in Ken Olsen. DEC managers knew from experience what to expect of one another and therefore were able to adjust for whatever contingencies might arise. If the software group was unreliable, the hardware engineer could develop backup plans to ensure that his schedule would be met.

Functional familiarity is crucial in understanding the importance of "Getting buy-in" versus merely reaching consensus. One can have consensus with low functional familiarity and then be surprised that things are not implemented as well as group members expected. A group can reach consensus in that no one will sabotage the decision, but some members may go along passively and fail to help when their help is needed. DEC's concept of *buy-in* meant actively agreeing that a given course of action was the correct way to go and therefore working to make it happen. That type of agreement required higher levels of functional familiarity. With growth it potentially gets harder and harder to calibrate whether you have consensus or active buy-in, because, with growing numbers of people and physical dispersion, functional familiarity begins to be lost. In later years people complained of the "DEC nod," which meant surface concurrence but lack of buy-in, thus making it hard to figure out how to operate.

DEC's first fifteen years proved to Ken Olsen and his managers that having a technical vision and organizing to maximize freedom and responsibility could create a viable and profitable business. The assumption that profits would result if you build good products and work with your customers was affirmed, making it unnecessary to worry about the more traditional business problems of marketing and cost control. The environment was turbulent, but functional familiarity was high enough to guarantee that the debate would lead to good decisions and continuing innovation.

STAGE 2. WITH SUCCESS AND GROWTH, DEC BECOMES A "COAT OF MANY COLORS"

The most striking aspect of the 1970s and 1980s was the growth of the organization from a small "extended family" to a large differentiated system consisting of many subsystems, loosely tied together by a culture and Ken Olsen's leadership. The sense of rapid, disjointed growth was felt inside the organization as controlled chaos—a wild ride fueled by one successful product after another and the sense that no matter how chaotic it felt, DEC could do no wrong. In 1977 DEC broke the $1 billion mark in sales and employed 36,000 people worldwide. By 1982 sales were $4 billion and the workforce had reached 67,000. In 1984 sales reached $5.6 billion, and the company maintained 660 offices in 47 countries, with 85,600 employees (Pearson 1992). By 1991 sales were $14 billion, and the workforce was 121,000.

DEC in 1980 was spread across nineteen buildings around Maynard and had created a fleet of helicopters and bus shuttles to facilitate easy contact and communication. DEC's egalitarian values were affirmed in its policy that even senior executives could not bump secretaries who had reserved a seat on a helicopter flight. The average age of the members of the Operations Committee in 1980 was 49, with a range of 40–55, and their immediate subordinates averaged 43, with a range of 34–55. It was still a young company but was rapidly maturing, both in age and experience.

Ken Olsen was pleased with the 30 to 40 percent growth rate at the time (though he was also worried about it) and was glad to have survived a recession in the early 1970s. He maintained his style of neutrality and devil's advocate stance, but his occasional emotional outbursts made it clear where his deeper values lay. DEC was running some thirty or more product lines with a structure focused primarily on products and secondarily on applications and markets, while engineering, manufacturing, sales, service, finance, and other corporate functions remained centralized. Fifty percent or more of sales were in Europe and the rest of the non-U.S. world, called "General International." Midlevel coordination was achieved through various committees and internal boards that met frequently to compensate for the growing physical distance between units. Product line managers were both independent and interdependent, tied together by their commitment to DEC's culture of freedom, openness, truth, and personal responsibility. As Jack Smith, DEC's de facto chief operating officer (COO) in the 1980s put it, what made DEC work so well was the close and trusting relationships among the various product line and functional managers and the relationships these managers had with Ken Olsen.

THE INEVITABLE AND OFTEN INVISIBLE CONSEQUENCES OF ORGANIZATIONAL GROWTH AND AGE

Growth is inevitable with economic success. Although one occasionally sees organizations that deliberately dissolve themselves after being successful, the more typical pattern is to develop motivation to continue to grow. In part this motivation reflects the growing concern of the members of the organization for their own economic growth and their growing sense of responsibility for themselves and their employees. For this reason, economic success not only breeds growth but also aging in the sense that the organization increasingly wants to survive. The major consequences of growth and aging are summarized below.

- *Loss of Functional Familiarity.* As organizations grow, age, and disperse geographically, fewer and fewer people are functionally familiar with one another; hence, work relationships become less and less predictable.

- *Loss of Personal, Face-to-Face Management.* Management processes change from personal interactions based on functional familiarity to more formalized systemic processes and more impersonal reward and control systems. Accountability and responsibility for managers remain the same, but the degree of control they have diminishes and becomes impersonal.

- *Increasing Differentiation.* Products, markets, geographies, and functions all become more differentiated and complex.

- *Growth of Subunits and Subcultures.* With differentiation the organization develops subgroups that eventually develop subcultures. The subcultures may or may not be aligned with the larger organization's culture. Commitment and loyalty increasingly shift away from the total organization to the subunit.

- *Coordination Mechanisms Change.* Coordination, integration, and alignment of subunits changes from an interpersonal to an intergroup process requiring more formal and impersonal mechanisms.

- *Measurement Mechanisms Change.* Measurement of costs, inventories, transfer pricing, and profitability has to be made consistent and equitable across the subunits.

- *Strategic Focus Becomes More Difficult.* With proliferation of products and markets it becomes more and more difficult to maintain strategic focus and allocate resources equitably to the subunits that are each fighting for "their fair share." Strategic focus often requires shutting down some products ("eating one's own children").

- *The Nature of Accountability Changes.* From measuring the credibility of an individual manager's explanation of his or her financial results, the process changes to one of finding appropriate formal metrics that can be applied equitably to groups and units. In a small organization, managers' explanations can be accepted; in a large, differentiated organization group metrics that fall below certain levels cause the manager to be automatically accountable, and explanations become irrelevant.

- *The Role of Functions and Central Services Changes.* With growth it becomes less clear which functions and services should remain centralized for reasons of economy and efficiency and which ones should be turned over to the subunits for reasons of proximity to customers, markets, or technologies.

- *Maintaining a Common Culture Becomes More Difficult.* Economic growth requires the hiring of additional people. Mechanisms must therefore be developed to select and train new people who will accept and learn the critical elements of the culture.

- *Growth of Responsibility for Self and Others Increases.* A feeling of youthful exuberance and creativity gradually turns into a feeling of adulthood and responsibility (for self and for others as the number of employees grows). This feeling of adult responsibility results both from personal aging and from growth in responsibility for others as the organization grows and subdivides. If the organization goes public, it takes on additional responsibilities to shareholders.

- *Self-Confidence (Arrogance?) Grows.* Uncertainty about the future turns into a feeling of success and growing confidence about the future and one's own role in creating that future.

- *The Family Becomes a Clan and Eventually, a Community or Society.* As numbers increase and the population ages the organization moves from a small-family climate in which the father figure has the power and wisdom to a large-clan climate in which children and cousins develop strong personalities and power centers of their own and eventually come to believe that they are wiser than the father figure, while still retaining a deep respect for that father figure. With the death of the father and further increase in size and dispersion, the organization becomes more like a loosely connected community and eventually becomes a society of "strangers."

- *The Core Technology Evolves.* As products and product lines become technically more complex and more differentiated, the nature of engineering work changes from cradle-to-grave responsibility that individual engineers had in the early small DEC to working on small pieces of large systems that have to be tightly coordinated if the final product is to succeed.

- *Cost Pressures Increase.* With success the organization attracts competition and stimulates technological evolution toward commodification.

- *Product Innovation Is Increasingly Replaced by Process Innovation.* To achieve the cost reductions of commodification, organizations increasingly have to invent more efficient processes.

- *The Nature of Leadership Changes.* Leadership becomes more distributed throughout the organization, and fewer and fewer employees personally know the top leaders, making it more and more important for those leaders to work through rituals, symbols, and image management.

The most significant of the organizational changes listed above is the loss of functional familiarity, or what Dennis Burke, the VP of human resources, described in 1975 as a shift from a trust culture to a power culture. This shift from trust to power is an inevitable consequence of growth because of the loss of functional familiarity. If one cannot predict the behavior of others on whom one is dependent, one must resort to what can best be thought of as political behavior. And that is what most alumni of DEC describe as the most salient characteristic of the mid- to late 1980s. Even as DEC was becoming more and more successful in the economic arena, it was becoming more political. The combination of values that leads both to a high rate of innovation and success and to a maturing of the empowered employees (who begin to realize that they do have wisdom of their own) also leads to a feeling that "Doing the right thing" means not only fighting with brothers and cousins but often challenging parental authority as well.

DEC's midlife can be thought of as a period of muscle flexing and testing, both within the organization and in the broader marketplace. Within the organization newly acquired managers from larger, older companies—like Pete Kaufmann in manufacturing and Andy Knowles, Julius Marcus, Roger Cady, Irwin Jacobs, and many others who had learned how to run successful product lines—gained the confidence to argue with Ken Olsen, with the Operations Committee, and, most important, with one another. In the broader market arena DEC developed the confidence to tackle IBM directly. In order to understand this whole evolution we must now review some of the less visible consequences of the growth and aging process.

INVISIBLE CONSEQUENCES:
INDIVIDUAL DEBATE BECOMES INTERGROUP DEBATE

As products and markets proliferated, the need for central coordination and priority setting increased, but Ken Olsen's philosophy of letting internal competition and the external market forces be the priority-setting mechanism held firm and forced managers to become effective politicians. When DEC was small these political battles were among individuals fighting for their individual points of view in a climate of rational debate and problem solving reminiscent of academia. With growth and success, these same managers now "owned" organizational units with many employees for whom they felt increasingly responsible. To give in to an argument now meant letting your organization down. Pure rationality was thus undermined by the bias that results from being responsible for others, from the need to protect one's turf and one's people, from becoming a representative of a group rather than an individual agent. On the surface, the debate and the process of getting buy-in appeared to be the same seeking of truth, but it was increasingly evident in Operations Committee meetings that managers were bringing forth proposals that were colored by their needs to protect their turf, their people, and their prior investments.

The meaning of *truth* in that intergroup context changed even though truth as an absolute value remained. As much intergroup research has shown, when groups compete with one another for increasingly scarce resources, they close ranks, externalize only information that is favorable to themselves, focus only on information from the others that is unfavorable to them, withhold selected information that would put them at a disadvantage, and reduce the amount of communication they have with the other groups while increasing internal communication (Schein 1987). Problem solving between group representatives declines, while negotiation to gain advantage increases. In that process, presenting only information favorable to oneself and detrimental to others becomes the normal process. I believe that Ken Olsen remained idealistic and did not realize that all through the 1980s communication among the key groups was deteriorating to the point where individual managers were, in effect, lying to him.

As frustration over the inability to marshal needed resources mounted, some groups lost motivation and didn't work as hard, while others isolated themselves, including, for example, Andy Knowles in his new facility at Marlboro, Stan Olsen in his new facility in New Hampshire, and various country managers in Europe. Product lines fought more overtly with sales over the allocation of sales resources to the product lines, as illustrated by conflict between Andy Knowles and Ted Johnson.

The conflict between Knowles and Johnson became so acrimonious that I was asked to meet with both of them to mediate. It turned out that the conflict between sales and the product lines went back to earlier times when Andy Knowles had written a memo to Ted Johnson on June 18, 1970, stating: "For the past weeks, the PDP-11 Steering Committee meetings have lacked sales department representation.

Since we are in the initial delivery/quote mode (options, peripherals, software), product line wise, it is essential that decisions are participated in by sales so that communications are concise and clear. Please have someone attend weekly (3:00 P.M., every Wednesday, Nick's new and beautiful conference room in beautiful downtown 5-2)."

In 1975 Andy Knowles headed the Components Group and noted that salespeople were chronically missing the staff meetings of his group. In a memo he sent to Ted Johnson on January 16, 1975, he first pointed out that salespeople had been present at only two out of the last twelve of the meetings and then said: "After four and a half years of this it still intrigues me how you and your line management acquire sufficient information and data on our businesses to do your job professionally. Having been through this before with the PDP-11 Steering Committee and now with the new group, I promise this will be my last written document on the subject."

Ted Johnson replied to suggest that Andy should structure his staff meetings around Ted's schedule, which precipitated a longer and angrier January 23, 1975, memo, which is reproduced in its entirety because it illustrates so well the issues that DEC managers were coping with during this growth period.

INTEROFFICE MEMORANDUM

TO: Ted Johnson

FROM: Andy Knowles

CC: Gerry Moore, Allen Michels, Ed Schein

SUBJ: ATTENDING COMPONENTS STAFF MEETINGS

I find your 1/20/75 memo on the subject to be incredible! For five years now I have been trying to get permanent sales representation at first the PDP-11 Steering Committee meetings, then the Small Computer Group staff meetings and now the Components Group Staff meetings. The motives on my part remain the same:

— Communications with your monolith on running the business

— Given an understanding of the business then the budget, planning hassle might be reduced since you would be in on the thinking behind our plan or plans

—Build an operating team, which would include Sales, Marketing, Engineering, Finance, and Manufacturing management regardless of who they worked for at the time.

My staff meetings are structured accordingly. We strategize, plan and decide on the running of the business there. The topics are meaty, timely and we visit Westfield [manufacturing] every 6 weeks to include them in our thinking, planning, etc. Soon we will include Puerto Rico every 6 months or so. And you, after your promises to me to participate (in the meeting with Ed Schein) and your failure again to follow through, now have the arrogance to ask me to structure my staff meetings around your time. Be serious! All the topics we discuss are important. Most issues have an impact on sales. It strikes me that if you were truly interested in being part of the team you would have done more in the 14+ weeks since our meetings with Ed Schein than write me that asinine 1/20/75 memo which only serves to frustrate me further by confirming my suspicions and hang-ups.

During the last woods meeting when we discussed organization you were again given a similar message by Win and Stan so I am not alone. If you can't assign a senior guy, full time, to interface with my group, attend my staff meetings, and line wise participate in the operating management team's running of the Components Business, don't bother to send anyone. I am not very patient when it comes to educating someone else every week, month or quarter when it is convenient to you and your group. Full attendance and permanence builds teams.

Starting the 11 product line in the Company was difficult. The main hassle was with sales. My hindsight notes that our failure to agree on a bookings budget, the first big year, set us back competitively more at the outset of the PDP 11 than anything else did. I never did order enough that year because of the difference in bookings goals of $10M. This resulted from, in my opinion, a lack of understanding in sales of the potential of the PDP 11. This lack of understanding resulted from the lack of a direct, permanent sales interface on the PDP 11 operating management team. So now the COMPONENTS GROUP startup is even more difficult. The major hassle has been with sales again. No wonder the monolith is bigger, there are no direct, permanent interfaces and limited understanding of what we are trying to do. Someday, when the book is written, we may learn from all this I hope.

This conflict reflected both growing pains and cultural assumptions. Sales resources were stretched thinner, so people in product line organizations got more frustrated. At the same time, people in the sales function were confident that they had enough understanding to allocate resources wisely. The conflict had severe consequences down in the trenches in that customers experienced disconnects in their dealings with DEC or were given conflicting information by the product line and the sales organizations. DEC developed a reputation of being very hard to deal with because of conflicting information, slow responses, and lack of coordination among the product lines that led to too many salespeople calling on the same customers, and slow order processing.

INVISIBLE CONSEQUENCES:
THE DILEMMA OF INTEGRATION GROWS

The conflicts described above were observed at senior management levels, and as we will see in the next chapter, efforts were made to resolve them, but the cultural assumption that each executive was "Doing the right thing" to the best of his or her ability not only made it difficult to develop more integrated systems but also resulted in a clear reluctance to enforce the systems once developed. In these situations Ken Olsen became de facto the ultimate point of resolution and integration, but his response was usually to let the key parties sort it out for themselves. Olsen would not tell Ted Johnson or Andy Knowles what either of them should do, either because he believed that his "highly paid senior executives" should be able to reach a logical solution by themselves, or perhaps because deep down he would admit that he did not know what the right solution was. On the other hand, though he usually tried to remain neutral, his personal biases were known, and his subordinates learned to varying degrees how to calibrate him and how to get their own way. This process could be effective as long as Olsen stayed formally in a neutral or devil's advocate role. He forced the quality of thinking to remain at a high level by supporting a climate of open challenge and only involved himself directly around specific issues such as the physical appearance of the computer.

But in the case of Andy Knowles's product line versus Ted Johnson's sales organization, it was Knowles who was the new kid on the block, with his money genes being neutralized by the engineering-based immune system. Ted Johnson was one of the original managers and thought he knew best how to handle things. Knowles had already attempted in 1974 to develop a practical personal computer system, but to convert DEC to a commodity type of organization—operating with lower margins, putting components together from other manufacturers rather than building their own, designing for lowest costs, and using open systems that would encourage a broad range of software development—went against the engineering culture grain in too many ways. DEC's success had been with sophisticated high-margin products for sophisticated customers using sophisticated designs. There was every reason to believe that continuing on this path was viable. Knowles was therefore in a situation where his proposals would have required a number of cultural changes that the old-timers were not about to agree to.

INVISIBLE CONSEQUENCES:
OPEN COMMUNICATION BECOMES MORE DIFFICULT

Not only is functional familiarity lost when organizations reach a certain size and degree of differentiation but upward and lateral communication in general becomes more difficult and time-consuming. On the one hand, the organization wants to be more efficient and speed up processes; on the other hand, the organization wants to operate with full information. In DEC the values were to listen to whoever had the relevant information, and that would often be someone way down in the organization and now geographically distant. With growth it became more time-consuming to get buy-in and build consensus across all the levels, with the consequence that some information from lower levels was lost or buy-in was assumed (hoped for) when it was not actually there. Hence, promises of support were not always honored, throwing schedules into turmoil. This bothered Ken Olsen tremendously, as he increasingly felt that what was presented at the Operations Committee meetings was not the original plans of the working-level engineers, whom he trusted, but the desires of various middle managers who he often felt were out of touch and not to be trusted. Decisions at the level of the Operations Committee were therefore often based more on intuition and second-guessing what the proposal was really about than on hard numbers or facts.

INVISIBLE CONSEQUENCES: EMPOWERMENT LEADS TO POWER CENTERS

To understand fully what the DEC organization became in midlife, one has to examine more carefully the consequences of what we so glibly call "empowerment." Olsen really meant it when he said that he hired the best and brightest and expected them to come up with proposals that, if approved, would be their responsibility to implement. In this climate all kinds of technical and organizational innovations flourished, most of them ideas that Olsen would not have had himself, and some that he would not even have approved of. In other words, empowerment in DEC was successful to an extraordinary degree in that people felt capable of "Doing the right thing," even if that meant insubordination or hiding what one was doing.

The main consequence of this kind of culture was that people developed self-confidence and became more and more willing to trust their own judgment. Combining that with a track record of success and growth led inevitably to powerful subunits that developed their own strategic agendas and subcultures. The first indication of that kind of process was the departure in 1968 of Ed DeCastro and a group of engineers to form Data General when their view of what the next product should be was not approved by DEC senior management. Later fateful examples were the continued work on the Alpha chip in spite of opposition from Ken Olsen and the continued work on large computer systems (the VAX 9000) in spite of the opposition of the Engineering Committee and most of the engineering community.

Olsen assumed (or hoped) that once you approve a project the proposer would hold himself or herself accountable. As previously mentioned, DEC never developed consistent centralized formal controls that would enable senior management to determine exactly how each of the many products was performing in the marketplace. There was talk of accountability, managers were brought in to report on results, and numbers were rolled up by products, markets, and functions, but this process was never formalized enough to give clear results. Proposals were not reviewed systematically to determine whether what was promised was actually achieved. Measurement of accountability was treated in the same experimental way that product development was, allowing the hiding of inefficiencies while sales skyrocketed. The finance, controller, and audit functions were present but not really respected as being intrinsic to the running of the organization. The senior job with the highest rate of turnover was the CFO job.

INVISIBLE CONSEQUENCES: SUCCESSION ISSUES BECOME SENSITIVE

The Operations Committee continued to be the place where all of the fundamental issues described above were surfaced and debated. DEC was full of bright people who saw what was happening in the marketplace and the turmoil inside the organization. Ken Olsen's commitment to openness led him to charge me, as the consultant to this committee, to regularly interview members, collect issues, and bring them back to the committee for discussion. After interviewing all the senior managers in 1972 and observing the rapid growth of DEC, it seemed clear to everyone that with continuing growth DEC would need an executive VP or chief operating officer. Olsen had far too many people reporting directly to him, and some formal processes were needed to manage the growing organization, yet it was clear that Olsen would not systematically enforce even the few formal processes that were in place.

Peter Kaufmann was the obvious choice for the COO role because he had shown himself to be a very effective and charismatic manager in building the worldwide manufacturing organization. He had the support of the other members of the Operations Committee and was willing to take a crack at the job. Win Hindle and I proposed this idea to Olsen. For reasons that were never entirely clear, Olsen perceived the suggested appointment as a threat to his own position, reacted very negatively to the idea, and misinterpreted it as a desire on Kaufmann's part to usurp power. Why did Olsen react so negatively? One speculation was that Olsen had perceived Harlan Anderson's efforts in the mid-1960s as being power seeking; another was that perhaps Olsen perceived any potential number-two person as a threat.

The problem of adding a COO remained unsolved. However, all of us had learned from this incident that Olsen was highly sensitive to perceived challenges to his power by any of his subordinates. He was himself conflicted about power in that he wanted to empower people, but those closest to him had to learn that in certain areas he wanted to retain complete control.

It became evident that distributing power widely below him also allowed Olsen to maintain control, something that he clearly needed. Kaufmann's position in the group continued to be strong for a few more years, but he had lost credibility with Olsen and eventually left the company in 1977, when he felt that his managerial approach was better suited to a small-company environment and that DEC had grown too large.

INVISIBLE CONSEQUENCES:
EXECUTIVE ANXIETY GROWS

My interviews of the Operations Committee revealed another set of "problems": the difficulty of managing the anxieties that attended rapid growth. Ken Olsen interfered more as he became more anxious, often undoing plans that were well under way. Whenever one group became too powerful, Olsen would find ways of challenging them so that power remained widely distributed. Gordon Bell was caught in a role conflict between being Olsen's senior consultant on engineering issues and being the head of a large engineering empire with a need to protect his people. As engineering became more powerful, Olsen wanted a stronger marketing group to tell engineering what to do, but marketing as a function was never allowed to develop strength and was, in fact, usually denigrated. Marketing VPs usually quit after short periods of time because they could not exercise any power.

One of my key roles as a consultant in the meetings was to help the group to understand that when Ken Olsen became very angry, it was usually a symptom of anxiety, and the way to deal with it was not to fight back but to develop insight. The group should try to decipher the source of the anxiety and figure out what they could do to reduce it. Once Olsen believed that others were worrying about the problem and doing something about it, he relaxed and his anger subsided.

As the organization grew, it became more difficult to deal with anxieties that involved executives' sense of responsibility to their groups. The prospect of having your individual project turned down was much less traumatic than having a project turned down that would require you to relocate a large number of employees, not to mention the loss of face involved in confronting them with the decision.

One of the critical lessons to be learned from these events is that growth and success can coexist with turmoil and problems. Some have even argued that it is the turmoil that permitted the creativity that DEC continued to display. For our purposes what is important to recognize is that the problems of growth and age are inevitable and that organizations have different ways of dealing with those problems. DEC stuck to its values of maximizing individual freedom and responsibility even if that produced a more or less controlled chaos.

CONCLUSION

In this chapter we have seen how success leads to growth and aging, and how those two processes influence a whole range of organizational phenomena. The most important of these phenomena is the inevitable loss of functional familiarity, the knowledge of others' work habits that makes them more or less predictable and hence manageable. Within the smaller units of the organization, functional familiarity remained high, strong subcultures formed, and effectiveness at the subgroup level therefore remained high. This is why DEC continued to be highly successful right through the 1980s. But the other inevitable consequence of growth—that individual debate becomes intergroup debate and conflict—created an increasingly political environment that the engineering culture was ill-equipped to handle. Remaining an extended family under the leadership of Ken Olsen as a father figure became more and more difficult as DEC differentiated into more units. Age and experience increased the sense of responsibility and personal confidence of the leaders in these units, causing the DEC of the 1980s to be more and more "a coat of many colors" that felt more and more chaotic and out of control.

eleven

Learning Efforts Reveal Cultural Strengths and Rigidities

The problems that surface with growth are invisible in the sense that they are unintentional, inevitable, and easy to overlook. Ken Olsen and DEC's senior management saw some of what was happening with success and growth, but they did not fully appreciate how difficult it would be to develop fixes that would work. In a sense, what was invisible to them was the strength of the culture they had created and the difficulties that arose when they attempted to make changes in a still growing and highly successful organization. But learning and experimentation were highly valued, and Ken Olsen's engineering background led to a tinkering mentality that suffused his thinking not only about products but about organization and management as well. He was willing to try all kinds of processes and mechanisms to address the various problems that arose as the technology and the organization evolved.

Experimentation seemed normal in the DEC culture throughout the 1980s, but it reflected more the engineering mentality of trying one thing after another than the scientific mentality of carefully reflecting on why certain experiments did not produce the expected results. Careful reflection was missing except at the Woods Meetings and in the context of various educational interventions that will be described in this chapter. Impulsive and intuitive tinkering was more the norm, especially in an environment where there were always multiple proposals for what to do coming from the various subcultures.

As a consequence, none of us saw that the constant tinkering with incentives, changing of organizational forms, redefining of roles, and trying of different management controls produced confusion in the now large and highly differentiated DEC organization. None of us realized that the response to negative information about the state of affairs could easily be discounted while financial performance remained high. None of us realized that the remedial efforts that will be described in this chapter were never pursued in a way that would make a difference. None of us saw at the time how powerful and stable some core elements of the culture had become.

Learning efforts on the part of DEC fell into two broad categories. From the beginning Ken Olsen and the Operations Committee were concerned about improving communication, teamwork, and human relations in general. This concern was reflected most clearly in bringing me on board as a consultant to that committee and in licensing me to do a variety of organization development projects such as those described in chapter 8. It was also reflected in bringing into the organization talented and forward-thinking executives who specialized in human resource policies and practices. Extensive supervisory training and support of all kinds of employee and executive development programs was one major result. It was as if Ken Olsen and the Operations Committee recognized that an organization founded by electrical engineers needed help in the human relations area.

The other broad category of learning efforts was the use of outside consultants throughout the organization. Ken Olsen was very open to outsider views, and all of the various segments of the DEC organization used outside consultants effectively. These two categories of learning were combined in various kinds of corporate seminars in which outside speakers were prominent and in the invitations to outsiders to attend Woods Meetings and make presentations on topics considered relevant. Exposure to outsider views and internal critiques was frequent, as we will see. However, the manner in which the information was handled and the remedies that were applied reveal the culture most clearly. One example was the hiring in 1974 of a consulting firm to examine some of the problems with organizational structure that arose with rapid growth.

THE MAC PROJECT

The Management Analysis Corporation (MAC) was a highly respected Cambridge consulting firm consisting of full-time consultants working closely with principals who were Harvard Business School professors and partners in MAC. The DEC project was to be coordinated by Professor Richard Vancil and was to examine DEC's organization. Ken Olsen asked me to be helpful to MAC and to facilitate whatever coordination might be needed. MAC did a thorough job of interviewing senior management and analyzing the data. What they heard and how they interpreted it were summarized in one of their memos:

Symptoms observed:

- Lack of clarity as to which salesman is in charge of a given customer
- Inability to price according to the different service requirements attached to products
- Budgeting difficulties in that as it goes through the echelons it comes out differently from what was originally planned
- PLMs [product line managers] frustrated by lack of clear authority
- Absence of long range plans, strategies
- Poor communication between technology, product and market developers
- Difficulty of coordinating decision making with overseas divisions
- Stock option compensation is a source of frustration

DEC has been a fast growing organization in an industry characterized by an annual 40% improvement of cost/performance. DEC follows two distinct strategies at the same time:

- One around OEM (at lowest cost) which implies the opening of new markets at a fast rate since small minicomputer life expectancy is only 2–3 years.

▪ One around end-user (at fixed cost) which implies increasing service capabilities.

DEC is characterized by a broad range of products from $1,000 to $150,000. The huge range of their market segments and of the product prices is increasing the problems of an organization that has reached a critical mass.

DEC is squeezed between a need for stronger integration at the top, to provide guidance and long-term directives, and a need for a finer decentralization into small sub-divisions, to provide more sensitivity to the market. Integration and decentralization needs are antagonistic and complementary. A balance between two forces is to be reached in order to permit long-term strategic planning to evolve. (MAC, internal memo, 1974)

In my role as liaison with the MAC project team I sat in on the diagnostic sessions and observed the evolution of the recommendation to empower a stronger marketing VP. I tried to argue that making any recommendation might be a problem given what I had learned about the DEC culture, and I advised that MAC should instead focus on clarifying the problems identified and the costs of not fixing them but let DEC wrestle through to its own solution. DEC managers with their academic orientation did not like anyone telling them what to do, as I had found many times over, but they did listen to data. The consulting company culture, however, demanded that a recommendation be made or "we did not do our job." Vancil and I debated this at length, but he was convinced that the recommendation for a marketing VP made so much sense and was so well backed up by the data that it clearly would be the thing to give first, backed up by fifty slides with supporting data and arguments.

The MAC report was given a two-hour slot at the beginning of one of the Operations Committee meetings. Professor Richard Vancil and one of his MAC colleagues were set with their slide presentation and, in the best tradition of management consultants, led with their primary recommendation—the creation of the marketing VP. Ken Olsen listened politely for a few minutes and then, before more than one or two of the slides could be presented, thanked the MAC group for their work and dismissed them!

Various written reports were later circulated, and individual managers concurred with much of what MAC had learned, but the primary recommendation went nowhere, and the power of all the data was lost in the shuffle. Of course, the MAC data basically confirmed what DEC already knew, but did so in a more thoroughly documented manner. Elaborate analytical effort by MAC had also gone into showing how the new structure with the new VP would actually work and would solve a lot of problems, but none of this could override the confidence that DEC management had in its own ability to solve problems. The major lesson of this story is that DEC management believed that they understood very well what they needed to do, even before the consultant told them. The problem was in not really wanting to implement that solution, given Ken Olsen's public lack of confidence in marketing.

A few weeks later Ken Olsen wrote a long memorandum to Richard Vancil terminating the consultation. In the memo he indicated what he had gotten out of the project, included a complicated chart showing the matrixed relationships of the product line managers and the central functions, spelled out the roles of three group vice presidents, and reinforced the philosophy of decentralization by empowering the product line managers to be marketers rather than centralizing that function. Some excerpts follow:

> People think we had a good Woods meeting. Things did not work out quite the way we expected them to and we did not accomplish all the things I had hoped. We did not take directly your suggested solutions, but I am convinced that we would not have accomplished this without your help. We also invented, or reinvented, our own solutions to traditional problems. We clarified many things and it seems to me we have possible answers to most of the problems that were bothering me.
>
> By charting the interfaces and, therefore, the responsibilities of the Product Line Manager, I think we have clarified his job and made it more possible, or maybe more mandatory that he have a staff to accomplish it. We have also given the Group Vice Presidents more responsibility in helping the Product Line Managers. Through the years the Group Vice Presidents have had the problem of little direct responsibility in

the running of the Product Lines. This comes about because everybody talks to everybody and works out all problems at all times at the lower levels and therefore leaves out the Vice Presidents. Now much of the decision making is simplified, formalized and done through the Group Vice Presidents.

We have always had the theory or philosophy at Digital that we allow free flow of information at all levels and between all levels, but decision making is formal. We have here formalized much of the decision making but in no way limited the free flow of information in any direction. . . . It is going to take us a while to understand what we have generated here and to understand the problems. Until we understand a little more, and we understand more of what we want to accomplish, I think we would like to stop our consulting contract until we can somewhat better define what we would like to do. (Ken Olsen, memo to Prof. Richard Vancil, Harvard Business School, January 9, 1975)

THE LESSONS OF THE MAC PROJECT

The first and most important lesson that I learned in the years subsequent to this diagnosis was that insight does not necessarily produce the right kind of action. I observed repeatedly in Woods Meetings that critical information was surfaced, discussed, analyzed, and then rationalized away. The points in many of my feedback memos and in the MAC analysis were not original observations—we were reflecting what senior management, including Ken Olsen, was telling us and complaining about. These points were discussed and debated, yet no new action was taken.

Too often we assume in our management literature that if we could just show people what is going on, they would act to fix things. We assume that insight leads to action. But just as therapists have learned that for various reasons patients often do not act on new insights, so one of the deep lessons of cultural dynamics is that if the remedy would require an organization to violate some of its deeply held cultural assumptions, that remedy will not be applied. Instead, the organization will rationalize that what it is doing will work out in the end, or it will apply quick fixes and organizational Band-Aids that provide an illusion of problem solving.

A second lesson is that Olsen really believed in decentralization of responsibility in that his letter argues for strengthening the product line managers, not the central marketing VP role. In retrospect this was a fateful decision because it eventually led to massive duplication of resources, as each product line hurried to beef up its own corporate functions and, in effect, build its own empire. What happened in the product lines when they beefed up their own financial organizations in order to remain on top of their jobs was now repeated in the marketing and sales areas.

Third, we saw again very clearly that Olsen and his key subordinates felt they knew better how to fix their problems than some outside consultant. Their knee-jerk rejection of MAC's formal recommendation made it difficult to examine more deeply the implications of what the MAC analysis showed. We all learned that in this culture and during a period of economic success, one could surface problems but could not really push them because, in a sense, everyone knew best what to do. Paradoxically, Ken Olsen feared periods of success because he believed that people became complacent during such periods. He would then challenge, confront, cajole, and stimulate his subordinates to action, but he did not realize that by not enforcing anything, by continuing to believe in self-management, he was colluding with this complacency.

The MAC project revealed how a group of outside analysts viewed the DEC of the mid-1970s. At the same time, Dennis Burke, who had been hired as VP of personnel and had done most of the management and supervisory training, wrote a memo to the Operations Committee in mid-1975 giving his internal assessment of the state of the company. He vividly highlighted all the factors mentioned in chapter 10:

DENNIS BURKE MEMO TO OPERATIONS COMMITTEE, JULY 22, 1975

DEC Culture. It is my opinion that DEC has subtly changed from a "trust culture" to a "power culture." In other words, position in the organization and ability to reward or punish is much more significant than personal relationships in getting things done. Roles and titles have replaced names, and persons. People place much greater value on being powerful than on being trusted. DEC is no longer a family of persons, but a group of units. These units are more or less personally involved in the real decision-making process. We have many meetings at DEC in order to create the "illusion of consensus." There is probably not any real consensus in most instances. Part of the reason for this is the difficulty of a committee being all-wise and knowing and making wonderful decisions in limited time based on limited facts.

Another negative consequence is that higher management hears only of problems, rather than of individual persons. These problems must become very serious before higher management knows about them itself. One final negative consequence is that if a culture is not dominated by trust, it is dominated by distrust. People are afraid to he honest because honesty may be interpreted as weakness and incompetence. Management does not communicate because knowledge is power and ignorance is weakness.

In my judgment, DEC tends at the present time to have a lower degree of trust and a higher degree of power in its culture than in the past. . . . At least five Vice Presidents have said to me personally that they think another Vice President, or key manager, in the corporation is "lying" or is "dishonest," "cannot be trusted," etc, when the reality of the matter was they simply were not communicating openly with each other in solving a problem which was in the best interests of the corporation.

I believe it is possible to have a very successful company, to have powerful managers use power ethically, and to place a high value on trust and honesty, and to place a lower value on status, roles and titles. The remarks that I make here ought to be put in context. Unlike most companies in American industry, DEC has shown a remarkable ability in maintaining a trust culture for such a long period of time and, despite our temporary problems and frustrations, we have the ability, if we have the will, to keep that kind of culture alive. I think now is the time to work this problem vigorously.

Most of the problems described by Dennis Burke can be attributed to the rapid growth, differentiation, and systematic empowerment of individuals and groups. What is remarkable in the DEC scenario is the willingness to be open and blunt about these problems and to attempt

to confront them. As in the case of the response to the MAC proposals, the primary response was to attempt to reinforce the values
around freedom, truth, and personal responsibility. More hierarchy
and more centralization were strongly resisted. Instead, a broader
arena for reflection and analysis was created through using Corporate
Seminars. These were usually two- to three-day off-site events for the
top eighty or so executives, carefully designed by consultants, staff, and
line managers to deal with current problems and to stimulate problem
solving throughout the organization. These sessions facilitated a certain amount of shared consensus on what problems had to be addressed but unfortunately rarely led to unified action in response to
such consensus.

THE 1976 CREATION OF A PERSONNEL COUNCIL
AND HIRING OF A SENIOR HR EXECUTIVE

Dennis Burke left the HR job in 1975. He had launched a number of
developmental projects, had built an effective supervisory training
program for engineers, and had created an executive development
program. But, as the above memo showed, he felt that the rapidly
growing company was outgrowing his own ability to continue to be effective. Win Hindle took over the HR function and created a Personnel
Council that would have both human resource staff managers and
senior line managers on it to set broad corporate HR policy. In 1977
an entire Woods Meeting was devoted to "organization and human resource planning" in which Olsen and the Operations Committee decided that a decentralized personnel organization with solid lines (on
the organization chart) to the product line and a dotted line to the corporate VP made the most sense. Personnel managers were to become
committed members of the product line organizations.

As the company continued to grow in size and importance it became evident to senior management and to Ken Olsen that some degree of centralization and formalization was necessary, especially in
the human resource systems. Dennis Burke had been the ideal HR executive for a rapidly growing adolescent company trying to develop its

own learning style, but as the company continued to grow it became clear that a different kind of HR executive would be needed, one who embodied the values that were now ingrained in the culture yet would have the experience and skill to build a mature HR system for a multibillion dollar corporation that was rapidly becoming a major player in the computing industry.

In the growing field of organization development, a number of companies and individual executives stood out as both state-of-the-art practitioners and articulate spokespersons for a value-driven kind of management system. One of these was Sheldon Davis, who had published papers on value-based management and who had a proven track record as the senior HR executive at TRW Systems. This organization and Davis's work within it were widely hailed as a model of what was possible in the context of large, technically based organizations. Davis was known to me and to most of the senior HR people within DEC, particularly those in the growing organization development community that was evolving within the company. Well-known academic consultants who were working on various aspects of DEC's management systems, such as Paul Lawrence and Richard Walton, were highly impressed by Davis's work. All of these forces conspired to make it inevitable that Shel Davis would be recruited to join DEC in a senior role.

Davis was attractive to DEC because he represented in his personal philosophy most of the values that Ken Olsen had infused into the organization. DEC was attractive to Shel Davis because it provided him new and larger challenges to implement his philosophy of how an organization should be run in a context where the right values were already in place. After much discussion and many interviews with Ken Olsen and others, Shel Davis was hired in 1978 to bring in the wisdom and discipline of running an HR system for a large, growing organization. It was thought of as a triumph for DEC to bring in a seasoned HR professional to centralize and organize the HR function and to help formalize that management system in general.

Under Davis the DEC organization development function became one of the largest, most active, and most effective internal consulting organizations of its kind in U.S. industry. Many of today's active practitioners in the organization development field had critical learning experiences within DEC and were responsible for some of DEC's most important innovations. It was this organization that made it possible for DEC to develop state-of-the-art models for enterprise integration and ultimately to create a group that successfully sold these services to external customers. Many of the innovations in the engineering and manufacturing organizations (see appendix B) were nurtured in the climate that Dennis Burke had created initially and that Davis and the organization development group evolved into a mature and effective function.

One of Shel Davis's major projects was to bring together the various external consultants who had been working in different parts of the organization with the internal consultants and organization development specialists. For the November 1978 two-day Woods Meeting of this group, he issued the following agenda, which reflects his perception of what DEC needed to focus on: "The following are some possible large issues, opportunities, and themes that we might decide to have as our current key focal points for the consulting team: (1) low trust matrix, (2) precocious organization, (3) lots of stressed people 'in over their heads' who need training and development and/or management and leadership, (4) adaptive organization (very rapid rate of change due to technological/product/market phenomena), and (5) management development and career planning" (Shel Davis, memo to Planning Team, November 9, 1978).

Two years later the consulting group meeting agenda items were very similar, reflecting some of the chronic problems of organizational growth: "1) Improve the structure of decision making, 2) sustain entrepreneurial spirit and feeling of excellence, 3) maintain strong position in exploding marketplace, 4) better planning and implementation, and 5) develop managers sufficient to sustain business plans."

The main output from the consulting group's planning meetings was to create the agenda for some of the Corporate Seminars that were designed to educate senior management and especially to expose Ken Olsen to outsiders' views. The HR function in conjunction with some of the outside consultants used these seminars to stimulate reflection on important organizational and other issues. The faculty was made up of prominent outsiders, some of whom had consulted with various parts of DEC and therefore knew something about the company's problems and issues. The seminars were usually two full days in length and involved lectures, discussion, and whatever else seemed appropriate in terms of the material. Faculty came primarily from Harvard, MIT, and Columbia and included Benson Shapiro, Richard Walton, Paul Lawrence, Ed Roberts, Tom Allen, Michael Scott-Morton, Eli Ginzberg, and Ed Schein. Faculty members worked with key internal consultants and HR managers such as Sue Lotz, Steve Jenks, and Shel Davis to design these seminars, give lectures, and run sessions. The aim was to make senior management, especially Ken Olsen and the Operations Committee, aware of different options for the organization and of the need to focus strategically.

WORKING ON KEN OLSEN

Shel Davis also developed a personal agenda based on his own value system. He deplored the way Ken Olsen vented his anger on people and decided that one of his personal projects would be to help Olsen to develop more constructive ways of dealing with his anxieties and angers. My own experiences along these lines had taught me that confronting Olsen directly on this matter would not work, so I counseled strongly against what Davis was trying to do. But Davis had strong values as well, and he could not abide what he saw as the sometimes brutal treatment of DEC managers and employees.

He tried many approaches to changing Olsen's behavior, from direct counseling to various kinds of games, but none were successful. In fact, the main impact of Davis's efforts to change Olsen's style of emotional expression was that Olsen turned against him and, in characteristic fashion, mandated that Davis move to some other job well removed from Olsen. He would not fire Davis, but he would banish him from Maynard. Davis moved to Europe and lived out his career fruitfully in that environment, but we all had learned a lesson once again. If you fly too close to the sun, your wings melt and you crash. Davis had succumbed to the Icarus Complex and paid a personal price in terms of ultimate career accomplishments.

TROUBLE IN THE FIELD

In the summer of 1976 Larry Portner, the vice president of software development, made a trip around the various field locations and wrote the following report. Portner was one of the early DEC employees and managers who could well be considered a member of the dominant coalition in that he represented the software function and had built that function within DEC. He was a highly respected member of the DEC family; hence, his comments show to what extent problems had crept into DEC's way of doing business. Excerpts from his report illustrate the flavor of DEC's self-analytic style and openness:

> The business is there, but sales resources/effectiveness need to be augmented to get it; DEC software and hardware lack "polish," but do the job; Watch out for H.P.; Distributed computing is where it is at; Something is wrong in the Engineering/Manufacturing interface; Our posture on UNIX needs to be updated; We haven't even scratched the surface of the market potential for mini-computers; The DEC sales force is a major strength.

> Specific Points

>> POLISH—A fairly uniform opinion among our customers was that our engineering lacks polish. This is true for both hardware and software. Our systems were described as working well, once you get them working, but extremely painful in the initial stages.

>> QUALITY ASSURANCE—This may be just a result of the recent excessive demand versus capacity, however, many comments along the lines that the system could never have worked when it left the factory—the cables were wrong, modules were missing, parts were bad, and so forth. Our image has suffered badly.

>> DISTRIBUTED COMPUTING—Everybody is interested in distributed computing, although they have slightly different ideas about what it really is. It nets out as implying the ability to incrementally distribute computing power, control, functionality and flexibility in inexpensive and appropriate increments as dictated by the needs

of the application. The computer company that can talk most coherently about this concept in a way that demonstrates a sensitivity to the needs and economics of the using community, and has the products to support this philosophy, is the computer company that will own the business in the future.

SECURE SYSTEMS—There is a rapidly growing interest in secure systems. While primarily driven by the intelligence community and government agencies, it could emerge more and more as an issue for the corporate data processors. I believe this piggybacks the whole concept of distributed computing. Once you unlock the door to the computer room and open up access to the system to remote terminals, or even worse, remote data bases, the whole issue of secure systems escalates in importance and interest.

UNIX—While the reasons are highly variable, I think it is clear that UNIX is making a significant impact on our customer base. It is apparent that UNIX fills a real gap in the 11 product set. I think we need to aggressively reconsider our posture and our strategy vis-a-vis UNIX. What is clear is that it's rapidly becoming a factor in the industry. One of the driving forces is clearly to provide vendor independence and I don't believe we can ignore that aspect. Our problem is to understand how we can provide equivalently attractive capabilities.

APPLICATIONS—I believe that there is relatively little payoff for us in getting more directly involved in applications. I view the payoff for us being much higher in doing a better job of applications tools. This divorces us from ultimate responsibility for the success of the application but provides the customer the raw material that he needs to reduce his applications development costs, plus gives him the flexibility to tailor his applications as his sophistication and the use of computers grows.

HIGH AVAILABILITY SYSTEMS— Again, as in distributed computing, high availability was a topic of great interest among the customer base. It covered the full spectrum of interest, from just better on-line diagnostics to redundant capabilities throughout the hardware system, and fault tolerant software complete with "warm" standby, failure prediction, audit trails, and the like; clearly an area where we have to pay more attention.

MANUFACTURING/ENGINEERING INTERFACE—Without any data to support it but based upon our decreasing price edge and my own observations of the DEC manufacturing process, I believe we need some serious attention to what I'll call the manufacturing/engineering interface. It's not clear to me whether we don't engineer the products for efficient manufacturing, or the communications in the transition of responsibility from engineering to manufacturing are not adequate, or whether our manufacturing process is just fundamentally in need of revamping. I believe that the engineering/manufacturing organizations must aggressively address this area.

BETTER QC [quality control]—We need much more focus on polishing the products before they leave our shop. In software this translates into reduced patch levels, automated patch distribution and insertion mechanisms, more attention to start-up procedures, and a much tighter liaison with Software Services. The hardware organization has an equivalent set of issues, and in particular, much higher emphasis must be placed on the final stages of manufacturing and system assembly and test.

SUPPORT—Something is seriously wrong or deficient in our ability to support our software products. It's not a simple issue at all and I suspect that the problems and the solutions lie in a much closer liaison between Software Development and the Software Services organization. A particular problem that I do believe exists is the lack of a clear process for effectively using the skills and availability of our field manpower to get maximum utility.

MANAGEMENT NEEDS TO KNOW WHAT IS GOING ON— I strongly recommend that senior engineering managers at several levels spend more time in the field talking to customers. This is the most valuable form of feedback we have and it's vital that direct knowledge of trends is attained for the people making the products and defining the strategy. I know from my personal experience that there is no way in the current DEC process that I could have acquired one fifth the insight. (Larry Portner, memo to Operations Committee, 1976)

With rapid growth and de facto geographical decentralization the Maynard headquarters organization and the various field units were increasingly out of alignment with one another, as the Portner memo points out. But the cultural norm that managers were expected to identify and fix their own problems made it difficult to gather good information. Within the Operations Committee the members were increasingly protecting their own empires and finding it more and more difficult to act as responsible corporate leaders, even if they believed much of what the Portner memo revealed.

After many observations of miscommunication in the Operations Committee and a further round of interviews of its members, I wrote a memo dealing with marketing. My own frustration showed in the degree to which I advocated solutions instead of just providing data.

> DEC has not resolved whether it wants to be driven by technology (engineers) or markets and hence creates an organization which forces the integration into a group (one of the committees) rather than an individual manager. Groups as integrators don't work because members do not take a corporate perspective, meetings are badly run and groups permit diffusion of responsibility. That, in combination with Ken's nondirective style increases the lack of coordination, increases decision time, and encourages internal competition. The functional groups get stronger by virtue of being centralized.
>
> The Product Line Manager should be the integrator with complete authority, but the co. does not really want him to be and hence undermines him. The Vancil solution would clearly give more power to marketing. In the present set-up it is not clear where marketing is being done and/or where it should be done—nowhere, everywhere, high up, low down, in a group or in a person. Marketing people are doing the wrong thing—worrying about detail of design instead of customer needs. Co. is not really doing marketing. Marketing thinking is being duplicated in PL [product lines], Sales, and Engineering and is not coordinated.
>
> Services for marketing such as research, pricing, advertising, etc. are too spread out across product lines, duplicate each other, fail to coordinate with each other, cost too much. No sense of where to segregate, create boundaries. PLM's [product line managers] vary too much in their talents, their orientation and their experience. (Ed Schein, memo to Operations Committee, 1977)

THE VIEW FROM MARKETING, ANDY KNOWLES

The message that there needed to be more centralized and coordinated marketing got through to some extent, leading to a reorganization in 1978. Andy Knowles, probably the most experienced general manager in the company at that time was offered the job of corporate marketing VP, which is what MAC had recommended several years earlier. He was coming off the successful management of the components business and felt that 1974 to 1978 were his most productive years. He wrote me a letter reminiscing about what followed that summarizes his retrospective feelings.

By 1978 the company was climbing the Fortune 500 ladder quite dramatically and was maturing in many ways. Why then was there so much dissatisfaction with the management of the company? One will never know. Was it a creation of the boss, perhaps? Or were the then fringe players jealous of success and desirous of undermining the overall management structure of the company. I believe it was a combination of both. The hidden agenda at Operations Committee meetings was very heavy. Early in 1978 it was decided to form an Office of the President composed of the President, Marketing Vice President and Operations Vice President. Building 10 in the Mill in Maynard was renovated completely and I reluctantly moved back to Maynard as VP of Marketing. The job looked good at first blush. The VP of Marketing was responsible for ensuring the company had product and market strategies, had policies and pricing for its products and customers. In addition to this the corporate advertising and public relations groups reported to the marketing VP, along with corporate planning and the environmental watchdogs. Also, as chairman of the Pricing and Policies Committee, and the Marketing Committee, it was felt the job had real clout. The job turned out to be a year and a half long nightmare.

My move to Maynard was completed in July and in that Spring I turned over the Components Group to Ed Kramer. For the first six months things were OK as we set up processes which were aimed at smoothly managing what was now a very large company. The whole notion of strategy, planning and control was foreign to major portions of the company. We were in dire need of a new advertising agency and major competitive threats were on the horizon. The new committees were in place and accepted but the major new product, VAX, was not. In fact, Europe had rejected VAX along with the 10/20 series of products. They were just not marketing or selling these products and were convinced these products were not needed for success. Europe was also convinced the dollar would be down forever. These were the problems my group and I focused on along with trying to zero in on what might be major, competitive, future threats.

I made my first big mistake in the marketing job by confronting Ken with the next problem for Digital—the Personal Computer. The first production personal computer in the company, the PDT (Programmed Data Terminal) had been pooh-poohed by Ken and his cronies to the point that people were not even allowed to use the term personal computer in presentations or memos. The sales department refused to lend Dan Bricklin [founder—Software Arts], a PDT to develop VISICALC! So he developed it on an Apple. Sad stories tell well, don't they? This confrontation was, I guess, the beginning of the end for me at Digital. Ken questioned my "vision." I questioned his continued heavy involvement in managing the company. His obsession with the commercial market was obvious to all. Why we let him develop DECMATE on the PDP-8, I will never know. The PDP-11 was the clear minicomputer winner. Developing word processing on 1965 technology played clearly into Wang's strategy. But what do marketing guys know anyway? Engineering must run Digital! Clearly, Ken wanted engineering to run the company and constantly berated marketing.

The issue of planning became somewhat of a joke. It was professed loudly that Digital wanted planning. When it came to putting the rubber on the road, upper management, led by the CEO, really didn't want an integrated, corporately approved, short or long range plan. How did this manifest itself? Well, the sales plan didn't have to match the business plan. Europe could sell to one plan and submit another filtered one to corporate. Profit goals did not have to add up so that the geographic rollup matched the corporate, product line totals. All plans were in dollars, no one paid a great deal of attention to the actual forecasting of products. The planning effort was never taken to the point where people were measured and rewarded or not against their plans. Sales was allowed to run against separate plans. The level of second guessing by the functional groups was encouraged. Everyone added overhead to deal with "the planners." The number of meetings and the level of frustration peaked around March of 1979. Massive volumes of product group plans were prepared which were, for the most part, ignored by the functional groups who were supposed to integrate into them. Engineering ignored marketing. It certainly wasn't fun to be at the center of that mess.

Then there was the subject of advertising, managed out of the Office of the President, and the product groups. Ken's disdain for advertising in particular, and marketing in general, is legendary. One of the beliefs he held dear was that "great products sell themselves." That might be true in some markets where a company has heavy presence and very high market share. But it certainly isn't true when your potential customers don't know you at all and don't even know you are in the business. It was a mistake to base DECMATE on the PDP-8 because that dead-ended it. The fact remains the DECMATE was a very good, albeit limited, stand alone word processor. The trouble was that only a very favored few in Merrimack knew it. Most potential customers didn't even know that DEC was in business or what a DECMATE was. There was just no visibility to the corporation outside of the technical arena or Wall Street. And, sadly, no one cared to challenge Ken's negative view of TV or massive print ad campaigns. Suggestions as to what we might do about corporate identity were scoffed at openly. DEC or Digital? We were not allowed to decide. The notion that Digital might go on national TV was sneered at. "Give them lots of good literature and the product will sell." So what did Wang do? Wang did precisely what we wanted to do using TV as a springboard. Years after the timeframe we are discussing, IBM established Charlie Chaplin as their lead salesman of PC's and for awhile cleaned everyone's clock, PC wise. If there is a simple message here it is that one must understand one's company's identity and its product's positioning in the potential customer's mind before discarding any line of attack to try to get this to change. Failure to do this will lead to disasters such as DECMATE. (Andy Knowles, letter, personal communication, September 25, 2000)

Needless to say, what comes through clearly is Knowles's frustration, as well as his attribution of many of the antimarketing biases to Ken Olsen. What is not so clear is that opposition to much of what Knowles wanted was more widespread, based on twenty years of success with high-margin products that did sell themselves. The cultural bias toward proprietary, high-quality, high-margin products that required high-margin services was thoroughly embedded and supported by a number of senior managers, notably Jack Shields, whose star was rising during these years. In looking at a culture at this stage, one must think in terms of a dominant coalition that maintained it, not a single leader.

PASSING ON THE CULTURE: BOOT CAMPS

With rapid growth there was a growing concern that newly hired managers and engineers would not understand how to work in the DEC culture. Ellen Feir, an MIT Sloan School alumna with organization development training, helped to design and run two- or three-day "boot camps" during which a selected group of "elders," managers with long DEC experience, would be available to answer questions, lecture, or do whatever else was appropriate to ensure that the new employees understood what they were getting into. The discussions often led to follow-on letters or memos capturing some of the spirit of the culture, as in the example below:

OPEN LETTER TO NEW MANAGERS FROM OLD MANAGERS

You are joining a team that
— has a great deal of pride
— has high standards
— believes in each other
— is humble and arrogant
— is all fucked up
— is fun
— needs you and recognizes the fine balance and value of individuality and interdependence
— recognizes an individual's responsibility for him/her self
— places a high value on trust
— enjoys a good fight
— places a high premium on face-to-face deals (a "laying-on-of-hands")

— that knows, understands, and can deal with fear

— considers mistakes a learning experience

— makes things happen

— uses horseplay and humor as a tension relief

— is sensitive to people problems

This team does not and will not accept:

— an observer (as opposed to a participant)

— success at the expense of others

— closed minds

— fragile egos

— passing the buck

— dishonesty

— complacency

— class distinctions

— saying the right words and not believing them (FRAUDS)

— CYA (burying the mistake)

— keeping your mouth shut about any issue that could sink us

There followed several pages of "what we learned about the culture from analyzing critical incidents," "Some rules for the road for new managers," and especially "Attributes of Personal Power in the DEC culture" written by graduates of the boot camp:

— Contacts

— Performance—track record

— Getting off on the right foot

— Proven technical strength

— Humble arrogance

— Keeping commitments

— Charisma

— Being in sync with the basic values of the culture

— Flexibility

— Trustworthiness

— Humor, ability to horse around, ability to laugh at yourself

— Broad view of the job

— Being very involved

— Having "old warriors" on your side

— Ability to re-open an issue, reconsider, and re-decide

Finally, a list of "unpardonable sins" that were "heresy" and that got you excommunicated:

— Do a really dumb thing three times in a row

— Deliberate dishonesty

— Not being trustworthy

— Compromising your integrity by "winning" through making someone else fail

At the end of the boot camp the new managers also got to write a letter to the old managers detailing their socialization experiences and their observations on entering DEC from recruitment to being on the job. The boot camps were used primarily in manufacturing, but to indicate how pervasive the culture was. Here is Peter DeLisi's account of entering DEC as a sales manager in 1977:

I joined Digital in July, 1977, the year in which the company achieved two major milestones—a $1 billion in sales and the introduction of the VAX computer. My first introduction to the company was the interview process. Although I had been aggressively recruited, it felt strangely like the courtship process in my parents' native Sicily. Everyone got to say whether they liked me or not—my prospective boss, his boss, his boss's boss, prospective peers, prospective subordinates, administrative support people and a few others thrown in for good measure. Later in my career, I was to learn the reason behind the extensive interview process—newcomers weren't just joining another company; they were joining the "Digital family," and therefore, had to be approved by the other significant members of this family.

Going to Digital after 11 years at IBM was quite a culture shock. Indeed, my immediate Digital manager had warned me that it would take at least a year to get over the shock. The two companies were as different as night from day. IBM was a large, well-managed company; Digital, by comparison, seemed small and very unsophisticated.

My first exposure to Digital executives was no exception. I heard Ken Olsen speak to a group of Digital employees and it was abundantly clear to me that he was no Tom J. Watson Jr. My reaction was one of bewilderment, as I tried to capture the main points of a talk that seemed to jump all over the place. I remember being seriously distressed that I had made the wrong career decision. I had left one of the world's truly great corporations to join one that showed absolutely no external class. And what's more, its leader talked in parables that I couldn't understand. But as I was to subsequently discover, underneath the apparent simplicity, and perhaps rambling style of this engineer from MIT, was an incredible wisdom.

Later, I was to experience the individual autonomy and empowerment that existed in the Digital culture. Once again, I was to contrast this with my IBM experience by making the observation that it seemed to me like a "good news-bad news" type story. The good news about IBM was that whatever responsibility you were given, you owned the whole thing. The bad news was that it was extremely small. The good news about Digital was that you could assume whatever responsibility you wished. The bad news was—so could everyone else. And as a result, lots of people ended up doing the same things.

I was to learn that it didn't make any difference where you were in the organization. If you saw an opportunity and you believed you had the talent to apply to it, you could make a proposal and be assigned the responsibility to carry it out. "He who proposes does," was more than an accepted practice; it was a deeply held value of the company.

In those early years, I also learned about "pushback." People in Digital seemed to fight a lot with one another. Shouting matches were a frequent occurrence and I came to conclude that Digital people didn't like one another. I was subsequently told by more senior members that it was OK to disagree with someone, because "truth" would ultimately prevail. These people didn't dislike one another; they just believed strongly in their point of view. In fact, I was told stories about people who had gone all the way to Ken Olsen and ultimately prevailed, because they were so strongly convinced of the merits of their argument.

Over the years, I'm ashamed to admit, I became quite fond of these heated exchanges. After one of these exchanges, one in which I almost came to blows with one of my peers, I was called in by my manager the next morning. Sensing that this time I had really exceeded the bounds of propriety, I thought about updating my resume. It was with great and pleasant surprise that I was told that my behavior the previous day had been admirable. I had stood up for what I believed in, and as a result, the whole group had benefited from the final conclusions that we had reached.

In those early years, I learned more about the family belief in Digital. In addition to the extensive interviews which I had experienced earlier, I was to learn about team play, consensus decision-making, and "buy-in." At first it appeared incongruous to me; people would fight like crazy over ideas, and yet, really seemed to care about teamwork. It wasn't just words. Teams existed at every level.

I also got my first lesson in the "veto power" of the Digital culture. Whereas it was true that the people in Digital were tremendously empowered, it was also true that they had to get the "buy-in" of all those affected by their proposed actions. This could lead to endless rounds of meetings, negotiations, and frustration. I was later to describe this phenomenon by complaining that, "It seems that everyone in Digital can say 'no,' but no one can say 'yes.'" (Peter DeLisi, memo, personal communication, 2001)

Clearly the culture was valued, was understood, and was sold to newcomers, even as the climate according to Dennis Burke, Larry Portner, and Andy Knowles was deteriorating. To understand this seeming inconsistency, it is necessary to understand that the boot camps were run primarily in the manufacturing organization and DeLisi was brought into the sales organization. Within the functional organizations the culture was still very strong. What Burke and others had detected was the growing distance between the subunits of the organization and the growing distrust between the product lines and the functions.

REFLECTIONS AND IMPLICATIONS

As I reflect on DEC's midlife what is striking is the energy and passion that went into trying to fix things by constant minor reorganizations and the introduction of various accounting and other management tools. But the basic cultural dynamic based on the engineering genes continued to drive the system. What got people energized was products, and while enough customers continued to love DEC's products there was little chance for the business values to take hold. Not only was the business/money gene missing in the cultural DNA, but the DEC organization's immune system generated antibodies that destroyed hybrids, mutants, or outsider influences that were not consistent with the existing cultural DNA.

This point has to be emphasized in order to understand why even Ken Olsen, who was very business oriented, was never successful in imposing a management system appropriate to DEC's rapid growth and changing market. He himself was conflicted around these issues in that he advocated good business and management practices but never insisted on the necessary trade-offs to bring them to fruition: setting priorities among projects instead of letting internal competition continue; imposing stricter cost controls, especially in the human resource area; articulating a clear corporate philosophy that would guide the increasingly decentralized organization; and reviewing people systematically to ensure a system of formal accountability. There were lots of ideas of how to fix things but little systematic follow-up.

From DeLisi's point of view, the main "learning failure" was the lack of recognition that a decentralized product line organization such as the one DEC had become required a more formal strategy process. DEC's management did not understand the role of strategy and therefore never learned the process for creating a strategy to give direction to the increasingly unfocused organization. In my view, it was the engineering culture and its faith in product innovation that made the dominant coalition continue to believe that good enough products would solve all the problems. And, of course, Bell's VAX strategy did just that throughout the 1980s. By the time that technical strategy had run its course; the organization was depleted and could not really recover to deal with the technological changes that had occurred.

Symptomatic of the growing problems was the departure of some of the early team. Nick Mazzarese, the first and most successful product line manager, retired at an early age in 1972, and Pete Kaufmann left after a very successful decade in 1977. Both men felt that the climate of growth was somehow changing the organization in ways that they did not like. On the other hand, the technical side thrived with the return of Gordon Bell in 1974 from his multiyear sabbatical at Carnegie Mellon University. Bell saw the need for new products beyond the PDP-8 and PDP-11 and to this end brought together a task force of his best and brightest engineers to launch the VAX strategy. Bell's ability to sell the VAX strategy in the face of considerable opposition—because it seemed to bet the whole company on one technical strategy—reflected the power of technical visions in this kind of culture.

The combination of Olsen's commitment to innovation and Gordon Bell's insight into computer architecture continued to nurture the climate of support for the many creative engineers that DEC had accumulated and enabled them to continue to grind out fabulous products that kept them going for the next two decades. One of the many ironies of the DEC story is that Ken Olsen always wanted to build a simple business with simple products that could be mail-ordered from a catalog. I heard him repeatedly wish for that even as DEC was evolving and supporting the sophisticated products for scientists and laboratories that were in no way capable of becoming commodities and as the company was undermining or failing to support peripherals, storage products, and other items that could be easily turned into commodities. Why did Ken Olsen not impose his wish on his organization? Because, in my opinion, of his own deepest convictions about giving people freedom and responsibility.

So Olsen ended up living with where his engineers led him. In a certain sense Olsen could see but could not understand at a deeper level that a large complex organization needed a different kind of management system than the one he had created. And Olsen could see but not fully grasp that the core technology underlying computing was fundamentally changing toward miniaturization, software, and commodities. What he could understand and respond to was the consistent positive feedback that the large installed base in many large organizations was providing on the elegance, utility, and quality of DEC products. And both sales and profits were continuing their meteoric rise. So why change?

In the next chapter we will examine several of the key events of the 1980s and how the handling of these events led to DEC's ultimate end.

twelve

The Turbulent 1980s: Peaking but Weakening

In the previous chapters we have seen how the technology stream and the organizational stream diverged and how the culture served both as a continuing source of growth and as a conservative force to prevent effective learning and adaptation. In the 1980s both of these processes became sharper. Most alumni feel that DEC reached its peak in 1987, but this very growth accentuated the forces described in the previous chapter and made it harder and harder for DEC to develop a coherent strategy that would permit it to deal with the changes in the technology and the market. On the surface DEC was peaking, but underneath, the company was weakening.

Detailed accounts of the main historical events in terms of technology, personalities, and external events that impacted DEC can be found in Pearson (1992) and Rifkin and Harrar (1988). In going over these details and my own consulting notes, it became clear to me that what DEC did in the 1980s that brought it both to its peak in 1987 and to its demise in 1998 is best understood in cultural terms. *What* DEC did is fairly obvious. *Why* DEC did what it did is far from obvious, because some of the alleged mistakes that DEC made are incomprehensible except in cultural terms. For these reasons I will review the events themselves fairly superficially and put more emphasis on analyzing and trying to explain the reasons behind those events.

REORGANIZATION AND CULTURE-CHANGE EFFORTS

Growth and geographic dispersion continued at a rapid rate. This created tension between geography managers, who wanted more autonomy, and product line managers, who operated out of Maynard. Even out in the country units the product lines had learned to protect themselves from being seen as irresponsible by building their own financial units, which led to duplication of effort and excessive expenses. Coordination between product lines, sales, engineering, and manufacturing became more and more difficult. In particular, Europe, which was contributing one-third of DEC's revenue, felt too much control from Maynard. This state of affairs led, among other things, to Jack Smith, then head of manufacturing, spending six months in the Geneva European headquarters in 1981 to get a feel for the place and to interview the individual country managers on whom DEC depended heavily. This move was also a developmental assignment for Smith, to enable him to become more familiar with the sales and marketing side of the business, since he had spent most of his career until then in manufacturing.

Smith reported back, and the Operations Committee decided on a major reorganization, which consisted of the following elements: (1) reduce the profit and loss responsibility of the product lines; (2) shift profit and loss responsibility to the geographies or, in effect, to the sales organization; (3) give the country managers more power; and (4) abandon the indirect channel of distribution, that is, abandon the OEMs. This reorganization was viewed by many as one of the major reasons for DEC's ultimate decline in that it abandoned the matrix model that had kept power balanced between the product lines and the functions and now gave too much power to the functions, specifically to Jack Shields and the sales organization that he took over completely in 1983.

This new organization, along with the newly formed Executive

Committee—Ken Olsen, Win Hindle, Jack Smith, and Jack Shields and an extended Operations Committee—was viewed by some as a necessary adaptation to size and growth and by others as "the worst decision DEC ever made." Problems with the new organization were eventually recognized, leading to the promulgation later of the New Management System, but, as Peter DeLisi notes, its impact in his area was mixed.

Digital recognized the problem with its lack of accountability. In an attempt to fix this problem, it implemented the "New Management System," a form of an internal market economy. The theory, as espoused by Russell Ackoff and others, is that an internal economy causes internal businesses to operate much as external businesses do, that is, to compete for business based on the value that they provide. This value is determined in the internal economy by establishing a price that is charged to other internal users for the products and services rendered.

In the application of this theory at Digital, the sales force became the center of operation. Individual account managers were assigned profit and loss responsibility for their respective account. The idea was that the sales force would buy products and services internally, mark them up with some appropriate margin, and then sell them to their customers. Two flaws that appeared early in the implementation were, first, that the sales force could not buy product on the outside. Therefore, market competitive forces did not prevail. Secondly, since every major function was being measured on profit and loss, each of them would add a markup to its products and services, with the result that by the time the sales force added up all the markups, the price to the customer was prohibitively expensive, and therefore noncompetitive.

As a result of this inflated markup, negotiations took place to get the internal functions to lower their price to the sales force, so that Digital could price the products and services competitively. Much time was spent on this activity, and perhaps this would have normally been a healthy way of learning, except for the cost pressures on everyone at Digital at the time. Cost pressures and eroding market share made the internal economy more than an exercise in organizational theory.

The internal market economy provided an accountability that had been lacking in Digital. It provided a way to measure individual achievement that had not been present since the product line days. The cost pressures on the company, together with a way to hold individuals accountable, unfortunately led to a preoccupation with measurements. The assignment of profit and loss responsibility to individual salespeople caused an inordinate amount of time to be spent fighting over who got credit for what and who got charged for what, rather than concentrating on the important aspects of growing the business. Perhaps more critically, the measurement of individual performance was strongly opposed to a culture that had always emphasized the good of the whole family, rather than that of its individual members. We were to learn how very difficult it is to get people to work together as team members when they are rewarded and held accountable for individual achievement. (DeLisi, memo, personal communication, 2000)

As the customer base changed, the nature of the sales job changed as well, creating greater tensions within the sales organization and greater anger in customers who were less and less patient with inconsistent communications from the company, mishandled order processing, and long delays in delivery that reflected lack of planning between sales and manufacturing. Ted Johnson was under increasing pressure as head of sales but was not able to give up many of the sales traditions that had made DEC unique, especially the tradition of a salaried (not commission-based) sales force. Bill Long was made head of sales in 1980; Johnson was moved into a corporate marketing job, which did not work out, so he left in 1982. Jack Shields had been spun out from under him in 1978 to run service and was put in charge of both sales and service in 1983.

JACK SHIELDS TAKES OVER SALES

Shields's managerial style had always been somewhat different from the empowerment style that Ken Olsen promulgated. The service organization needed discipline and responsiveness. To achieve this, Shields emphasized acceptance of authority and loyalty. Pushing back was less acceptable in the service organization. Shields also trained a cadre of competent managers, many of whom were promoted into important higher-level jobs within sales and service, leading some senior managers to feel that Shields was deliberately populating the higher levels with his people and that this was done for power-grabbing reasons rather than to put the most competent people in these jobs. It also led to the later opinion that the sales function was dominated by people who brought with them a service mentality that led them to prefer higher pricing, higher profit margins, adding services to the established customer base instead of aggressively seeking new customers, vertical integration instead of buying components, holding on to proprietary products, and avoiding low-end commodities that would ultimately cannibalize the high-margin high end. In effect, the subculture of service came to dominate key elements of strategic thinking as Shields gained more power.

From a cultural point of view, the decision to give Shields more power could be viewed as an experiment that DEC was conducting in changing the culture from complete openness of debate to a more centralized process of decision making and the expectation that decisions, once made, would be accepted and implemented. "Do the right thing" would have to evolve to "Do what headquarters has decided" in the interests of timeliness and coordination. Shields could get away with making such a change because he was in the culture and of the culture. He had the respect of senior management and Ken Olsen based on his track record. He knew and understood the culture, but he also knew how to be more disciplined within that culture.

Unfortunately the chemistry between Shields and Olsen deteriorated, primarily because Shields viewed his 1983 promotion to head of sales and service as a clear indicator that he was a "contender." He improved his life style with the purchase of a more expensive house and the increased use of limos and chauffeurs for commuting. Nothing could have been more offensive to Ken Olsen, who still maintained his attitudes of frugality and, more important, believed that once a person became self-centered in this manner, he could not possibly deliver good work for the company. At an unconscious level there could also have been the tendency that Olsen had shown before of undermining people who had become powerful, even if he was himself responsible for giving them that power. In any case, once Shields had displayed his ambition, he began to lose favor, and he eventually left in 1991.

From a financial management point of view, the reorganization was regarded by many as a serious mistake, especially the abandonment of the product line model and the indirect channels of distribution. From a cultural point of view it made sense because Ken Olsen was attempting to curb what he thought was the growing power and autonomy of the many product line units by centralizing the functions and giving them more control. In that way he could maintain more control, something that became more and more important as the organization grew and differentiated. However, as discussed in chapter 10, with the growth of the many autonomous units and their growing subcultures based on their own successes, Olsen was actually beginning to lose control, and other powerful managers were beginning to second-guess him, ignore him, or even go around him in the later 1980s and early 1990s.

Through the 1980s, then, DEC became more centralized functionally, with Smith running engineering and manufacturing while Shields ran sales and service. People described DEC as increasingly stovepiped and referred to Jack and Jack as the "twin towers." A whole generation of key product line managers such as Julius Marcus, John Leng, Andy Knowles, Irwin Jacobs, Roger Cady, and Stan Olsen left in 1982 and 1983. The Operations Committee became a broad group called together occasionally, while more centralized control fell to the Executive Committee.

On the positive side, the new organization allowed Europe to flourish. For Olsen it provided an opportunity to grow into a new and somewhat unfamiliar role: to attempt a more active leadership with his new slogan, "One Company, One Strategy, One Message." Until this period Olsen had not felt the need to control directly because the "Truth through conflict" and "Do the right thing" assumptions produced decisions that satisfied him and allowed the company to flourish. What Olsen did not realize, and what would haunt him more and more, was that twenty-five years of empowering others left them feeling they knew better what was wanted anyway, with the result that he could not assert control in the way he wanted to. The process of second-guessing him, discounting him, even openly or behind his back disrespecting him, was well under way. As has been noted over and over again, the people under and around Olsen loved him and stood in awe of him, but they increasingly trusted their own judgment more than his. Though Olsen gained prominence in subsequent years and continued to make strong efforts to control, or at least to guide, DEC, it was increasingly clear to me that DEC was more and more out of control and at the mercy of rampant intergroup competition and political infighting. As many of the departing managers and engineers said, it was harder and harder to tell the truth in this environment. For DEC as a total business, this climate proved too toxic.

In the meantime, Gordon Bell was successfully selling to senior management the more integrated VAX strategy that put more emphasis on high-margin proprietary products on which high service charges could be loaded. This product strategy conflicted with the market's increasing desire for low-cost nonproprietary commodities. The OEMs would want low-cost hardware on which they could build a variety of applications. But DEC's success had been in the high-margin end, and Jack Shields had built a very successful service business with the high-margin model. It also offended Ken Olsen and others that in going through OEMs, they were leaving money on the table that DEC could collect if it went to direct channels only. Was this evidence that there was a money gene operating in DEC after all? Not really, in that the motivation to protect the high-margin products was based more on "protecting the family jewels" than anything else. If they had continued through OEMs, the proprietary technology would have had to be shared and, at that time, the VAX and its VMS operating system were viewed as being a far superior and more elegant product. Culturally one could clearly see here the arrogance that resulted from decades of success with this product strategy.

DEC LAUNCHES THREE PCS

Early in 1980 DEC decided it had to accept the reality of the PC and enter that market with its own products. Ken Olsen was alleged to have described the IBM PC as "a piece of junk" and to have said he "would have fired the engineer who designed that." So it is not surprising that DEC set out to produce a more elegant product. They already had a desktop word processor in the DECMATE to which some computing power could be added. A number of proposals had been made over the years for products that would in effect be PCs, but these had always been turned down. When pressure to come up with something competitive finally forced Olsen and the Operations Committee to move forward, several different proposals were approved: the Professional, to be developed by Avram Miller; the Rainbow, to be developed by Barry Folsom; and the DECMATE, to be developed by Dick Loveland. In all three cases it was implicitly assumed that the DEC product would be of higher quality and that the market would pay a premium for that.

Bob Supnik, one of DEC's senior engineers, was an observer of the decisions around the three PCs that DEC decided to build. His analysis of this bit of history highlights the conflict between technology and culture very poignantly.

> I was already in Hudson [DEC's semiconductor factory] by that time, finishing up the last PDP11 we did, the J11, and then starting the MicroVAX project. I was peripherally involved primarily through the Semiconductor Group's interactions with Avram Miller. I think what was happening was a fundamental misreading of the market's willingness to accept proprietary products. The PC is the first instance of the market saying we don't want personal computers, we want the IBM personal computer; we'll take it from anybody who will provide it, but we want that standard, i.e. we don't want VHS and Beta Max and everything, we just want VHS, thank you.
>
> I think the company as a whole misread what the state of the market was—that the IBM PC was just the first entrant, that there was going to be an Apple Mac and there would be other entrants in this growing marketplace. I don't think you can blame Ken or others for missing the fact that this is the first instance in what's called the tornado phenomenon of Geoff Moore, where the market coheres around a standard. Everybody who's part of that standard just gets dragged off into it by their coattails, and everyone who tries to fight it is destroyed. That had never happened before. (Supnik, interview by author, June 24, 2002)

Note that this comment reflects Paul Kampas's analysis in chapter 9 of what happens when the market chooses a dominant design. Once that has happened, the door is opened for all kinds of category-killer companies to enter with faster and cheaper clones of the dominant design. Supnik continues:

> The market was not going to take a proprietary personal computer from Digital. It had made up its mind. And I think where you can fault Ken is not for the first round of PCs but for the second round. Following the debacle of the Pro 350 and the Rainbow, the engineers had no illusions about the market, and the very next proposal from Engineering was a PC clone. Make a clone of the latest IBM machine, stay on their coattails, give it the Digital values of sturdiness and good industrial design, clean up the packaging and cabling, but fundamentally build a bit for bit, bug for bug copy of the IBM PC. It was called the DEC PC25 and 50 proposal. Now this is '84. Compaq has not been founded or is just being founded, and the proposal was to do exactly what Compaq was going to do—a fast clone. But Ken killed it; DEC is not a copycat.
>
> When this proposal was being debated, there was no one in Engineering who thought that making a clone was a bad idea or the wrong thing to do. Everyone said yes, this is obviously what you do, the market has gone here, and you do what the market says. . . . Digital did have design, assembly and test, and distribution processes tailored to high volume projects, namely, terminal products. This proposal was effectively coming as an extension to the terminal group. We did terminals, okay so we'll do PCs. The design and manufacturing processes were there, what wasn't there was the willingness to have it be an IBM compatible PC from Digital, something that Ken would embrace fully in 1991. (Bob Supnik, interview by author, June 24, 2002)

Note that it was the deep assumption about product quality and DEC's role as an innovator that was being challenged by the engineering groups proposing a clone. So even though all three PC entries failed to become successful products, the assumptions about what a product should be held firm. DEC would not compromise on quality or elegance, and DEC would not be a copycat. And this assumption was validated by the continuing success of the VAX strategy and networking with Ethernet.

GORDON BELL'S DEPARTURE AND ITS CONSEQUENCES

As DEC grew and became differentiated into various functional and product empires, it became schizophrenic. Organizational health and toxic forces were running side by side, and the toxic forces were perceived but denied, rationalized, or absorbed by selected members who in turn became sick, notably Gordon Bell, whose heart attack in 1983 seemed clearly related to the stress levels that were building up within DEC. Bell had built a world-class engineering organization but ran into increasing difficulty with Ken Olsen and was beginning to be viewed as too much of an empire builder, leading to a plan to give engineering to Jack Smith in the early 1980s. Bell resented this plan, and arguments with Olsen became more acrimonious. He had a heart attack during a skiing trip in Colorado but survived because of the heroic efforts of several DEC colleagues, notably Bob Puffer, who was trained in cardiopulmonary resuscitation (CPR). However, this health crisis made him realize that he must move on, so he and Bob Puffer started a new venture of their own called Encore.

Puffer in a June 2002 letter describes these times:

> Since I was there from 1969 through 1983 (became a VP and officer in 1974) I did not see the battle of the fiefdoms play out in the late 80's. But clearly in 1983 there was a great deal of senior level discontent and the departure of a number of officers. As much as we loved the company we were all sensing that Ken was losing control, we were getting too large to coordinate in our traditional way, and the various interpretations of doing what was right were tying us in knots. I left to do a start up with Gordon Bell (Encore), with the aspiration of building another Digital on a smaller scale. Although Encore survived for a decade (without any of its founders, save one), it was a business and cultural failure and an unpleasant personal experience which led those DECies there to a better appreciation of the working environment we had left. (Bob Puffer, letter, personal communication, June 2002)

Gordon Bell ended up on the West Coast working with Microsoft, and Puffer ended up in Coriolis, a New England networking company. With Gordon Bell's departure in 1983, a huge vacuum was created. Bell had the intellectual power and track record to pull together the various parts of engineering. Some felt he was the only true systems engineer and that his replacements were all more component oriented. With his departure the door was opened to more fighting among the engineering groups. Jack Smith was the senior vice president to whom engineering was now reporting, and he chose to manage it by creating a task force under the chairmanship of Bill Strecker, who was acknowledged at that point to be the most visionary of the senior engineering group, though everyone missed Bell's intellectual power and willingness to focus. This group, known as the STF (for "Strategy" or "Systems" Task Force) was colloquially called the Strecker Task Force and consisted of most of the senior technical talent in the company. It was their job to recommend which projects should be pursued, though, as Olsen often complained, they had a lot of power and very little responsibility; hence, their decisions were a priori suspect in Olsen's view.

A senior member of the STF provides some context in a 2001 interview:

> And then the so-called Strecker Task Force came into being. It was officially known as the Strategy Task Force. After Gordon decided to leave, there was no formal authority for settling disputes within Engineering about allocation of resources or budgets. At first, things were prospering enough you could just take every request and say yes. But even by '84, '85 after the company had spent a significant amount of money on its unsuccessful quest to do personal computers, there were already issues of we can't do everything. So this mechanism was devised to get the company's leading technologists together and to have them grade the requests (at least in a technology sense) to see which ones made sense and which ones didn't, which ones added up to a coherent strategy, and which ones were marching off in a different direction.
>
> Bill chaired this from the moment it was formed; that's why it was called the Strecker Task Force. For the first couple of years the STF not only made technology recommendations, but it also settled the engineering budget, which was a useful and completely thankless task to do. Bill made an increasing number of enemies as this went on. By '88 there was pretty much undeclared warfare about whether the STF had the right to set budgets or whether the VPs, the business VPs or the product line VPs or the engineering group VPs, would have that ulti-

mate authority. This all came to a head over a project called Aquarius, which was a very ambitious program to build a VAX out of the same kind of technology that IBM mainframes were built out of—water-cooled, multi-chip ECL [emitter-coupled logic] gate arrays. With the exception of the people who were working on the project, every engineer in Digital thought it was ill-advised.

Whether or not this decision was "ill-advised," DEC went ahead and produced a state-of-the-art large computer system, the VAX 9000, which was announced in October 1989 and shipped in June 1990. It was considered a marvel of technological innovation, a heroic accomplishment, a project that cost too much, and, in the end, a product that failed in the marketplace. One view of this failure is that smaller and cheaper machines would soon outperform it. Another view is that the lack of support in making the 9000 a complete system was responsible for its failure. What is significant is that the decisions to move forward and the explanations of outcomes were all biased and continue to this day to be controversial. Why the VAX 9000 project went ahead is related to another major set of events to be analyzed: the decision to compete with IBM.

TURMOIL IN THE ENGINEERING ORGANIZATION: COMPETITION WITH IBM, AND PRISM, AQUARIUS, AND ALPHA

Engineering was a large empire with many fiefdoms within it, and the culture of freedom and empowerment ensured that each of these fiefdoms would fight for what it thought to be the right future for DEC. New technologies such as Reduced Instruction Set Computer (RISC) chips were evolving, the market was moving toward accepting a dominant design, and semiconductors and miniaturization were threatening to turn the whole industry upside down. Competition with IBM was talked about already in the 1970s, but a more explicit strategic decision to compete directly with IBM was not articulated until the early 1980s and was attributed primarily to Jack Shields.

In appendix D Peter DeLisi describes the competition with IBM as follows:

Product leadership had carried Digital for over three decades, but the turning point was between 1986 and 1988. During these two years, Digital hired 26,800 people to go head-to-head with IBM. Looking back, we see that the growth that they anticipated did not materialize. Unbeknownst to anyone in the industry at the time, the computer business was entering a flat period of growth in anticipation of the future emerging client/server and networking type businesses. Saddled with the increased cost of 26,800 people, Digital needed to cut cost and become much more efficient. It needed to move the company from product leadership to operational excellence. It could also have reduced manpower, but in a no layoff company, this was impossible.

Why take on IBM? As one senior engineer, Jesse Lipcon, analyzed the question, both IBM and DEC had fallen prey to a belief in a business model that emphasized a full line of products, high margins, proprietary systems, emphasis on vertical integration (making everything versus buying), and heavy reliance on service revenues. The great success with a large installed customer base allowed high "monopolistic" service charges and made it difficult to disaggregate the portion of service cost that should be charged as part of the initial cost of the product (creating the high margins) versus charging for services later as an independent item (driving costs of the basic products down). From the point of view of this business model, low-end commodities were seen to be an intrinsic threat to the high-margin, high-end machines because they might perform as well but at a much lower cost. Therefore, low-cost commodities had to be avoided, and their avoidance had led to the dismantling of the indirect channels of distribution.

The controversial decision to build a high-end VAX, the VAX 9000 (dubbed Aquarius), was seen by most alumni to be part of the marketing-driven strategy to compete with IBM, ignoring the technical skepticism expressed by the STF. DEC had successfully built high-end computers. The VAX 8600, dubbed Venus, was behind schedule but under Bob Glorioso's leadership was completed and introduced in 1984. A successor and faster model, the 8650, was approved and built. The 9000 project was the logical next step, except that the technology was getting more complex and semiconductors were becoming more and more efficient. A natural disagreement therefore arose within the engineering community between those pursuing the "compete with IBM and build the 9000 strategy" and the group that wanted to bet on new and smaller chips and the new RISC technology. Glorioso noted that "the 9000 group felt that they had been asked to come up with a system solution that would compete with IBM in the general business area and transaction processing in particular. The 9000 was to be only one leg of that strategy that included Clusters, Storage, Networking, Data Bases, System Management, Development Tools and Services into a complete offering. That was a customer/market view that my group was charged with and was trying to accomplish. The problem was the rest of the company and STF in particular were looking at Components. I believe that the Component view is what hampered the potential for success with Alpha as well" (Bob Glorioso, interview by author, 1999).

How this played out in relation to DEC's own engineering efforts after the departure of Gordon Bell is described by one of DEC's senior development engineers in a 2001 interview:

> This was the period, '85–'86, when the first DECWorld's were happening. This is when Ken is appearing on the cover of Fortune magazine as entrepreneur of the century. This is the time when BEAT IBM replaced beat the minicomputer vendors as the company's mantra. There was a very significant shift in '85–'86. IBM became the official enemy rather than Sun or Data General, or any of the people we were used to competing with. In fact I remember very distinctly when Bill Strecker came to the STF and said this. He was greeted with dead silence by all the assembled engineers. . . . The general reaction was dismay: are you out of your mind, we're tiny compared to IBM, we don't have the global product nor do we have the distribution channels, why are we abandoning our traditional customer base on a suicide charge? But this is the year of those famous bow ties of Number One in 2007, because somebody had projected DEC's growth and IBM's growth and it crossed in 2007. The company was filled with hubris from its success. People didn't realize that it was the apogee and not just a point on a slope.

RISC technology began to surface in the academic community in the late seventies. The first experimental machines were built in 1982 through 1984 at Stanford and Berkeley and then at DEC's own Western

Research Lab. At first there was general skepticism in DEC Engineering about RISC, because all of the papers were written around trivial test cases. Most engineers believed that it works for this five line program but it's not going to work on transaction processing.

In 1986, when the Western Research Lab finished its machine, there was a fly-off between the Lab's RISC system and the then-current top-of-the-line VAX, the 8800. The conclusion was, for a given investment in hardware, RISC technology is going to outperform VAX technology by at least 2-1. Once that came out, the mood in Engineering shifted from skepticism to what are we going to do?

A lot of people floated proposals for RISC technology. The Semiconductor Group floated one, Dave Cutler [in Seattle] floated one, the Large Computer Group had one. All of them were underfunded and without coherence. Finally, Jack Smith said we're only going to have one RISC program, and Dave Cutler is going to run it. Dave took charge of it in '85, and it was called Prism. Engineering fell into line behind it, and all the other projects stopped.

But Dave unfortunately had been bitten by the large machine bug. Somewhere along the line he wanted to build hardware, and his group didn't have the skills to do the chips. Because VLSI [very-large-scale integration] design was very specialized and sort of a black art, the Hudson Semiconductor Group was it for the company. Dave didn't want to just build a system out of something that somebody else built. He wanted his own. So he concluded he'd have to build a big machine out of the ECL technology that was being used by both the Argonaut group (the next midrange VAX) and the Aquarius group. Now there were three large machine projects all fighting for funding starting in about '86. There was outright warfare among all these groups. The Aquarius people felt that whoever else was trying to build a large machine was on their turf and taking their budget, and the Argonaut team felt that if you were going to build something you should build a VAX. Things just fractured.

In the meantime the Hudson Semiconductor Group was trying to build a silicon version of Prism. This all came to a head in late '87, early '88 when it was clear that there just wasn't enough money to complete these machines. The executive group got together, and they somehow reached the conclusion that the machine they would drop would be Dave Cutler's machine. That was okay because there was still the silicon chip to continue the RISC program. Dave was upset but he wasn't so upset that he was going jump ship.

Starting at the beginning of '88, a group of workstation engineers under Carol Peters in Palo Alto decided that Prism, the chip, was taking too long and the company needed to be in the UNIX RISC workstation business immediately. They struck a deal to pick up an existing RISC chip from the MIPS Company. They went back to the Executive Committee in April of '88 and said look if you guys are just doing RISC because you want to run UNIX, skip this proprietary architecture and just do MIPS; give us the go ahead today and we'll have a product in nine months. That really put the cat among the pigeons, because Dave Cutler's Prism effort was not just the silicon chip, it was a new operating system. If the Prism chip went away, then the whole operating system went away, and everything Dave had done for two years was suddenly gone.

The MIPS proposal was debated for three months. In June of '88 there was a climactic meeting in front of the Executive Committee about whether to do the MIPS based workstation or to continue with Prism. The issue was drawn very simply—Prism was going to take about another year to finish, it wouldn't have been out until early 1990. A product based on the MIPS chip could come out in the beginning of '89. Ken's view was if it's only UNIX, it doesn't really matter to the future of the company, let's do what's cheap and expedient, let's go with the outside vendor. He cancelled the Prism program altogether. Dave Cutler left the company taking that new operating system with him, and that became Microsoft NT.

The fiefdoms not only fought for resources but also they saw the same events rather differently. Bob Glorioso, who had had most of his projects cut even though he had brought the Venus project to completion, became head of the information systems business with Joe Zeh as head of the Aquarius project when Ken Olsen decided to reinstate the group in spite of STF objections. In a 1992 internal memorandum he wrote about these decisions in a very different way:

> The folks in Seattle in Dave Cutler's organization, and the folks in Hudson in the Semiconductor group, managed by Jeff Kalb, worked closely together to deliver the 32 bit RISC system based on the original work done in Marlboro [in Glorioso's organization]. As they evolved

very nicely in Seattle, the opportunity arose to purchase an existing chip
. . . from MIPS Computers in California. MIPS people came by with lots
of slides and promises of several next generation products immediately
on the heels of the first product. They also claimed to have all the software compilers completed, debugged, and fully operational, an area
where we felt we were behind. The firm belief that we couldn't do
anything right and everybody else could, led to a mass hysteria type
reaction that resulted in Bob Supnik, the champion of Prism, standing
up before the Executive Committee and stating "we should go with
MIPS." . . . With Bob's strong recommendation . . . the decision was
made to go forth with MIPS.

The result is history. MIPS did deliver their first part, late. Their
compilers were a disaster and had to be totally rewritten by Digital
and follow-on products were not months late but years late and ultimately MIPS was bought by Silicon Graphics and disappeared from
the scene. In the meantime, the Prism part was delivered on time, with
better performance by the way, and the software had to be rewritten for
MIPS anyway, but the decision had already been made. We lost it. Our
workstation business would never recover from this decision. (Bob
Glorioso, internal memo, 1992)

Different interpretations of the events surrounding the evolution of
key products were par for the course, depending on which fiefdom was
writing the history. And, in particular, major issues arose around the
evolution of the VAX 9000 and the Alpha chip. A senior engineer who
preferred not to be named stated in a 2001 interview:

Bob Glorioso and Joe Zeh were the business and engineering leaders.
The reason everyone else thought it was wrong to build the VAX 9000
was that they could see that the progress of little tiny semiconductor
chips was such that in the early nineties it would be possible to build
more powerful machines out of microprocessors. So why invest a couple
billion dollars, a huge amount of money for a product that would liter-
ally be out of a future by 1990–92? Gordon Bell had actually drawn all
this out in 1980 in a famous graph of microprocessor performance versus mainframes and supercomputers predicting when they would cross.
So every year the STF would try and clip the spending wings of this
large mainframe project, and every year Bob Glorioso would take his

case to Ken and to his fellow VPs and say these engineers have no right to tell us business people what to do.

Bob Glorioso, coming off his success with the Venus product, saw things differently: He did not view it as a VPs against the STF or engineers issue, but as a "Do the right thing" issue.

We fought for what we believed our customers wanted as we learned from our marketing work. I took my staff out to customers about twice a year and each one met with a customer at least once a month. We even had a program where senior engineers in our group attended a customer meeting at least once a year.

The Venus product was desperately needed. The company was in a lull (1983–84), stock prices were down, revenues were not growing, it was a tough time for the company without a follow on to the 780 [the first member of the VAX family introduced in 1977]. There was a 785 put out but its performance was only marginally better than the 780. We started shipping Venus at the end of December of '84 and we still had our heads down because we had to get revenue and we shipped 500 in six months. It was worth about a billion dollars of revenue and that pulled the company out of the doldrums. And the beginning of '85 was the beginning of the end in my estimation, from my narrow point of view. . . .

BJ [Bill Johnson] was my boss at the time. During this time that we had to get the 500 units of the VAX 8600 (Venus) out the door, was also the beginning of the first STF committee meetings for funding for the next year. I told BJ that I don't have any time to deal with this, and to please make sure my group gets dealt with properly. You have to take care of me because there's no way I can take care of the company and take care of myself at the same time. I just can't do it. This was really intense, dealing with problem after problem. We had a manufacturing organization that didn't understand how to deal with this new technology. I used my engineering organization to backfill manufacturing to get them bootstrapped and it took a lot of energy to do that. But working together, engineering and manufacturing, we got it done. Getting 500 units out in six months was hard work. BJ said, I'll take care of you, don't worry about it. I drove up to BJ's staff meeting in Nashua, I'll never forget this, and we got our budgets handed to us. And my budget

was virtually zero. All my new projects were cancelled and I had to dismantle this large organization that had just broken its back delivering
needed revenue.

In the meantime they had given me this group in California that was
doing a new architecture, RISC. Not only that, but they made me a vice
president—it was totally mixed signals. So I said, okay, you want me to
dismantle the group, I'm a good soldier, great, I'll do it. I was angry but
I'll do what I have to do. You guys are making the wrong decisions but
that's your decision not mine.

The only thing that changed through this period was as my group
was about to be disbanded Ken called me at home one night and asked
what's happening. I told him and he said, well why don't you propose
this and why don't you propose that. I started dusting off the things I
had proposed before and pushed them back into the system and somehow they got funded. So I know Ken supported them. What got funded
was some R&D on the next generation high performance system that
ultimately became Aquarius, Clusters, System Management Software
and the follow on to the 8600, which we had pretty much in the bag,
a performance improvement called the 8650. Most of the 8600's and
8650's went out in clusters, so we'd sell them in groups of two and three
which was even better. The average system sale was over a million
dollars. . . . But all the work in California was cancelled and that group
ultimately went off and formed the core of MIPS in Silicon Graphics
and other Silicon Valley firms. (Bob Glorioso, memo, personal communication, and interview by author, 2001)

I experienced the impact of this discussion directly in my role as
consultant to the Operations Committee in that Ken would talk to me
at length about the positive values he saw in the Aquarius project, but
I would hear from others that not only was it the wrong project but
that the business projections of what the product would cost and how
many of the machines would actually be sold were distorted. Some
even felt that the data were outright falsified with various motives
being attributed to the Aquarius team that were not complimentary. At
the same time I was asked by Paul McGowan, who was Glorioso's organization development consultant, to develop ways of improving
teamwork and management within the various groups that Glorioso

had working for him in the information systems business group—clusters, transaction processing, fault tolerant systems, systems management software, a high-end services group, and Aquarius within it. It was McGowan who provided at that time a most salient metaphor of teamwork. He said, "You know what kind of a team DEC is; it is a track team," referring to his observations of what DEC had become as the various fiefdoms evolved. This beautifully captured the image of the separate performers, each trying to win in their event but with very little coordination or support across events. I also recall that it was virtually impossible to get any hard facts about any of these projects because each group that I talked to was clearly in the business of protecting its own interests and therefore was prepared to bad-mouth other groups while embellishing its self-image. The commitment to "truth" and an open debate to reach "truth" were no longer in evidence.

Olsen believed that the Alpha group, which was developing a very fast state-of-the-art chip that was intended to be DEC's next major product after the VAX, was "jealous" and that they and others were withholding support from the Aquarius team, thus slowing up the product's development. Glorioso clearly felt this lack of support and stated that Strecker made promises for software products paid for out of Glorioso's budget that were not honored. I also got involved in consulting with the software group and witnessed there the struggle of allocating limited resources across too many projects. It is not clear whether this disadvantaged the VAX 9000 in particular or whether it made all of the projects late. What was clear was that the software group was in turmoil and that DEC had not realized the ultimate importance of software in the evolution of computing.

To complicate matters, the Alpha team was rushing to finish what they considered to be the product that would save the company in the post-VAX generation, and Olsen believed that they were using money that was allocated to other projects, and doing so in an underhanded way. One of Olsen's chronic complaints about Alpha was that its development costs were so high that it could never pay for itself once it was finally marketed. In the same way, the anti-Aquarius folks felt that the money spent on that project was a waste, since the new technologies that were developed from it were only relevant to products that had become obsolete. One senior member of the STF analyzed the problem as follows:

> I think that the project [Aquarius] started as one thing and it kind of got out of hand. Probably when it was first conceived of in '84, '85 it would have been a machine that cost about $100,000 and would have been much lower priced and therefore would have sold more units. But they were caught in a bind. They started here and then as the project began to develop they were forced into what I would call very heroic technology. They were fundamentally using the kind of technology that normally was left to Seymour Cray to develop. And once you do that your costs and your schedules go out the window. So I would venture that they got caught in an escalating technology spiral that drove the project out of control both in terms of costs and schedules, and didn't know how to get off.

Glorioso, on the other hand, comments that

> it was never a 100k machine. Our target was the 500k system. The technology for Aquarius actually got simpler as we progressed. It started as a water-cooled machine, hence Aquarius, and we later invented a better and much less expensive way to cool it with air. The basic interconnect technology that we used was an outgrowth of Gordon's investment in Gene Amdahl's company, Trilogy, which failed. We took the learning from that and created a new and much better multi-chip interconnect technology that worked very well. This was mostly in place at the end of the "research" phase of the project—the point where major funds are committed. Little changed after that. I believe it was viewed as heroic by those who were caught in or by the "coalition."

Olsen's role is also seen differently by the different factions. One senior engineer noted in a 2001 interview:

> Ken was not comfortable with the new semiconductor technology that we did. I can remember a discussion in 1989—Aquarius is almost ready to go but it's clear that the next chip that we're building called N-VAX is going to be just as fast and Aquarius cost $300,000 to build and this chip cost $300. And Ken called me up and said is this really right, this chip

you're developing is as fast as Aquarius? And I said, yes, Ken, it is and within two years it will be even faster because the technology just makes the chips faster, you almost don't have to do anything. And he said I just don't understand it, I don't see how this is possible, how this one chip can replace these racks of electronics, I just don't get it, was what he said to me. It was very, very poignant.

Glorioso, on the other hand, felt that "a chip does not a total system make, especially in 1989. The difference between the system and the component views again. Note that even the later high performance VAX and Alpha systems made with 'Single Chip CPUs [central processing units]' in the early 90s sold for business applications were still large racks of electronics. The real shrink has come in the last 6 or 7 years!"

From Glorioso's point of view, the issue was not costs, technology, or schedule. He has pointed out in letters to me that the VAX 9000 was not much later than most DEC products and that the costs were not that out of line given the technological problems that had to be solved. He felt the need for the 9000 arose out of a concern for customers and what they wanted and needed. His view was that most of the engineering group had insufficient customer contact to realize what customers wanted and needed. From his point of view, had the project gotten more support early, especially in the software area, and had it gotten more sales and marketing support, it might well have paid for itself. But the irony, in the end, is that neither the VAX 9000 nor the Alpha chip that was to be DEC's future came out soon enough, because resources were spread thin, and groups fought with one another and undermined one another, thereby slowing all development.

In fact, the Alpha project illustrated how projects that were viewed as "Doing the right thing" could flourish without a great deal of formal support. Bob Supnik noted that the Alpha team operated without major support or a clear location within engineering:

> I organized Alpha as a program with me as program manager. This had never worked before in Digital; it had been tried many times, never worked. You may remember the old saying that Digital ran

by the golden rule, which was, "he that has the gold makes the rules."
Yet the Alpha Program was a team of maybe a half dozen people with
never more than a million and a half bucks to speak of. But the time was
right to try and get people aligned around a common effort at engineering. I was very fortunate to hook up with Peter Conklin, who brought
a fervor for organization by alignment or enrollment that was truly
unique. And we really did run Alpha just as a program. It never resided
centrally in any organization, it was never really owned by any VP. It
evolved from this small core team of six or eight people to spanning
about 105 to 110 projects coordinated by the program team. It outlasted
Ken and a bunch of organizational changes and all kinds of chaos in the
first layoffs. When we shipped Alpha, we shipped a new architecture, a
new chip, four systems, three operating systems, 30 products with field
training and the whole works, at the end of '92. It was kind of a defining
experience for me. (Bob Supnik, interview by author, 2001)

Another fundamental element of the DEC culture was at work in
the Alpha team and was considered to be instrumental in producing
the success that this team had in spite of roadblocks and opposition.
Ralph Katz, a professor in the management of research and development area at Northeastern University, interviewed members of the
Alpha team and concluded among other things:

> Members of Alpha were experienced individuals who could function in-
> dependently and who did not need a lot of direction, hand-holding, or
> cheerleading. They were not preoccupied with their individual careers;
> they were more interested in having their peers within the engineering
> community see them as being one of the world's best design teams.
> Ambition, promotion, and monetary rewards were not the principal
> driving forces. Recognition and acceptance of their accomplishments
> by their technical peers and by society was, for them, the true test of
> their creative abilities.
>
> Although team members had very different backgrounds, experi-
> ences, and technical strengths, they were stimulated and motivated by
> common criteria. In the words of one Alpha member, "We see eye-to-
> eye on so many things." This diversity of talent but singular mindset
> materialized within Alpha not through any formalized staffing process
> but as a consequence of Digitial's fluid boundaries and self-selection to

projects. It is an organic process that may look messy and may lead to unproductive outcomes, but which can also result in synergistic groups where the individual talents become greatly amplified through mutual stimulation and challenge. . . .

A number of important behavioral norms was also established and reinforced by the Alpha team. It was expected, for example, that each one would inform other members as soon as he/she realized that he/she could not make a given deadline or milestone. It was acceptable to be in trouble; it was not acceptable to surprise people. Individuals were expected not to "grind away," but to go for help. There was zero tolerance for trying to "bull" through a problem or discussion. It was important for team members to be tenacious and not to give up easily, but it was also essential to realize when he/she was no longer being productive. Pushing and working hard were okay, but it was important to have fun. Humor and good-natured teasing were commonplace occurrences. (Katz 1993, pp. 224–26)

These norms were almost exactly the ones that Ken Olsen fostered when DEC was founded in the late 1950s, and once again the theme of having fun and being creative surface as central themes. Glorioso commented that

this was not unlike how other projects worked in many different groups. These norms were one of the positive things that did migrate through the engineering organization. The values as well as the design tools and project management philosophy were shared and moved quite rapidly between organizations. For example, when Demmer's group had technical problems with its chips, I sent a team over to train them to use our chips, and the timing tools we used in Marlboro were created in and supported by the folks in Hudson. We pioneered using software management techniques for hardware projects, and that spread quickly. It is too bad we could not capitalize on this spirit and approach.

KEN OLSEN'S MANAGERIAL STYLE CHANGES

Sometime in the 1980s Ken Olsen changed his style. In the 1960s and 1970s Olsen was scrupulously neutral and tended to play devil's advocate rather than advocating his own biases. In the 1980s the major change that people saw in him was that his biases became more overt and that he used his power to further those biases rather than to further diversity. In 1983 this became blatant in the decision to announce that DEC was "One Company with One Strategy and One Message," even though this was far from the reality.

A number of factors seemed to contribute to these changes. One of these was DEC's increasing visibility and the attention it attracted from the press. As DEC became more successful it inevitably attracted business press questions and criticisms about strategy and tactics. Ken Olsen was not comfortable with the press in the first place, and when criticisms or pointed questions arose, he was often abrupt and impatient. He came to believe that the press did not really want to understand what DEC was trying to do, and his engineering mentality made him feel he should not have to play a public relations role. It is a basic assumption of the engineering culture that "good work should speak for itself" and an engineer "should not have to sell himself." Public relations and image building are forms of "lying" and are thus to be avoided.

A second factor was the declining health and death in 1987 of Olsen's mentor, General Georges Doriot. Doriot had been the original investor and had through the years been one of the few people who could advise Olsen. Many observers speculated that Doriot played a key advisory role during the 1970s and into the 1980s and that with his death Olsen felt more on his own and felt the need to take charge more aggressively.

A third factor along the same lines was the departure of Gordon Bell, who represented a balancing force in the DEC dominant coalition. Whereas Olsen's strengths were in creating management processes that stimulated innovation, Bell's strengths were clearly in the technology of computing and systems engineering. Many observers felt that in Bell's absence Olsen became more active in engineering decisions, but there was no one in engineering who could really argue with Olsen in the way that Bell had; hence, Olsen's interventions were seen increasingly as disruptive rather than helpful.

A fourth factor was Olsen's own growing sense of confidence. In

1986 *Fortune* had named Olsen the Entrepreneur of the Century, and in 1987 *Business Week* named DEC the eighth most successful corporation in the United States. Olsen appeared to be in control, with a strong vision and a rosy future. He became, on the one hand, more directive and, on the other hand, more anxious, disappointed, and eventually cynical about the fact that the various empires under him fought destructively rather than solving their problems. Olsen apparently believed that the kind of culture he had created would scale up and did not clearly see the consequences of success and growth. Peter DeLisi saw the need for an integrative strategy process and wrote an articulate letter to Olsen proposing more emphasis on strategy, but the answer indicated that Olsen neither understood nor felt the need for the kind of strategy process that DeLisi was advocating.

The lack of the business gene, or money gene, at the top of the organization led to further difficulties in that many of the more business- and marketing-oriented managers left in frustration. Engineering was also losing good people with the departure of Bob Puffer, Dick Clayton, Larry Portner, and Jeff Kalb. Especially problematic was the departure of Bernie Lacroute and Barry Folsom to Sun Microsystems and Dave Cutler to Microsoft. For most of them the climate at the top of the organization had become too disorganized, too unpredictable, and lacking in strategy.

CONCLUSION

I have tried in this chapter to show concretely how the very positive innovative culture could at one and the same time grind out fabulous new products and develop such strong internal animosities that groups would accuse one another of lying, cheating, and misuse of resources. Groups were pulling apart rather than pulling together, and no one was strong enough, as Gordon Bell had been, to pull the diverging strands together into a coherent strategy. I consider this to be a highly important point in that it highlights what can happen in a knowledge-based organization. Neither strong concepts nor formal hierarchy produced enough consensus to allocate resources and energy wisely in terms of the rapid adjustments that the organization had to make to keep up with market and technology changes. By the time Olsen's style changed to being more of an advocate, the groups had already become too strong, were prepared to ignore what Olsen wanted, and fought among themselves. The culture of empowerment was alive and well, but its negative consequences for DEC the business entity were becoming clearer and clearer.

thirteen

The Beginning of the End

KEN OLSEN'S FINAL EFFORTS TO SAVE DEC

DEC's end did not come with either a bang or a whimper. Rather, it was a long drawn-out process consisting of several years of success mixed with occasional crises, recognition in the late 1980s that a new way of managing had to be found, intense efforts to market new products, networking and systems integration through large fairs, finally the acceptance of open standards and commodities, recognition of the need to downsize, two painful years of nonprofitability (1991 and 1992), and Ken Olsen's resignation in late 1992.

The board promoted Bob Palmer, vice president of semiconductors, who then spent six years trying to bring DEC back to profitability by selling off some units, imposing a more disciplined way of managing, and changing elements of the culture by bringing in outsiders in senior management roles. The formal DEC era ended in 1998 with the sale of the company to the Compaq Corporation. My direct involvement ended in 1992, so I can only provide limited secondhand data about the later years, but I interviewed many ex-DEC managers while they were working at Compaq.

On the surface DEC did everything right in the late 1980s and early 1990s. From the mid-1980s DEC exploited its own need for networking, its geographically distributed organizations, and its multiple computer lines by building an effective interconnect system with Ethernet. The essence of the DEC approach was a peer-to-peer network that did not go through any central computer, a feature that DEC managers touted as making their network more reliable and more congruent with their egalitarian culture. On the hardware side a steady stream of new low-end, midrange, and high-end VAXs were introduced with interconnect capacities, including a whole line of UNIX-based systems. Major changes were made in the manufacturing area acknowledging the technological changes toward semiconductors. The enterprise integration effort was launched in recognition of the fact that organizations needed systemic solutions, not individual pieces of hardware and software. Innovations in how to deal with all the different customer segments continued to be made, especially through the large product fairs.

LARGE PRODUCT FAIRS

Ed Kramer was involved in the creation of these events.

> Instead of each product line having a worldwide sales meeting, I recommended in 1983 having one humungous meeting of every salesman in the entire company at one time, over a long weekend in Boston. At this meeting each product line would set up an exhibition and hold sales seminars—in effect, a trade show for the DEC sales force. Ken liked the idea and we kicked it off that fall at the old Hines Convention Center. Ken and I visited the exhibit floor during the setup and we were both enormously impressed with the professionalism of the displays and their breadth and scope. The exhibit area had been named "DECtown."
>
> Ken asked if I thought we should invite some customers. That was truly an epiphany! I thought it was a fantastic suggestion, and although the meeting was only days away, I scurried around to see if we could open it to customers at some point. The sales meeting was a landmark event in DEC history (and Boston's). We had over 8000 attendees on the evening of the big party (held at UMass Columbia Point Campus). It took 300–400 school buses to move everyone, Massport redirected air traffic at Logan that evening to keep from disturbing the entertainment

(Peter, Paul and Mary). Overall, it was one of the most inspirational events I've ever attended. Ken was beaming when he came to the podium and addressed the multitudes who gave him a standing ovation. At the tail end of the sales meeting, we had customers attend. There were many more customers clamoring to attend than we could accommodate on such short notice. Salesmen in attendance were so impressed by the exhibits they began frantically calling their customers to "come on down." The hands-down success of that impromptu event led the Ops Committee to immediately approve a larger expanded DECtown event for the next year, renamed DECworld, and focused primarily on key accounts who would be accompanied by their salesperson.

This gave me the opportunity to propose an already proven success as an alternative to those god-awful industry trade shows—the One Company Trade Show. I ran the first couple of them and they later (after I left) became extravaganzas and cost tens of millions to put on. DEC even rented the QE2 and had it come to Boston to be used as hotel space, since there weren't enough hotel rooms in the area to handle the event. The concept of a one company trade show was very powerful for an organization such as DEC with such a huge range of products. It was awesome for a customer to enter a monstrous exhibit hall filled entirely with DEC products. It was about the best marketing/promotional idea I had ever seen and it came to fruition. All DEC employees were invited and given time to attend. It was a most impressive experience and something that every DEC employee could be proud of and relate to.

In the first few years of DECworld, I never heard a negative comment from a customer or salesman. The engineers had the chance to showcase their products, but it was really a marketing and sales driven event. Engineers had their own chance to exhibit to customers—at DECUS meetings. I lost track of DECworld after I left in 1987, but it likely became less relevant as commoditization of computing solutions and PCs took over the industry. (Ed Kramer, letter, personal communication, August 25, 2002)

DECworlds continued until 1992. They not only gave DEC visibility with customers but also played an important role in giving DEC employees a continued sense of identity and coherence. The 1992 DECworld was a three-week extravaganza which, according to DEC reporters, was "the largest single vendor-customer symposium in the information technology industry. Thousands of enthusiastic employees, over a three-week period, captivated 30,000 plus customers with an array of high-tech solutions to everyday business problems" (*Decworld*, 1992, vol. 1, no. 1).

Note, however, that this coherence was based on products and innovations. Pride and loyalty were tied to product elegance, quality, and novelty, not to specific metrics of business performance.

ENTERPRISE INTEGRATION AND ORGANIZATIONAL CONSULTING

One of the ironies of organizational life is that organizations will often tout and espouse that which is their own weak spot. We see this at the national level in the United States in the obsession with teamwork and team building. A pragmatic society of rugged individualists will always regard group activities, meetings, and teamwork as a necessity to get the job done, not something of intrinsic value. Hence, books on team building outsell most other books on organization development, a kind of silent testimony acknowledging where we are underdeveloped. DEC's evolution of Enterprise Integration Services and its extensive use of organization development specialists as internal consultants throughout the organization can be seen in the same vein—as acknowledgment of the increasing difficulty of integrating the vast number of entrepreneurial units that characterized the DEC of the late 1980s.

An internal Organization Consulting Group (OCG) under Ben Fordham brought together specialists in organization development and related fields to provide consulting services to current and future customers to help them think through their enterprise integration problems. Members of this group met from time to time with organization development consultants from the other parts of DEC in a Woods Meeting to deal with DEC's own integration problems. This group attempted to pull together a broader picture of what was happening in DEC by opening cross-group communication channels and defining "truth" in an organization in which truth had become harder and harder to identify. I worked closely with this group, which provided a deeper insight into what was happening than was possible to obtain in the increasingly isolated Executive Committee.

One of the important 1987 and 1988 tasks of the OCG was to provide the skills and manpower to conduct broad interview surveys across the top management. It was culturally congruent for Ken Olsen and the Executive Committee to identify issues and develop strategy by such broad surveys. I had done that when the company was smaller. The OCG was fulfilling the same function for the now much larger organization. The questions asked in 1988 and the main answers they received in the survey were as follows:

1. Five years from now, what business will we be in?

We'll have a full line of distributed processing products, integrated with new and faster products, a full line of services, and Enterprise Integration Services.

2. What will be our competitive advantage?

Who we are—flexible, responsive, entrepreneurial, and value differences.

3. How should we be organized to support this business?

Become less functionally driven, get closer to customers, more top level support for fostering interdependence.

4. Do you think our culture and values are congruent/appropriate?

The fundamental Digital culture promotes doing whatever is required to meet the customer's need within the values of honesty, integrity, and highest quality. People experience an inability to do that. They report being immobilized by fear, experience infighting at senior levels, see a decrease in creativity and risk-taking, a premature squelching of good ideas, out of date processes and standards, redundancy, excess bureaucracy, and an influx of managers who do not value the fundamental culture.

5. What will be our major internal and external challenges?

Our greatest challenge will be ourselves. We have grown to become a very large company with a costly infrastructure that is inappropriate.

6. What factors will be critical to our success?

External forces are requiring internal changes. What should drive our internal changes should be our marketplace, not history or inertia.

7. What strategies will we need to employ to ensure Digital's future worldwide leadership?

We need truly to become an international player . . . learn other languages . . . ensure international membership on our most senior committees.

8. What do you and other senior managers need to begin doing now to ensure that this future scenario will become a reality?

Create and/or take advantage of opportunities to meet together in open cross-functional forums to share ideas, grapple with issues, and influence strategic decisions . . . [in order to] break through habitual stove-piped thinking to refresh and revitalize us (OCG meeting agenda for Woods Meeting, 1988).

The goal of the interviews was to get a large number of managers thinking about these issues, and clearly they were. The managers' diagnosis of what ailed DEC was right in line with what I and others had observed. DEC was paralyzed and floundering. Problems within the functional stovepipes were readily perceived and worked, but cross-functional problems remained invisible. The OCG was in a good position to diagnose what was missing in the DEC structure, namely, effective lateral communication mechanisms across the functions and geographies. The electronic network, some committees, and corporate meetings were the only structures available for lateral communication and problem identification. The OCG realized that it could be an additional structure to gather information and bring together people who were known to be working on similar problems from across the entire organization.

To implement this concept, the OCG surveyed its own activities with the goal of identifying interdependencies so that it could bring together those managers who needed to work together. OCG could then also run educational interventions that would bring people together who needed to communicate in an open forum. A new series of Corporate Seminars would focus on "DEC innovations in working with customers," "Creative uses of information technology and networking," "How to manage the complex interdependent organization of the future," and "Controlling costs and maintaining efficiency." Olsen took the advice seriously of bringing top groups together and launched several extended Woods Meetings.

COORDINATION EFFORTS THROUGH EXTENDED WOODS MEETINGS

To regain control and a sense of direction, Olsen and the Executive Committee decided to bring large groups of senior managers together to achieve consensus on how DEC would proceed. In 1989 the focus of the three-day summer Woods Meeting was the way in which DEC managed marketing and customer relations, stimulated by Olsen's telling the planning committee that he was worried about the following problems: (1) "We are the worst company to deal with. Our customers wouldn't have anything to do with us if they had any choice." (2) "Our salespeople are frustrated, overwhelmed with red tape, rules, micro-management, and grossly inefficient." (3) "Three quarters of our products never make a profit and don't even return their investment."

The top forty or so DEC executives were flown up to Heald Pond, Ken Olsen's hideaway in Maine, to hear a customer and marketing analysis by consultant Regis McKenna, followed by small-group discussion and plenary sessions to (1) determine company goals, (2) identify changes to the organization and its processes to ensure a more effective company, and (3) get to know one another better and thus work together more effectively. By getting away for three full days in an isolated area that could be reached only by plane to Greenfield with a half-hour helicopter ride from there, it was hoped that a sense of working together to fix DEC's problems could be achieved. I helped to plan and facilitate this meeting and thought the discussions were meaningful and that they achieved the goals of increasing concern for customers and clarifying the responsibilities of the Operations Committee. However, as was so often the case in working with DEC executives in the 1980s, the face-to-face commitment at these joint meetings did not override the commitments these same executives had made to their groups back home.

In the meantime, to compensate for the growing power of the functional groups and to ensure that DEC "got closer to its customers," the spirit of the product line structure was resurrected by identifying business units and empowering them to propose their own budgets and, if approved, to be held accountable for them. This idea was the essence of the New Management System that was touted as being a state-of-the-art way to manage a decentralized networked organization such as DEC tried to be. Business units representing products, industries, applications, and services were to be profit centers and to link closely with the account managers who had the immediate customer contact. They were matrixed to the major functions of sales, manufacturing, engineering, finance, and service, whose explicit mandate was to "support the business units, i.e. everyone works for the customer." The new principle that was widely published was "Business units run the company."

A three-day Woods Meeting for the top forty executives was held in York, Maine, in March 1990 to review DEC's organization and discuss the details of how the new business unit concept would work. To stimulate the discussion, questions were circulated on "why are we losing money?" with possible answers being "lateness in shifting away from being a proprietary hardware vendor," "the sheer number of products that confuses both sales and customers," "the difficulty of doing business with DEC," and "the Alpha strategy not being clear to sales or customers." During the meeting, summaries were circulated of what the OCG had learned in its most recent round of interviews. Again the discussion was lively and meaningful, but it was not at all clear what follow-up there would be.

In these meetings Olsen played his old role of stimulating discussion, entering only now and then, but making his "dreams" clear in memos and impassioned speeches. What was often lacking, however, was any connection between Olsen's wish and some organizational process that would make it happen. It was as if Olsen still saw himself as the father/teacher who wanted his children/students to get the point and solve the problem. If his communications did not produce the desired result, he would express disappointment in his children/students but not deal with them directly. Instead he would find some other engineer or manager who did get the message and empower him or her unilaterally. This process would not only upset the more formally appointed executives in these areas but would signal that entrepreneurial activity was still favored more than playing by formal rules.

Olsen, of course, also disdained the formal rules because they had grown up as a response to the intergroup warfare that was going on. In his 1989 Woods Meeting he circulated a memo from a geography manager that showed that a $4,000 requisition to fix up an area in which customers would meet salespeople required twelve approval signatures. Complaints from the field about unnecessary reporting, fire drills, and too many measurements being applied to everything were circulating freely, including an amusing but poignant anonymous memo called "If I Were Captain," which brutally caricatured the degree of bureaucratization that had crept in.

The disastrous economic situation of zero profit in 1990 and an impending huge loss in 1991 led to a different kind of Woods Meeting in the summer of 1991. A professor who specialized in strategy and change, Sumantra Ghoshal, was recruited from the London Business School to lecture and then facilitate the meeting toward some kind of consensus on how to manage the turnaround back to profitability. Small-group discussions were to focus both on meeting short-run budgeted goals and on identifying what DEC would need to do to restore its vitality and leadership position. Group reports were handed in, summarized, and then discussed in plenary sessions to identify action steps to cure DEC's ills. Many ideas were proposed and debated, but what stands out most clearly in my memory of this meeting is Bill Demmer's periodic entry into the fray with a loud but clear "Alpha! Alpha will save us."

Olsen had by this time launched the New Management System and was lobbying quietly for its adoption. He was not too optimistic about the Woods Meeting outcome and sent a memo to the planners suggesting two more Woods Meetings that summer with outside professors John Kotter of the Harvard Business School, to talk about change management, and Sumantra Ghoshal, to return and push senior management harder to find remedial measures. The business unit concept was increasingly accepted, but postmeeting interviews indicated skepticism that the Executive Committee would allow enough time for people to learn how to use the new system before they changed it again. The old fear of perpetual tinkering with the organization and never allowing any system to work its way through was alive and well.

DOWNSIZING AND THE ROLE OF THE BOARD

The perception of DEC senior managers was that throughout these times of turmoil, the board did not act effectively as problems emerged and that the explanation of that ineffectiveness lay ultimately in how the board was initially selected. When DEC was first formed, the fashion was to have on one's board well-respected leaders in business and in the community. Ken Olsen was a powerful founder who became used to telling his board what to do; they could not fight back because the board did not contain anyone with sufficient technical credentials to really argue with him. Only his initial investor, General Doriot, seemed to have genuine influence on Olsen. With Doriot's death a vacuum was created that no one else on the board could fill. With hindsight, Doriot should have selected for the board some people who both understood the technology and had the personal strength to influence Ken Olsen.

The 1973 board consisted of the following people:

Vernon Alden, chairman of the board, The Boston Company

William Congleton, general partner, The Palmer Organization

Georges Doriot, chairman of the board, American Research and Development Corporation (AR&D)

Arnaud de Vitry, chairman of the board, Dunlop, S.A., France

William McLean, president, Stevens Institute of Technology

Dorothy Rowe, senior VP, treasurer and secretary, AR&D

No substantial changes were made until Philip Caldwell, chairman of the board and CEO of the Ford Motor Company was added in 1981; and in the late 1980s and early 1990s the following members were added: Robert Everett, retired president of MITRE Corporation; Tom Phillips, CEO of Raytheon; Colby Chandler, retired chairman and CEO of Kodak; and Tom Gerrity, ex-CEO of Index and currently dean of the Wharton School. Of this group only Bob Everett really understood some of the technical issues that Olsen was facing and tried to involve himself in solving some of them.

Ken Olsen had been asked to be on the board of Polaroid and the Ford Motor Company. Olsen saw what was happening to Edwin Land at Polaroid as Land's vision of what was possible and desirable became less reliable (for example, the instant movie camera). He saw Polaroid struggling to get Land into a research role so that the business problems could be managed by professional managers. Olsen often said to me that he would never allow himself to get into the position that Land ended up in, yet tragically that is exactly what happened.

Because Olsen was on the Ford board, the idea arose that Philip Caldwell should be given a place on the DEC board, and that took place in 1981. Apparently neither Olsen nor Doriot realized that Caldwell would bring the business gene with him, but in the late 1980s pressure came from Caldwell to begin downsizing, something that went against one of Olsen's deepest values. Olsen promptly lost confidence in Caldwell because he saw him as "only wanting to cut people" and not appreciating DEC's values and assumptions. We don't know where Doriot stood or how much influence he had in the middle 1980s because his health was already failing (he died in 1987). One of the criticisms of Doriot is that he never brought other strong people onto the board but did it all himself. Once Doriot died, it became "Olsen's board."

DEC managers, particularly in manufacturing, were well aware that changes in the technology of computing—from building, assembling, and testing hardware to baking chips—required far fewer people and different skills. They recognized that DEC had far too much capacity in the hardware factory arena. This kind of downsizing was seen as necessary by Olsen and therefore was not resisted. The pressure from the board that Olsen perceived and deplored was to downsize without regard to the technological or other issues.

Ted Sares, working for John Sims in the personnel organization, was charged with developing some programs for dealing with this excess of people. He recalls:

> So downsizing first started on a purely *voluntary* basis in Phoenix, Albuquerque, and Tempe manufacturing areas in the mid-80's. Employees were offered 13 weeks to leave during a 13-week period. This rather simple approach proved extremely successful and helped make each of these three plants leaner and more productive.
>
> Business was great from 85–89 so no downsizing took place. Things got serious again in 1989. Again the methodology was all purely voluntary but quite extensive and very, very generous throughout North America and later in Asia (Japan and Korea first) and then GIA [General International Area]. Europe (Ireland first) came last.
>
> In 1991, we did our first layoff (it involved some office people in Maynard). This was like opening the door because we started to do it everywhere and with very decent packages. We closed Enfield, Springfield, Phoenix, and a number of other facilities.
>
> In the Spring of 1992, we called a halt to everything in the US for about 3 months while we did SERP (the Special Early Retirement Program I developed with my task force). This was, of course, voluntary and resulted in 3,200 employees selecting it out of about 7,000. After SERP, DEC went back into layoffs with a vengeance closing plants and downsizing throughout the world. (Ted Sares, memo, personal communication, 2002)

As has previously been pointed out, it greatly bothered Ken Olsen that downsizing through layoffs was necessary, that DEC could not grow its way out of its inefficiencies or let natural attrition take care of it. Olsen remained upbeat and optimistic about DEC's future but felt increasingly alienated from a board that seemed to him obsessed only with downsizing instead of seeing the potential for growth.

THE LAST ACT

Ken Olsen became increasingly cynical about the failure of his senior management to fix the problems of coordination, to loosen the bureaucracy that had grown up, and to adopt and use the New Management System. A final effort was made in the Woods Meeting of 1992 to get the top management group to find coherence, but surface agreement did not translate into effective remedial action.

Especially problematic was the growing conflict between Olsen and large segments of his engineering organization. Some resented that Olsen was continuing to support the VAX 9000, which they felt would never pay for itself. Others were upset that Olsen did not appreciate the Alpha group and saw it as raiding money from other projects. A number of senior engineers lost confidence in Olsen's judgment, and it is alleged that they went around him to various board members to complain. These complaints might have been discounted by the board but for the fact that board members themselves were increasingly worried about, and upset with, Olsen's own complaints about his senior management at board meetings and his apparent inability to fix DEC's problems. The situation deteriorated and led to Ken Olsen's fairly abrupt resignation in late 1992.

The board elected Bob Palmer to take over as CEO, because he was perceived to be "level-headed and in control." DEC the company gradually returned to profitability by selling off some units, continuing with massive layoffs, and instituting a more disciplined management system with a number of outsiders hired into key senior executive slots, but DEC the culture was on the wane. Most of the managers and employees I talked with prior to the sale to Compaq said the culture was being killed by the new executives, leading many of those who were not fired to leave voluntarily. What Palmer could or should have done is widely disputed, ranging from assertions that had he handled things differently DEC would have survived and thrived to assertions that he was handed a sinking ship and could only do what he did to "get DEC ready to be sold."

The main impact on DEC employees whom I talked to during the early and middle 1990s was demoralization and the perception that the way in which the layoffs occurred was way out of line with the DEC culture. Many perceived the layoffs as capricious, unfair, and poorly communicated. Palmer's more aggressive layoffs policy was, of course, expected, but by then the perception was that the DEC culture was being destroyed anyway.

HOW TO THINK ABOUT THE END

The events of 1991–92 were fairly vivid and clear to observers both inside and outside the company. The best way to think about them is to realize that Ken Olsen believed to the end in his values and in the culture he had created. What he did not realize was that critical elements of that culture (for example, being truthful with one another) had eroded seriously and that clinging to other elements (for example, continuing to believe that the various groups under him could solve their own problems) was, in a real sense, the final and proximate reason for DEC's failure as a company. I say failure "as a company" because even as DEC was failing to maintain profitability there was widespread consensus that the way DEC worked, its culture, was the way people wanted to continue to work.

The sense of freedom, the entrepreneurial spirit, the commitment to innovation, and the sense of empowerment were alive and well in various groups within DEC right to the end. The Woods Meetings of 1991 and 1992 affirmed all the original DEC values. But there was no mechanism to bring the groups into alignment with one another. Olsen continued to believe that responsible, empowered executives could do that for themselves if he gave them processes to do it. They clearly could not. But even more telling is the fact that even if Olsen had tried to impose order from above, the groups were now too powerful and would not have accepted it. In fact, there were rumors and allegations that some of these groups were actually plotting ways to overthrow Olsen in the late 1980s and early 1990s because they felt that the direction in which he wanted to go was out of line with their own strategic visions.

The absence of the business gene showed up clearly in these later years in that there were many indicators that DEC's continued commitment to innovation and its belief that the market should weed out successes and failures was too costly. Inefficiencies of all sorts were visible and were acknowledged but were not dealt with. DEC was supporting too many projects, products, and people. DEC could not put management processes in place that would set priorities, weed out deadwood, stop product lines that were unprofitable, resolve issues between competing engineering groups and between engineering and marketing, make cost containment a priority, abandon vertical integration, and so on.

Many of my interviewees speculated that had DEC focused in those later years on networking or been able to bring out the VAX 9000 or the Alpha chip sooner, it might have survived and continued to grow. But the intergroup conflict and loss of confidence in one another had reached levels by the late 1980s that made each of those alternatives unworkable.

It is tempting to ask whether an earlier board intervention might have led to a different outcome. That intervention would have been to remove Olsen sooner and to replace him with a different kind of manager. A number of people speculated on how nice it might have been if Olsen could have retired in 1987 when he was named the "entrepreneur of the century." Whether someone could have been found either inside or outside of DEC who could have replaced him, preserved the culture, and yet created a viable business is hard to judge. My own hunch is that an executive with more of a business gene would have found it difficult to reverse the strategy that DEC had embarked on of being a vertically integrated supplier of the complete line of computing solutions built around networking capability and enterprise integration. As Paul Kampas's analysis shows, the transformation of DEC into an organization that could operate in the new computing environment concentrating on commodities would have required a very different genetic structure in its culture, one that might not have been achievable with the existing cast of characters (see chapter 9 and Kampas 2003).

On the matter of preserving the entrepreneurial culture, another intriguing speculation is in order. We will never know exactly why Compaq wanted to acquire DEC. Theories range from wanting the powerful service and enterprise integration organization to simply wanting to show who was the winner. However, an intriguing thought is that one major reason why HP wanted Compaq is that they wanted what was left of the entrepreneurial culture of innovation that DEC folks brought with them in order to stimulate more innovative activity within HP. In a few years a researcher might want to track whether some of the key executives at HP might turn out to have come from DEC.

part three

Lessons and Legacies

Many of the lessons and legacies of Digital Equipment Corporation have been woven into the various chapters of part II. What remains to be done in the last two chapters and in the appendixes is to focus more specifically on lessons and legacies and to examine their implications for organization and management theory. In particular, the DEC story has tremendous implications for technical entrepreneurship and the role of boards of directors in helping to manage the evolution of technically driven organizations. The DEC story also illustrates in great detail what organization theories talk about in the abstract: the consequences of success, growth, and aging.

Management theories do not sufficiently take into account how different it is to be a leader in a small-family climate where functional familiarity is high from what it is to be a leader in a larger, older, highly differentiated organization where functional familiarity extends only to the one or two layers immediately above and below a given manager.

Communication theories do not sufficiently differentiate the nature of the communication process among individuals of goodwill, on the one hand, from that among representatives of groups who are protecting the people whom they feel responsible for and accountable to, on the other hand. Truth was valued throughout DEC's history, but the very nature of "truth" changed as DEC grew and became differentiated into many subgroups.

Organizational culture theories do not distinguish sufficiently between different types of culture: corporate cultures; subgroup cultures based on growth, differentiation, and organizational age; and occupational cultures that infuse both the corporate and the subgroup cultures. In many respects the "wars" within DEC were wars between engineering, marketing, and finance, but none of these groups saw itself as a culture having to deal with other cultures. We assume that such groups can simply solve their problems without taking seriously that to do so would require some real intercultural understanding.

241

Goodwill and good intentions are not enough when cultural misunderstanding is involved. Serious dialogue and reflection become necessary processes.

Management how-to books oversimplify in implying that some magic number of steps or a few principles will apply across the broad spectrum of different types of organizations, with different cultures, at different stages of development. If there is one overarching lesson in the DEC story, it is that the interaction of technology, organization, and culture produces a very complex stew and that the best way for others to learn from the story is to reflect deeply on how their own organization resolves its issues.

But lessons can be drawn, so in chapter 14 we will review a variety of these lessons, and in chapter 15 we will explore some of DEC's legacies.

fourteen

Obvious Lessons
and Subtle Lessons

The analysis of the DEC story teaches us two things about how the world works. First, the lessons of history can be viewed on various levels—there are obvious lessons to be learned that are fairly clear based on events, but, more important, there are subtle lessons to be learned by trying to explain why the obvious events occurred. Second, the events of history are highly interactive. The search for root causes is flawed because it implies that there is a root cause, when, in fact, the events may have occurred for a multiplicity of reasons. For example, it is obvious that one of the reasons DEC failed is that it did not respond to the shifting market away from minicomputers to personal computers. But why did DEC not make this shift? Many senior DEC managers and engineers saw the shift in the market, saw the need to respond to it, and came out with a variety of products to compete with the PC but never could make the trade-offs that would have had to be made to be competitive because such changes were not supported by the cultural DNA.

Not only were the genes that would have worked toward commercial survival basically missing in the DNA but the set of values and beliefs that created the technical innovation–oriented culture was so strong that it created an immune system that basically undermined or ejected any manager who proposed business solutions that would have required more cost control, different forms of manufacturing, more open architecture, and the cutting off of many other innovative projects. The subtle lesson is that once established, a culture operates invisibly and powerfully to support some kinds of actions and to prevent other kinds. Add to that the political fighting between successful engineering groups, the sales and service bias toward more elegant and higher-margin products, and Ken Olsen's belief that internal competition is good and that the market should decide, and you begin to understand why DEC missed the PC market.

In this chapter we will review the obvious and subtle lessons that the DEC story teaches us, but we should keep in mind that all of the forces and events described are interrelated and worked in combination with one another.

LESSON 1. *Don't judge a company by its public face.* Neither DEC's strengths nor its weaknesses were visible from the outside. There is no way one could tell from its track record of growth to $14 billion when and where the causes lay for either its innovative strengths or its business weaknesses. Elements of the culture were certainly visible, and the enthusiasm of DEC's employees sent a clear message of strength. But those cultural elements and that enthusiasm were still visible in 1992 when DEC was in deep economic trouble. In fact, during the Woods Meetings that summer, enthusiasm and optimism were still running high. It would have been difficult for an outsider to anticipate the rapidity of DEC's decline as a business, and it would have been equally difficult to anticipate how strongly DEC alumni felt about the positive side of their culture.

LESSON 2. *A culture of innovation does not scale up; functional familiarity and "Truth through debate" are lost with size; "Do the right thing" becomes dysfunctional; managerial sense of responsibility changes with age and maturity; buy-in becomes superficial agreement.* This is perhaps the most powerful lesson of the story. Many organizations start out without business genes because they have a strong and relevant technical vision that produces innovative products that succeed in the marketplace. That vision can be strong enough to provide success and growth for a considerable period of time, in DEC's case for thirty years. But the very cultural elements that guarantee a continuous stream of innovation—the philosophy of empowering people, holding them responsible, depending on open and truthful communication, forcing broad consensus and buy-in in decision making, and ultimately trusting people at all levels to do the right thing—depends on people knowing and trusting one another, operating, in a sense, as an extended large family.

Once functional familiarity, in the sense of knowing how others work, is lost because of size and differentiation into geographical, functional, and marketing subgroups, new coordination mechanisms have to be adopted that inevitably limit the amount of power that was originally granted. As the subgroups become more powerful, their managers cease to operate as individual actors in the consensus process and function increasingly as representatives protecting their people and turf. As the organization matures, resources are likely to become scarce, forcing groups to compete. As intergroup competition grows, communication and commitment to truth are eroded.

As organizations and their employees grow and age, youthful "irresponsibility" turns into mature responsibility and the protection of the now older workforce. Managerial attention increasingly comes to be focused on internal matters and decreasingly on technical challenge and market analysis. The fun associated with youthful innovation and the creation of a new industry wanes as the industry matures, becomes more competitive, and more commodified. The need to protect one's turf, to be responsible for thousands of employees, to continue to provide returns to shareholders, and to protect the community all creep in as new concerns that can undermine creative innovative thrusts. The desire to take risks declines because with age and increasing responsibility one has more to lose than to gain.

The difference between agreement and buy-in is crucial. Agreement is passively going along and not sabotaging. Buy-in is active agreement and support. Olsen's genius was in creating a culture of buy-in. DEC's concept of *buy-in* meant actively agreeing that a given course of action was the correct way to go and therefore working actively to make it happen. With growth there is the potential that it gets harder and harder to calibrate whether you have only agreement or active buy-in. And, paradoxically, formal written contracts are not as good a guarantee of commitment as face-to-face enthusiastic agreement.

LESSON 3. *If a culture of innovation works only at a certain small size, the organization must either find a way to break away small units that continue to innovate or abandon innovation as a strategic priority.* Ken Olsen's philosophy of giving financial responsibility to product lines and small business units was correct for maintaining innovation, but DEC did not solve the problem of how to keep those units functionally lean, on the one hand, or to keep the powerful centralized functions from overmanaging, on the other hand. Autonomous divisions were resisted for a variety of reasons—too much duplication of resources, lack of good general managers, and unwillingness to give up centralized control—so DEC attempted to work with a complex matrix of business units and functions.

Ken Olsen and some of his staff developed the New Management System to create a large network that would continue to make the matrix workable. Indeed they argued that such a management system of coordinating through the network the work of many autonomous nodes was the management system that would be needed in all future knowledge-based companies. It is not clear whether the failure of that network within DEC resulted from conceptual flaws in the design or from the undermining of this process by central functional units who wanted to maintain their power.

LESSON 4. *A culture that breeds success and growth over a considerable time becomes stable and embedded even if it contains dysfunctional elements; changing the culture means changing key people who are the culture carriers.* DEC's weakness as an organization, its tragic flaw, was its total imprisonment in some elements of its incredible culture of innovation. Some elements of that culture—such as assumptions about lifetime employment, growth as the solution to inefficiencies, and the ability of competing units to solve their own coordination problems—made it difficult for DEC to become competitive as a business. The culture remained strong in the sense of continuing to espouse the assumptions by which DEC wanted to continue to operate, but the practical implementation of those assumptions was impossible in some cases and dysfunctional in others.

When a culture becomes strongly entrenched because of decades of success, it cannot change without massive changes of people who are the culture carriers. The cultural assumptions that supported technical innovation were widely spread throughout the DEC organization, so that individual managers who made a more business-oriented argument met resistance at all levels. In the early 1990s Ken Olsen says he attempted to inject more business-oriented values and better accounting methods, yet he felt defeated at every turn, partly because the ideas seemed to others at this stage of DEC's evolution as unworkable and because by then the various subcultures were fighting with one another and resisting centralized measurements that might have exposed their biased protection of turf. There was no tradition of decentralization with clear accountability; hence, efforts to make managers more accountable always fell short. The subtle lesson is that once culture takes hold even the leader can become quite impotent. And the irony of the situation is that the managers who were subverting Olsen's New Management System were claiming to do so based on the same cultural principles, that is, "Do the right thing." They felt they knew better.

When Bob Palmer took over he found himself replacing many of the top managers because his no-excuses, more disciplined management principles challenged some of the DEC culture's sacred cows. In many cases these managers or employees left on their own because they felt that "Palmer is changing the culture," and they did not want to live in the new culture.

LESSON 5. *Cultures are sometimes stronger than organizations.* A culture can survive even though the organization dies. The kind of culture that DEC created and by which it operated until nearly its end in the mid-1990s was appreciated and loved by almost everyone who grew up in it. The values that Olsen infused in the employees remained after they left DEC and were strongly touted as "the" way to run a company. Many of the managers and engineers who started in DEC eventually populated the entire computer industry, becoming senior technical people or managers at HP, Sun, Apple, Microsoft, Data General, Compaq, and a host of smaller companies. The DEC legacy is very strong even though DEC the company does not exist any longer.

LESSON 6. *A successful technical vision will eventually create its own competition and, therefore, changes in technology and in the market conditions; dominant designs will emerge and commodification will occur.* No matter how unique or powerful an innovation is, no matter how much monopolistic control or patent protection an organization has, the innovation will eventually stimulate enough competition to force the innovator to evolve process innovations toward becoming more efficient. Competition, technological evolution, and changing market conditions will eventually lead to the acceptance of a dominant design and commodification of the products. The organization is then faced with the choice of whether to continue as an innovator or transform itself into an efficient business. The subtle lesson is that if the business gene is missing, this choice will inevitably be made toward attempting to remain in the innovator role, even when economic disaster is inevitable.

LESSON 7. *Successful growth based on a technical vision will hide business problems and inefficiencies until an economic crisis reveals them or until the business gene is switched on; recognition of those problems will not necessarily produce remedial action.* The subtle lesson here is that the organization may not realize how inefficient it is because the technical visionaries and innovators are neither sensitive to, nor motivated by, business problems and inefficiencies. Employees who highlight such problems are either ignored or rejected, and the problems are rationalized as being fixable through continued growth.

Another subtle lesson is that seeing and accepting a problem as a problem does not guarantee the ability or willingness to do something about it. Insight is not enough if the cultural DNA does not support the changes that would be needed to act on the insight. Every problem that consultants and academics identified as being present in DEC was also recognized and extensively discussed within DEC. Many groups were formed to deal with such problems as they were identified. For example, it was obvious to everyone that DEC's early success had enabled it to operate inefficiently. Growth was sufficient to absorb whatever inefficiencies arose. The excess of people that was identified in the 1990s was recognized and downsizing programs were launched.

But Ken Olsen was intensely moral in his commitment to employees and customers. His unwillingness to abandon customers by going to new kinds of computers and his unwillingness to lay off employees were the result of strongly held non-negotiable values. These values coexisted with business values, so the painful trade-offs that would have had to be made to improve profit levels by cutting costs and abandoning certain projects could never be made without a great deal of ambivalence. This ambivalence not only undermined the efforts to downsize and improve costs but also created demoralizing tensions as different groups within DEC fought to maintain their own resources.

Furthermore, dealing with the business problems requires switching from the "fun" of innovation and growth to the "hard work" of creating a business strategy process, of becoming cost conscious, of changing organizational routines toward efficiency, of laying off deadwood or obsolete technical talent, of developing more precise measures of economic return that could lead to the killing of some products (eating your own children), of modifying the basic processes in engineering and manufacturing to respond to changing technology, and of allocating increasingly scarce resources. For the manager who has the business gene, these tasks can be fun, but for the manager who is the technical visionary/innovator the fun is in creation. Many observers of DEC pointed out that DEC management had neither the inclination nor the skill to do this hard transformational work.

LESSON 8. *If a growing business lacks the business gene, the board must act to introduce that gene.* The technology gene is clearly enough to start a company on the road to success, but at some point trade-offs will be required that will not be made unless the business gene is present. It is unlikely that the members of the innovative culture will perceive this necessity as long as they are having fun, or if they perceive it, that they will act on it. By the time they recognize the problem—for example, DEC in the early 1990s—it is probably too late to do anything. The board, acting on behalf of the shareholders, must then intervene to introduce the business gene into the organization's cultural DNA. How this is done will depend on local circumstances, but the board may be the only entity that sees the problem early enough to take effective remedial action.

In first-generation companies, entrepreneurs should in principle worry about succession and the development of future general managers, but they rarely do. We assume that founders can manage their own departures, yet rarely does this happen. It is not really surprising that successful "fathers" are threatened by upstart "sons" and eventually come to believe in their own omniscience. Ken Olsen repeatedly said that he would not fall into the trap that he saw Edwin Land fall into at Polaroid of hanging on to power too long. Yet he repeated the exact same pattern, convinced until the end that if his new management and accounting systems had been adopted, the company would have been back on the road to profitability. What Olsen could not see was how unworkable many of his ideas were and how strong the various subunits had become, to the point that they often discounted or actually subverted many of his ideas in the late stages of DEC's history.

LESSON 9. *If you try to do everything, you may end up not doing anything very well.* If resources are spread too thin, nothing succeeds. The obvious lesson is that DEC's innovative products arrived too late, when the market had already adopted a dominant design. The subtle lesson is that if the organization tries to do everything, it may fail across the board. Alpha was two years late because of foot-dragging and failure to commit to it. Aquarius was too late and too expensive because the engineering community never favored it and withheld resources. All-in-1 was a great desktop PC–type office program that never got full support to market it effectively. DEC tried to be a player across the whole range of computing products, and did have good products in all these areas because it had the resources to support them all during its growth period, but the company never focused or set priorities when resources became scarce and when development costs increased because of technical complexity.

LESSON 10. *How the market evolves may not reflect either the best technology or the most obvious logic.* A logical progression can be seen from interactive computing on large machines, to minicomputers, to networking of minicomputers and building them with smaller semi-conductors. What the market said that did not seem logical to many in DEC was the desire to have a cheap desktop machine that would provide a variety of services to an individual with or without a network. In a way it is ironic that the DEC vision for interactive computing implied individual work but that somewhere along the line the full implications of that vision were lost.

DEC's published mission in 1990 read as follows: "Digital will be recognized as the best provider of quality integrated information systems, networks and services to support customers worldwide." The emphasis was clearly on networks and tying the elements of a customer's organization together rather than providing stand-alone computing capabilities to anyone and everyone. What the market wanted proved to be different from what DEC "logically" decided it needed to provide. Why DEC did not pursue its own mission more aggressively and develop the Internet is a puzzle except in the context of the previous lesson, that DEC continued to try to do everything and never got sufficiently focused on networking. An alternative cultural explanation offered by Paul Kampas is that DEC never gave up on its need to have proprietary products.

LESSON 11. *A technical vision that is right for its time can blind you to technical evolution.* In the DEC culture of innovation it was the vision of the minicomputer that was a dominant gene. Not only did DEC have a complete engineering mentality, but within that mentality it was dominated by a technical vision built around the minicomputer. But the minicomputer was still a large machine, so when miniaturization occurred, it was hard for Ken Olsen to grasp that small machines built with chips could be faster and cheaper than the minicomputer. Many observers felt that DEC not only lacked the business gene but also was obsessed with the vision of the minicomputer.

LESSON 12. *The value of "listening to your customers" depends upon which customers you choose to listen to.* A company can start out to be very customer oriented yet fail to detect market changes because it continues to listen to and respond to only one customer segment. DEC's philosophy from its very beginning was to be intensely customer focused, and it held this philosophy as a moral obligation. The sales function was there to help sophisticated customers figure out their problems and to involve customers in the solution. Anytime a customer had a problem, sales was ready to help, which led to a great many separate projects all over the organization. Customers were organized into a users' group (DECUS), and this group continued to love DEC products. DEC managers paid constant attention to them and therefore believed sincerely that the company was highly customer oriented.

But because of the engineering and innovation bias, only the most sophisticated and "interesting" customers drew attention in an elitist paternalistic way: "if you were smart, we would listen to you and take care of you; if you were 'dumb,' we would take care of you but not listen to you." When the market became primarily mainstream users, DEC would not listen even when the customers screamed about poor order processing, schedule delays, and product problems.

Furthermore, because resources were not infinite, many projects that "good" customers wanted and that DEC promised to work on could not get immediate support, which meant schedule delays and impatient customers. DEC salespeople could always say with conviction that a given project was still alive, but the schedule might slip, sometimes by a matter of years. Keeping the project alive and thereby ultimately solving the customer's problem was often seen as far more important than meeting an arbitrary schedule. The subtle lesson is that a successful company has to pay more attention to its critics and to the customers it loses. It is dangerous to listen only to the customers who love you.

LESSON 13. *The type of governance system an organization uses must evolve as the organization matures.* Warren Bennis once wrote that "democracy is inevitable," referring to the degree to which large bureaucratic organizations are increasingly finding it necessary to empower their employees. The DEC story suggests a reverse twist on this prediction: "hierarchy is inevitable." DEC worked very well for a couple of decades with a minimum of hierarchy, but as it grew and aged, the negotiations in the matrix structure became more difficult as functional familiarity was lost among the players and as shrinking resources required more prioritizing.

Hierarchy may not be the only solution, or it may have to metamorphose into other forms, but some coordination or integration mechanism must evolve as the organization grows and differentiates—an effective strategy-building process is one such mechanism; charismatic leadership is another.

LESSON 14. *The events and forces act in unison.* It should be emphasized that one cannot understand either an organization's success or its failure without thinking systemically and considering a number of factors in combination. All organizations are systems of forces that derive from their technical environment, their own growth dynamics, and their cultural DNA. It is pointless to look for one or two simple reasons why DEC behaved as it did. All of the factors listed above played a key role and interacted strongly with one another. The key is to understand clearly that organizations are complex systems that ultimately derive from the values and beliefs of the founders and early leaders. Putting the DEC culture into a box or labeling it as a certain kind of culture is highly illusory because to understand DEC one must understand the subtle interaction between the cultural elements and how they formed into a paradigm of mutually reinforcing nonnegotiable and tacit assumptions.

LESSON 15. *Knowledge workers cannot make efficient decisions together.* One of the most striking phenomena of DEC's later years is that key senior people, on both the technical and executive ends, were calling one another liars and were not trusting one another; each was totally convinced that he or she had the right answer for the future. At the same time, they blamed DEC's demise on the "lack of any decision making at the top." From my outsider's perspective, and having seen decision making in academia that is anything but efficient in the short run (though it may be very effective in the long run), I cannot see what kind of decision making would have resolved the deep disagreements that existed among the senior technical and executive people in the late 1980s. Perhaps some powerful intellect such as Gordon Bell could have achieved some consensus, but wishing for such a person does not produce one. If a powerful executive had demanded more discipline and efficiency, many of these knowledge workers would have screamed foul and claimed that their culture was being destroyed.

If it is true that more and more companies are becoming complex networks of knowledge workers, and if those knowledge workers become representatives of groups that they lead, those companies will have major difficulties making efficient decisions and maintaining any kind of discipline in the implementation of decisions. What is possible among a small group of knowledge workers debating their different points of view to some clear decision that everyone buys into is less and less possible as each of these knowledge workers is successful, builds an empire under himself or herself, and enters the debate with a growing need to protect his or her own turf. The freedom that made the building of such a culture of innovation possible leads inevitably both to intergroup conflict and to a strong commitment to that culture.

When all is said and done, the basic reason why DEC ended up where it did was that the evolution of the technology required transformations in the organization that the culture did not encourage or allow. The judgment of whether that was a desirable or undesirable outcome is a separate issue. Perhaps a culture such as DEC had should survive, as it has in its alumni. Is it worth changing such a culture to preserve the business entity? One aspect of the DEC legacy is to leave us with this tough question. What is, in the end, more valuable—a culture that is ennobling but economically unstable or a stable economic entity that changes its culture to whatever is needed to survive?

fifteen

The Lasting Legacy of Digital Equipment Corporation

How does one capture the legacy of an organization that existed for forty years? In part of this chapter and in appendix A we will review the obvious legacy, the technical contribution that DEC made to the world of computing. Perhaps more significant, however, is DEC's contribution to the careers and lives of its alumni. As I indicated in the first chapter, one of the reasons for writing this story is that so many ex-DEC people say that working in DEC was the high spot of their careers and that "Doing the right thing" was a key value that informed their entire approach to their jobs.

MANAGERIAL INNOVATIONS AND CAREER IMPACTS

Michael Horner, who was employed primarily in Europe, included the following note in a recent e-mail:

> I am writing this from the building which used to house "DEC Europe" HQ. In this building this evening there will be a cheese and wine party as part of a series of "ex Decies" events and typically between 100 and 200 people turn up! Remember there has been no DEC since 1998 and many left [in] 1993 or earlier, 10 years ago. I find this amazing. . . . I

want to share the "Sunflower Story" applied to the termination of DEC as an enterprise. In the "strong" version of the story, the end of DEC was planned by Ken and he somehow put many of the free spirits he had attracted into the company (and helped them to develop themselves), under such unpleasant conditions that they chose to leave. In the same way that a sunflower spurts out its seeds at the end of Summer, these people seeds took the DEC culture with them and influence the whole of business today. In the "weak" Sunflower story Ken did not do it intentionally but unconsciously. It is evident that the end result is in fact true and the DEC culture continues to influence business worldwide. In systems thinking, DEC outgrew being an enterprise. It emerged to the next level to become an influence in the world business ecology. The legal entity of DEC had to give up being an enterprise to become an important part of business culture. This point is not made just to have a happy ending but is a serious point and indicates there may be other examples of enterprises that became so successful that they had to emerge to the next level. (Mike Horner, e-mail, personal communication, September 9, 2002)

Not only are people nostalgic about their days at DEC, but they carry forward the model of management, particularly "Do the right thing," that Ken Olsen created as a model to be emulated and reproduced wherever they go. I believe that the essence of this model is that Olsen treated people as responsible adults, something that most organizations fail to do. Giving people freedom and responsibility *and meaning it even if they abuse it* is the critical ingredient. We have seen in the previous chapters the difficulty of scaling this management philosophy up into a large, highly differentiated organization, but in spite of those difficulties, all the levels within the DEC hierarchy attempted to continue to work in this open manner. Olsen never gave up on his faith in people, and that faith carried forward in the thousands of ex-DECies. Alumni meetings and parties can be found all over the world from time to time, always emphasizing how exciting and fun it was to work in DEC and how sad it was to see DEC run into difficulty.

In chapter 7 Tracy Gibbons explored in some detail how the DEC culture fostered leadership and these lasting positive feelings. Peter DeLisi expresses it as follows:

As I think about the question of what DEC taught me about leadership, I'm more inclined to think about the "DEC Magic." What is it that makes us so passionate about the company years after its demise? The leadership question is still a valid one to ask, but I learned a lot from DEC about what leadership is not.

DEC was a fun place to work. We had a lot of "freedom." Coming from IBM and a previous history of top-down authority-centered institutions, I found that this newly-found freedom was intoxicating. You mentioned people coming from behind the Iron Curtain to democracy.

Today, I was thinking about the family analogy once again. DEC was a family in which the siblings were very talented and could do almost anything they wanted. Like some modern families, the children were indulged with the latest toys and had little or no discipline or controls on them. It's fun to be in that kind of family where you have almost unlimited freedom to do whatever you want. Sure the siblings sometimes fought with one another, but there was respect there and there was respect for the patriarch.

I guess none of us would seriously think about raising a family in which the kids did whatever they wanted and there was no discipline, no limits set, and no punishment for "misbehavior." And we wouldn't probably encourage the kids to fight with one another, just so truth will ultimately prevail. But, isn't that what DEC kind of did? What happens in this type of family as both the patriarch and the children grow older? Does the previous lack of discipline finally show up and produce indulged, arrogant people?

Back to the "magic." We learned that anything is possible in DEC. You didn't have to have the responsibility assigned to you in order to do something from the breadth of your talents. "He who proposes does." In most companies, what you accomplish is the direct result of work skills. I have never thought of it this way before, but in DEC, what you accomplished could be the result of a personal talent, or interest, or previous experience. You could truly leverage your whole person if you saw something to be done that you felt uniquely qualified to perform. I personally experienced this "magic" when I did the Corporate Leaders Forum, a responsibility that belonged to another group, but because of my interest and background I could "propose and do." (Peter DeLisi, memo, personal communication, 2001)

Bob Glorioso, now president and CEO of Marathon Technologies Corporation, says:

> I think I learned a great deal from DEC. The most important was how to manage complexity in both technology projects and organizations and how to treat and manage people. I also learned a lesson in failure that when things get difficult, people will easily move from working for the company's interest to working for their own interest even if it means the company will go down. (Bob Glorioso, memo, personal communication, 2002)

Win Hindle, who was Ken Olsen's administrative assistant and rose to the position of executive vice president, summarizes this arena well by linking management philosophy to the political process.

> I am basing my comment on the first 25 years of the company, or through the early 80's. The qualities I mention here are the result of the philosophy of Ken Olsen, Digital's founder. I believe that Digital was one of the early companies to adopt a "democratic" form of organization and governance. Digital cared deeply for all of its employees and its communities, yet maintained an unrelenting insistence on profits. The setting in an old run-down mill building with sparkling new equipment emphasized the importance of products and people over posh surroundings. There were no status symbols—rewards and promotions were based on proven capabilities on the job.
>
> One of my earliest feelings about the company was that people really liked to work there. They felt proud because their neighbors would say "You are really lucky to be working for such a fine company." And they knew it was true because they had opportunity and challenge while working beside very capable co-workers. In addition Digital reached out to local communities by contributing equipment and money and encouraging employees to help in the community.
>
> The program to encourage stock ownership in Digital also reflected the company's democratic philosophy. In other firms stock options went primarily to top executives. Shares of Digital stock were awarded for special contributions to all employees.
>
> Employees who had tragedies were encouraged to take care of their families and return to work when they had their personal life under control. The result was an amazing loyalty on the part of employees,

appreciating what the company felt were the appropriate priorities in their lives.

One of the practices of Digital was to be sure that customers not only knew the product specifications but also really understood what they were buying. The company went to extraordinary lengths to assure that customers were satisfied. Not every product arrived on time, nor worked perfectly when it arrived, but the organization never gave up on ultimately satisfying the customer. It took a company dedicated to strong ethical principles to assure that every employee understood this objective.

These "democratic" principles created a sometimes chaotic environment in which decisions were slow in coming because they required consultation among a wide group of people. But, as in our American democracy, the results were most often the right outcomes. The strong loyalty felt by ex-employees of Digital is testament to the wonderful qualities that created this legacy. (Win Hindle, memo, personal communication, 2002)

DOING THE RIGHT THING AND DIVERSITY

Many alumni have pointed out that "Doing the right thing" in combination with the other values noted above led to a climate in which diversity flourished, because it was recognized that paying attention to the needs of others would also enhance personal growth and make DEC a better company. Ken's management philosophy stimulated innovations in affirmative action, education, and community development. DEC started a variety of initiatives in the 1970s, particularly in the manufacturing space under the leadership of Pete Kaufmann. Kaufmann saw the need in 1969, saying that "we have to do something in the many communities in which we work and for the many people who are 'left behind.'"

As Bill Hanson pointed out in an interview, it was the "Do the right thing" philosophy that enabled the DEC managers to innovate because it allowed them to integrate their own sense of personal growth with doing things for others and making DEC a better company. Ken Olsen created the climate, and Pete Kaufmann recognized the need and stimulated others to action. Managers like Hanson, Jack Smith, and John Sims responded not only by developing the specific programs to hire talented minorities but also by building factories in Roxbury and Springfield, Massachusetts, in neighborhoods that were almost exclusively African American.

The strong belief that plants should be managed by locals allowed the company to build plants not only around the United States but also in Puerto Rico, Taiwan, Singapore, Ireland, and other parts of the world. Hanson pointed that DEC always wanted to be valued by the communities in which they built factories and that communities in Arizona, Colorado, California, and New Hampshire were willing to rezone areas to enable DEC to come in.

Goals and timetables were set for the hiring of females and minorities. Vigorous training in the handling of minorities was instituted for managers and supervisors, and efforts were made to create core groups of whites, minorities, and females to take responsibility for the implementation of ambitious affirmative action plans. If no management personnel were available for these core groups, employees were recruited for them.

Support groups of all kinds were encouraged for women employees and for gays and lesbians, thus sending a strong message that no form of discrimination would be tolerated. Managers who violated these antidiscrimination policies were terminated. These DEC programs gave a key start to African American managers such as Dorothy Terrell, whose career is briefly described in chapter 7. John Sims, who became a senior vice president and member of DEC's Executive Committee, was one of the highest-placed African American executives in the United States in the 1970s and 1980s.

Closely connected to the emphasis on affirmative action was a support for education. Through the efforts of Ken Olsen's wife and the Olsen Foundation, a number of initiatives were launched. A junior college technical education program, the first of its kind, was established for computer technologists. This program linked forty-two junior colleges, which were asked to recruit minorities and females to make up at least 50 percent of their classes. With the cooperation of Freedom House in Boston and teachers from MIT and Harvard, an inner-city college program was formed that picked high school students in the eleventh and twelfth grades who had average grades and supported them with self-confidence-building programs and placed them in college skills–development programs that helped them to get placed in some of the best schools in the country. A support team for each student was created consisting of a counselor from Freedom House and a student support group from a college or university. This program eventually graduated 484 out of 500 students that were placed, enabling most of them to go on to graduate school and successful professional careers.

In summary, this democratic environment produced a large number of important innovations in technology, community relations, affirmative action, human resource practices, sales training and compensation systems, and manufacturing. One could almost say that the DEC environment was a pure case of how an organization that wants to innovate across the board should organize itself. It also exemplifies what can be achieved when you have a socially responsible CEO.

THE NATURE OF COMPUTING

DEC changed the face of computing both in terms of the actual technology of computing equipment and, perhaps more important, in terms of the concepts of how a user and a computer could and would relate to each other. The concept of *interactive computing* was born in the early DEC, and one of DEC's legacies was, therefore, the empowerment of the individual computer user.

Bob Metcalfe, the inventor of Ethernet and founder of 3Com, put it as follows:

> Success has many fathers, but failure is an orphan, sure, but I'm here to testify that we beneficiaries of modern information technology owe much, if not everything, to DEC. DEC is of course Digital Equipment Corporation, which in its later years insisted on being called Digital, which I guess was DEC's idea of marketing. IBM was at least sensible enough not to change its name to International.

Of course DEC is not dead. DEC merged into Compaq, which in turn merged into HP, through which DEC lives on. And DEC's legacy lives on. DEC was the leader in interactive minicomputing. This was the information technology wave that followed IBM's mainframe batch data processing and that preceded Intel-Microsoft's personal computing and later Cisco's Internet computing.

How big is DEC's legacy? Huge.

Start with Microsoft's Windows NT/2000, which was developed under the leadership of Dave Cutler, DEC operating system guru. Basically, Windows is DEC's VMS rewritten for Intel microprocessors. Of course Windows has much more of a graphical user interface than VMS, but then DEC probably started the GUI movement with the PDP-1, when Gates was in diapers.

I'm part of the DEC legacy. In my day, I programmed IBM computers (7094, 1130, 1401), Honeywell computers (1215, Multics), and Univac computers (M460, 1108). But, my heart belongs to DEC computers (PDP-8S, PDP-6, PDP-10, DECsystem-20, PDP-11, VAX).

In 1968, while still an MIT undergraduate, I wrote a paper for DEC's user group (DECUS) about my Project ASC—the application of small computers in education. DEC had lent me a PDP-8S for my work at MIT in teaching computers to high school students. Right afterward, my PDP-8S was stolen. Instead of making me pay them back the $30,000 a PDP-8S cost, DEC turned my misfortune into a promotion: "DEC has made the first computer small enough to be stolen."

Just before inventing Ethernet, I built my first high-speed network interface using DEC modules for the PDP-6/10. It ran continuously for the next 13 years. I have it now in my home office. I wrote my first operating system software for DEC computers, including my first Internet protocol software. So, Ethernet is just one small part of DEC's legacy.

We cloned a PDP-10 at the Xerox Palo Alto Research Center in about 1972. I built the hardware that connected that clone, MAXC, to the early Internet, to the first Ethernet (with Dave Boggs), and to the first laser printer (with Ron Rider). When it came time for Ethernet to leave Xerox, it was DEC's VP of Engineering Gordon Bell who approved our first Ethernet paper for publication, through the Communications of the ACM. It was with Gordon in 1979 that we had the idea to make Ethernet an open standard by forming an open collaboration among DEC, Intel, and Xerox. Without DEC, the IEEE would never have made

Ethernet its 802.3 standard. And through the 1980s, DEC's distributed processing boomed using networking including especially Ethernet.

Not that I don't love Intel, Microsoft, Cisco, IBM, and HP, and 3Com, but I miss DEC. (Bob Metcalfe, memo, personal communication, December 15, 2002)

Bob Supnik, one of DEC's key engineers put it this way:

DEC's legacy consists of three things: technology, people, and business. In the technology space, DEC's achievements included:

— The first minicomputer.

— The first commercial timesharing system.

— The first commercial peer-to-peer network (DECnet)—and the first seamless integration of networking into standard operating systems (VMS).

— The first >100Mhz microprocessors—and the fastest microprocessors for a decade.

— The most influential processor architectures (PDP11, VAX) and operating systems (RSX, VMS) from 1970 to 1990—every major CPU architecture after the PDP11 (including the Intel x86) shows its influence, until the advent of RISC systems—and RSX and VMS are the design precursors to Windows NT (now Windows 2000 and XP).

In the people space, DEC's legacy consisted of both the people who worked at the company, and the people who grew up on its equipment. Most people learning computers between 1970 and 1985 learned on DEC gear—hence the enduring interest in PDP11's and VAX's, long after they have ceased to be manufactured. And DEC itself trained hundreds of thousands of engineers, sales people, service people, technicians, manufacturing staff, etc—an alumni group that is spread across the industry, bringing DEC's values to many different companies and projects.

And finally, in business, DEC left a legacy both positive and negative. On the positive side, DEC was a business innovator—the first commercial company on the Internet, the first company to use indirect channels. And on the negative side, the awful object lessons from its fall—that inflexibility in the face of rapidly changing competitive conditions is ultimately fatal. (Bob Supnik, memo, personal communication, February 10, 2003)

In a 2002 memo, one alumnus wrote about it as follows:

DEC popularized "personal" computers, although it wasn't called that and it wasn't for home use. The concept was for a researcher or engineer to be able to justify the purchase of a computer dedicated to his own tasks/project. Computers were not used as personal productivity tools in the sense of today's word processors, spreadsheets and simulation tools, but used to automate tasks or functions not done by computers since they were always considered too expensive to be dedicated to relatively simple tasks. Up to that point "hard-wired" logic was used and had to be rewired/redesigned each time the task changed. The ability to use an inexpensive programmable computer where only software needed modification to change the execution of the task was a bold concept. You made the hardware investment once and just did software changes thereafter. At that time, the largest expense for computerization projects was the cost of the hardware.

This "dedicated" systems concept led DEC to focus on the "user" (an individual engineer or scientist) as a key decision maker; heretofore engineers and researchers spent somewhat lesser amounts of money but on hard wired logic components. In the late 60's, with the advent of the PDP-5/PDP-8 family of computers, engineers and researchers started submitting purchase requests for computers (an unpopular thing in organizations where the financial folks felt computers were their province). DEC called its computers Programmable Data Processors (PDP), which even as a thinly-veiled disguise, was usually enough to allow users to get purchase approval and get around restrictions on who was authorized to buy computers. DEC did an excellent job in catering to the "user," since users were "compadres"—other engineers and scientists.

In my view, DEC was very successful against entrenched vendors/ competitors like IBM because (among other things) IBM's sales strategy was to focus on senior management and encourage centralized computing resources. DEC flanked IBM by encouraging distributed/ decentralized computing and empowering the user, fostering a permanent change in marketing and product focus that exists to this day.

In a 2002 memo, another alumnus noted the importance of DEC to hackers.

Before the killer micro revolution of the late 1980s, hackerdom was closely symbiotic with DEC's pioneering time-sharing machines. The first of the group of hacker cultures nucleated around the PDP-1. Subsequently, the PDP-6, PDP-10, PDP-20, PDP-11 and VAX were all foci of large and important hackerdoms, and DEC machines long dominated the ARPANET and Internet machine population.

DEC was the technological leader of the minicomputer era (roughly 1967 to 1987), but its failure to embrace microcomputers and Unix early cost it heavily in profits and prestige after silicon got cheap. However, the microprocessor design tradition owes a heavy debt to the PDP-11 instruction set, and every one of the major general-purpose microcomputer operating systems so far (CP/M, MS-DOS, Unix, OS/2) were either genetically descended from a DEC OS, or incubated on DEC hardware or both.

Accordingly, DEC is still regarded with a certain wry affection even among many hackers too young to have grown up on DEC machines. The contrast with IBM is instructive.

In a recent article another aspect of the technological legacy is highlighted.

Next month, Intel will bring its hyperthreading technology to desktops, another advance in the chip world that can be traced to Digital Equipment Corporation. Although Digital often floundered when trying to sell its own chips, the defunct computing giant left behind technologies and engineers that are at the core of many recent and coming advances.

"There is all this cool technology coming out on PCs that came from Digital," said Dean McCarron, principal analyst at Mercury Research. . . . Technologies with Digital genes march on, including HyperTransport, a high-speed method of chip interconnection championed by AMD; a future version of Intel's Itanium family of processors; and low-power chips for cell phones and handhelds from both those companies. . . .

The threading work will likely leave a lasting impact, as it remains one of the areas of chip architecture where substantial performance gains can likely be achieved without major penalties. With hyperthreading, a chip can run two parts of an application at once, boosting performance by up to 30 percent. The gains come because the application can take advantage of different parts of the chip at the same time.

Digital also built a state-of-the-art chip fabrication facility in Hudson, Mass., that manufactured Alpha chips and StrongArms, an energy efficient chip for cell phones, which rarely, if ever, ran at full capacity.

Toward the end of the decade, the intellectual exodus began. In May 1997, the company filed a lawsuit alleging that Intel's then-future Itanium chip violated 10 Alpha patents. Despite the public rancor, the two companies settled the suit by October. Intel obtained the Hudson fab [semiconductor fabrication factory] and the rights to make StrongArm, while Digital got $700 million. The two also entered into a 10-year cross-licensing arrangement.

Simultaneously, Intel hired a number of the Digital engineers and gradually began to incorporate the company's technology into its own product lines. The StrongArm became the foundation of Intel's IXA network processor line for telecommunications equipment. The XScale chip, used in the latest Power PC handhelds and Sony's Clie, derived from StrongArm as well.

A deal between Compaq and Intel in June 2001 led to a further brain transfer. Engineers acquired from Compaq in that deal are now working on compilers for Itanium and future versions of the chip, including "Chivano." . . . Hammer, the next big chip from AMD, also derives design principles from Alpha, said Brookwood, and many Alpha alumni work on the chip. One of the performance enhancements is an integrated memory controller, an idea touted years earlier on Alpha. (Kanellos 2002).

POPULATING THE COMPUTING WORLD

A third legacy that is highlighted in the above article is the populating of the computing and information technology industry with DEC alumni going all the way back to the formation of Data General by Ed DeCastro and three key engineers in 1967. Others include Bernie Lacroute, SUN Microsystems, where he became executive vice-president; Dave Cutler and eventually Gordon Bell, Microsoft; Grant Saviers, CEO of Adaptec; Carol Bartz, CEO of Autodesk; Bob Glorioso, CEO of Marathon; Jack Smith and Bill Strecker, Flagship Ventures; Dick Clayton, Thinking Machines and eventually Sycamore Ventures; Sam Fuller, head of research at Analog Devices; Jeff Kalb, California Micro Devices; Stan Olsen, Gulf Lakes Corporation, a highly successful real estate venture in Florida; Bob Supnik, Nauticus Networks in a senior engineering role; and Pier Carlo Falotti.

One DEC alumnus decided that relationships among ex-DECies should be maintained and created an alumni association that facilitates meetings and publishes a directory to facilitate contact among the alumni. In June 1996 the *New York Times* published an article entitled "Divorced from the Job, Still Wedded to the Culture," which emphasized how much ex-DEC employees like to get together and how much they rely on one another for job contacts.

> Corporate culture, with its invisible, immeasurable power to shape lives and communities, has always been a poorly understood force in business, management experts say. When it has been studied, it has largely been over whether a company's idiosyncratic totems and taboos were beneficial or detrimental to its bottom line.
>
> But the story of life after Digital suggests something even more complicated and powerful: that the mixture of values and assumptions that makes up a corporate culture may be capable of existing on its own beyond the life-support system in which it evolved, and that in this case at least, downsizing, often considered destructive, may have been an agent of that new creation. . . .
>
> The matrix system, as it evolved at Digital, was essentially an overlapping series of circles, each of which was a semiautonomous business unit, but which also required the cooperation of other circles within the company to accomplish any goal. So being connected on the job made it feel natural and comforting to stay connected upon leaving.

INTELLECTUAL OUTPUT

A fourth legacy is the intellectual output of ex-DEC employees and consultants who worked with DEC. Most notable are the following books by DEC authors and consultants who drew heavily on DEC as a case study.

Amidon, D. M. (1997). *Innovation strategy for the knowledge economy: The KEN awakening.*

Amidon, D. M. (2003). *The innovation superhighway.*

Kanter, R. M. (1983). *The change masters.*

Kunda, G. (1992). *Engineering culture: Control and commitment in a high-tech corporation.*

Lipnack, J., and J. Stamps. (1982). *Networking: The first report and directory.*

Lipnack, J., and J. Stamps. (1986). *The networking book: People connecting with people.*

Lipnack, J., and J. Stamps. (1993). *The TeamNet factor: Bringing the power of boundary crossing into the heart of your business.*

Lipnack, J., and J. Stamps. (1994). *The age of the network: Organizing principles for the twenty-first century.*

Savage, C. M. (1990). *Fifth generation management: Integrating enterprises through human networking.*

Schein, E. H. (1967, 1988). *Process consultation.* Vol 1. 2nd ed.

Schein, E. H. (1987). *Process consultation.* Vol. 2, *Lessons for managers and consultants.*

Schein, E. H. (1992). *Organizational culture and leadership.* 2nd ed.

Schein, E. H. (1999a). *The corporate culture survival guide.*

Schein, E. H. (1999b). *Process consultation revisited.*

THE FINAL WORD

So DEC lives on—in the lives and memories of its alumni, in its customers who still own DEC equipment, and in organization and management theory—as one of the prime examples of what is possible in the human and technical arena. Many people we have talked to feel that DEC was a company ahead of its time in how it organized. It remains to be seen whether the DEC model will be reproduced in the knowledge-based organizations of the future or whether DEC represents only one step in the slow evolution of management theory and practice.

DEC's Technical Legacy

For the reader who is more interested in technical detail, I asked several of DEC's key engineers to write about what they considered DEC's technical contributions to have been. The points below are an amalgamation of their various comments.

Interactive computing. Starting with the PDP-1, DEC computers were interactive, allowing immediate direct response to the user's commands for computational results without waiting for a long (potentially overnight) batch job queue. Interaction also included connection to lab experiments and eventually manufacturing processes for real-time control. The capability to easily and tightly interconnect computers to both people and other processes led directly to the first minicomputer that in turn enabled the OEM market and the ability to use computers widely.

Graphical user interfaces. Although the graphical user interface could be viewed as a subset of the above, it should be separated out because of its far-reaching effect on how computing is done, even today. Again starting with the PDP-1, DEC computers offered graphical displays to further their interactive nature. Evidence of this is the first computer game, *Spacewar*, developed on the PDP-1 at MIT (Steve Russell, Alan Kotok et al.). From the simple point-by-point directed beam display of the PDP-1 to the more complex (but still directed beam) vector graphics pioneered on the PDP-11–based GT40 to the advanced raster graphics on VAX-based and Alpha-based worksta- tions, DEC was out in front.

Computer architecture advances. DEC pioneered the most influential processor architectures (PDP-11, VAX) and operating systems (RSX, VMS) from 1970 to 1990—every major CPU architecture after the PDP-11 (including the Intel x86) shows its influence, until the advent of RISC systems—and RSX and VMS are the design precursors to Windows NT (now Windows 2000 and XP). The PDP-11 (clean or- thogonal instruction set, register-based addressing modes), VAX (the "ultimate" CISC architecture and premier 32-bit architecture), and Alpha (premier 64-bit RISC architecture) all led in the development of advanced computer architecture. If imitation is a measure of suc- cess, the PDP-11 was the most widely imitated architecture of the early 1970s (including the Motorola 68000, National 16000, and Intel 8086), the VAX the most widely imitated architecture of the late 1970s and early 1980s, while Alpha's jump to 64-bit was copied by IBM, HP, and Sun.

Operating systems technology. DEC's OS8 and RT11 were the pre- cursors of the early single-user operating systems prevalent on PCs. DEC's PDP-10 and -20 operating systems pioneered the development of time-sharing. DEC's RSX11-M and VMS were the leading general- purpose operating systems of the 1970s and 1980s and led directly to Microsoft's Windows NT of the 1990s, since all efforts were led by David Cutler.

Microprocessor design. DEC's microprocessor teams developed high- speed design technology that revolutionized the performance of CMOS CPUs. From 1988 until disbanded, DEC's microprocessor group delivered the highest performance microprocessors, both CISC and RISC, in the industry, including the first chips to run at more than 100 MHz, 200 MHz, and 500 MHz. The legacy of that design group can be seen in today's performance-oriented chips like the Pentium IV as well as high-performance embedded chips like the Broadcom 1250.

Affordable computing. Starting with the PDP-8 (the first minicomputer), DEC made computing affordable, thereby enabling the OEM market model, with the first computer under $20,000 (the PDP-8) and then under $10,000 (the PDP-8/S).

Clustering. VMS clustering capabilities were the leading implementation of the primary mechanism for scalability and high availability widely used in today's servers. Clusters introduced in the early 1980s led IBM Sysplex by a decade and UNIX clusters c2000 by two decades! Clusters are the only fully scalable computer structures.

Compiler technology. Though here it is not clear whether DEC was an innovator or just an excellent exploiter of available technology, DEC's compilers, particularly Fortran but later C and C++, were generally acknowledged as the best in the industry. The excellence of VAX Fortran that exploited the larger address space was a key factor leading to early VAX success and dominance in technical computing. The superior optimization technology in DEC's Fortran and C compilers was a (perhaps the) major factor in achieving and sustaining Alpha's performance lead throughout the 1990s.

Storage architecture. One view is that DEC's HSC50 storage controller series and CI interconnect pioneered the use of SAN (storage area network) technology. Another view is that DEC's HSC50 storage controller series pioneered the concept of an intelligent, autonomous storage subsystem and is the direct ancestor of today's EMC Symmetrix or IBM Shark. The central model of storage for scalable computers was adopted by Oracle and dominated throughout the early 2000s.

Networking and VAX Notes. DEC built the first commercial time-sharing system as a way to get interactive computing to a larger number of users. These systems fed the ARPA (Advanced Research Projects Agency) community in the 1970s through the mid-1980s. Although developed concurrently with ARPAnet (and its TCP/IP protocol suite, which eventually took over), DECnet was for many years the most advanced and widely used networking software in the industry, and it pioneered most of the networking usage models prevalent today. DEC pioneered peer-to-peer networking and was the first company to integrate it as an essential part of its operating systems and products.

In June 1980, Digital was using VAX Notes, a collaborative networking tool, to develop products with its engineers and suppliers. This was fully thirteen years prior to the release of Lotus Notes by Lotus Corporation. VAX Notes was more than a networking tool, however. It was also a community-building device; among the many ways Digital used VAX Notes was to conduct cultural discussions. VAX Notes was also an early form of knowledge access. Long before knowledge management became a popular initiative, people in Digital realized that a many-to-many computer dialogue represented the potential for people to learn from one another. In this manner, it was clearly different from the traditional data and information exchanges that had previously been conducted over communications networks.

DEC Manufacturing

CONTRIBUTIONS MADE AND LESSONS LEARNED

Michael Sonduck

I joined DEC in the Maynard plant in 1976 to help the company grow as organization development manager. DEC employed twenty-five thousand people in 1976, about fifteen thousand of them in manufacturing. Employment had grown at an average compound rate of 34 percent a year for the prior ten years. There were already manufacturing plants in Maynard, Massachusetts (1957); San German, Puerto Rico (1968); Westminster, Massachusetts (1970); Mountain View, California (1970); Westfield, Massachusetts (1971); Taiwan, Republic of China (1972); Kanata, Canada (1972); Springfield, Massachusetts (1972); Aguadilla, Puerto Rico (1973); and Marlborough, Massachusetts (purchased from RCA in 1973). DEC was manufacturing computers and almost all the component parts, printers, video displays, and core memory, eventually becoming the largest manufacturer of core memory in the world. The company was still servicing every computer in use by its customers.

By the end of the next year, there were thirty thousand PDP-8s installed, fifty thousand LA36 printers, and the PDP-11/70 ramp (increase in demand for the product) had begun, with one thousand already installed. There were thirty-six thousand employees in 1977, a growth of 44 percent in one year! Although manufacturing was still growing (eight more plants would be added in the United States and Europe over the next five years), the culture was well established within the larger DEC world.

Peter Kaufmann had been running manufacturing since arriving from Beckman Instruments in 1966. Manufacturing plants were divided into three groups. Bill Hanson, who had worked for Kaufmann at Beckman and joined DEC in 1967, led volume manufacturing. Jack Smith, who joined DEC as one of the first technicians in 1958, led systems–final assembly and test. Henry LeMaire, who joined DEC in 1972 (and died in 1977), led semiconductor and memory components manufacturing.

New manufacturing capacity and employees were being added at rates unheard of in billion-dollar corporations. This, in turn, required the development of systems, methods, and approaches for managing, introducing, and building product, hiring people, tracking inventory, moving goods and people, and so forth to be invented on the spur of the moment, often by people who had never done it before. Many of the basic tasks of manufacturing, production planning, inventory control, cost accounting, personnel management, and hiring were done differently in each group, if not in each plant. Steep learning curves were commonplace. There was almost no attention to career growth in the traditional upward-mobility sense because most managers were young (twenty-five to thirty-five years old), early in their careers, and many got a new position every eighteen months or less. The deeply ingrained belief in "hiring the best people and letting them prove themselves" led to the requirement to learn, at the steepest rate possible. This belief was the human corollary to the requirement to grow the manufacturing organization as quickly as possible to keep pace with the demand for very successful products.

The growth of manufacturing and of DEC in general led to my being there in the first place. My functional boss, Ellen Karp, was relatively new to her job as head of organization development for manufacturing. She had been with DEC for several years in other parts of the company and was brought into manufacturing to help deal with the growth. Her early analysis was that if the company continued to grow at the rate it was,

DEC manufacturing would end up employing almost every able-bodied adult in Massachusetts before long! There was no supervisory or management development in manufacturing and no systematic organization development or planned change effort either. Karp and her boss, John Sims, who headed personnel for manufacturing, convinced Kaufmann that manufacturing needed a supervisory training program in the plants in order to provide enough supervisors and managers to maintain the rate of growth. They also shared the sense that manufacturing needed a more organized and planned approach to growth.

Kaufmann agreed that Karp could hire a group of organization development specialists on the basis of the need for supervisory training, not on the basis of planned growth. Having some training background became a requirement for the position. I would subsequently learn that striking a balance between the explicit goals of training and the implicit goals of planned change was a hallmark of selling of ideas at DEC. Everyone was expected to be an entrepreneur when it came to ideas. This translated in the DEC folklore into "tin cupping," which meant that if you could sell your idea of how to improve something, you could do it. This led to an important management practice that governed innovation in manufacturing. The people with the most responsibility, who always were the plant managers, had the ultimate authority on innovation—technical, managerial, or organizational.

My experience illustrates several underlying notions that governed DEC manufacturing at that time and for a long time to come: local control, high autonomy, individual responsibility (push-back), diffuse authority, and collective decision making (buy-in).

Even though Karp and Sims had convinced Kaufmann that having a cadre of specialists in management training and planned change was a good idea, it was still up to the individual plant managers to decide whether it was a good idea in each plant. Coupled with the employment interview process, this became my first exposure to the DEC matrix management system. During my interviews I met more than ten DEC managers from throughout not only the Maynard plant, which had the position vacancy, but also manufacturing personnel and organization development groups in other parts of the company. In retrospect the buy-in this created about my joining DEC was the embodiment of the hire-the-best-person philosophy I mentioned earlier. Once I was taken into the DEC family, I would be expected to deliver extraordinary results and prosper in a confusing, seemingly unstructured organizational environment. They needed to be sure I'd make it!

I ended up in Maynard as the first organization development specialist in manufacturing. Karp and Sims represented personnel and were charged with developing approaches to growing the manufacturing organization worldwide. They were functional managers. Locally there was a personnel manager in the Maynard plant, Ted Campbell, who worked for the plant manager *and* reported up to Sims through a group personnel manager. To get anything important done, the local manager had to satisfy the needs of the plant, because that was where the financial resources remained, *and* satisfy the needs of his or her functional manager, because that was where the professional recognition and opportunity for professional growth were controlled. For me that meant that to be successful in Maynard I had to balance the manufacturing-wide need for training and the local need for improvement. More important, the responsibility to understand and strike that balance lay with me, not with my bosses. That kept the natural tendency toward bureaucracy from overdeveloping. I couldn't push a decision up, and I had to manage the decision making (buy-in) process to gain agreement among my bosses and other interested parties. To me this was political democracy in action in a business setting.

As I went to work on the problem of determining the training needs of manufacturing supervisors (which seemed the only real choice), I learned several lessons that in retrospect were learned by everyone who came to DEC and wanted to succeed. First, DEC was full of "experts," and everyone who wanted to offer an opinion had to be listened to. Therefore, it was important to build a coalition of opinion leaders if my idea was to become reality. Second, there was lots of help available, inside and outside the company, that I could access if I could find it. I didn't need permission, budget, authorization, and so forth. I only needed my own resourcefulness and the collective weight of the opinion leaders. Third, small ideas are better than grand ideas. To get the support of plant managers, who had the resources for implementation, I needed to be able to tell them how my solution would address issues in their plant, now!

Over its almost forty years as an independent company, DEC assembled and tested computers made up of parts the company manufactured in its own plants, including printed circuit boards, metal housings, core memory, integrated circuits, modules, cables, and wire harnesses. At its peak there were more than twenty manufacturing and assembly plants in ten countries employing over sixty thousand people. From the very beginning when a small team of engineers, who were also the builders and assemblers, designed, manufactured, sold, and delivered memory modules until the end of its life as an independent company, DEC built things.

Given this long, rich history, it is fair to ask what contribution manufacturing made to what we have described as the DEC culture. Interviews with many of those responsible for leading DEC manufacturing over this period as well as my own direct observation leads to several conclusions:

1. Although DEC experimented with a number of cutting-edge manufacturing concepts during its history, the company never made world-class contributions to manufacturing technology.

2. The foremost contribution of DEC manufacturing was to enable the products envisioned by its engineers to be reliably (in most cases) produced and delivered. DEC was never a low-cost producer. That was not a goal during most of its history. When it did become a goal during the final phase of its life cycle, it was met with only moderate success.

3. The manufacturing organization evolved over time in response to the company's need for products and the underlying ethos of DEC. As an organization, it was often cumbersome, Balkanized, and inefficient when viewed from the larger corporate level.

4. The most significant contribution of DEC manufacturing was to the lives, learning, and development of the men and women who worked as part of it, and especially to those who attempted to lead it.

One of the keys to understanding DEC, its evolution, success, and decline, is to see the different organizational subcultures that were operative in the company. Each waxed and waned over the life of the company. At different times DEC was dominated by its engineering subculture. Although engineering was always important at DEC, there were periods when the influence of the subcultures of the marketing organizations or field service organization was strongly felt in the company.

DEC's worldwide manufacturing organization had a distinct subculture all its own. From its beginning in 1957 with "Gloria's Girls" (the group of women managed by Gloria Parazzo who were the first factory workers at DEC) assembling module boards in the Maynard Mill to the most sophisticated VLSI clean rooms of the late 1990s, you always knew when you were in a DEC manufacturing plant. The characteristics that defined these operational entities and resulted in their distinct identity also set them apart from other parts of DEC, as well as from other manufacturing companies in general.

Manufacturing under Kaufmann was a culture of experimentation, of desire to excel. The machismo that resulted from achieving more than any organization had achieved before contributed to an almost unfettered desire to do even more, daily. The origin of this culture lay with Kaufmann himself. Recruited from Beckman Instruments, he joined DEC in 1966. He was the first professional manufacturing manager the company hired. Like so many others at DEC, he was the first at something. Jack Smith, who much later came to head manufacturing himself, was the first wire-wrapper (a technician who built a part of the computer by hand in the early days). It is important to understand this characteristic of "firstness." On the surface one could see it as arrogance, the ultimate adolescent desire to be number one. At DEC it was that and more. It was being driven by the need to produce and deliver huge quantities of sophisticated equipment to eager, hungry customers. It was also being driven by the internal competition of the engineers with the builders (manufacturing). If the engineers could design it, we could build it!

DEC manufacturing was, in my opinion, an oligarchy and a meritocracy. The "firstness" drove the meritocracy. It didn't matter whether one had experience doing something before; what mattered was that one was serious, committed, dedicated, and smart enough to think through the problem and propose a solution and see it through to its conclusion, whether ultimately it worked or not. This was true because of the volumes of product that customers demanded. It was a market-driven economy of manufacturing. As long as customers wanted more and more, DEC manufacturing was bound and determined to build it and deliver it. It didn't matter whether that translated into more plants than any other computer manufacturer had ever built; more square footage bought, planned, built, and opened per year than anyone else had ever done before; more résumés reviewed than anyone had ever done before; more air miles flown than any company had ever done before. These were necessities, not goals. They were what it took to get the job done.

In a more closely controlled, centrally planned and managed company these outcomes would have appeared to seasoned executives as ridiculous hyperbole. Kaufmann created a management culture that was anything but controlled, planned, and centrally managed. This was no accident. It was based on a belief, a fundamental belief that if you gathered smart people who were committed to the same thing you were committed to and gave them their head, even though mistakes would be made, the end result would be better than any other possible result.

There were significant positive and negative consequences—many of which would become harbingers of the ultimate decline of the company. Along with strong local control to ensure commitment came insularity to new ideas, especially when they were developed elsewhere. Along with the belief that brainpower would overcome brawn came the resulting overhiring (more is better). Along with experimentation came waste, which ultimately turned into excess cost. Along with a meritocracy came an oligarchy of smartness and "firstness," which resulted in pushing aside, pushing out, and not listening to new ideas that came much later. Ultimately DEC manufacturing was an organization designed to experiment with ways to achieve what no other had ever done. Once that was accomplished, it was unable to refine itself into the finely tuned organization that was needed to become the low-cost producer.

DEC, the First
Knowledge Organization

A 1991 MEMO BY DEBRA ROGERS AMIDON

INTEROFFICE MEMORANDUM

TO: Ken Olsen
DATE: 28 February 1991
FROM: Debra Rogers
SUBJECT: Origins of the "Knowledge-Based Firm"
ROUGH DRAFT

What Ken Olsen created in 1957 is historic in industrial management. He brought the research environment of an academic institution into a commercial enterprise. With the organizational insight from General Georges Doriot and the participation of his initial management team, he established a unique organization which we will describe as dynamic (i.e., the "D-Form"). This is not to diminish his technical contribution to the industry; but, rather, to define and position DIGITAL Equipment Corporation with the managerial leadership which leverages intellectual capital as a strategic resource in global enterprise management.

Since its inception, the Corporation has been an enigma organizationally. In some cases, experts refer to "the DIGITAL mystique." Others define it in simplistic terms as organized chaos . . . or the chaotic organization. In fact, it is neither. It is a networked, "knowledge-leverage" form of learning organization positioned for 21st century sustained profitable growth.

Perhaps DIGITAL would be better thought of as a "knowledge-utility" or a "global innovation system." It has a managerial foundation that preceded appropriate labels, language, defined concepts and principles simply because its origins were so ahead of its time. Now they are more defined.

Over the past few years we have veered from effectively capitalizing on the strength of our corporate managerial jewels. This may be due to the complexity of managing a large-scale enterprise amidst a turbulent evolving global economy. It may be the reality of restructuring amidst imposed resource constraints. Whatever the cause, the result is the same. We have reverted, in many cases, to some of the traditional, hierarchical management practice that hinders the DIGITAL type of "knowledge flow" said to be the competitive advantage of the future.

It is time to reaffirm our roots, including our sense of purpose, in a transformation strategy that will simultaneously preserve the best of our unique competencies and (re)align our strengths. Our vision ought to position us for transitional collaborative leadership. This paper is intended to document the historic role of DIGITAL in establishing the new era of industrial management similar to what Alfred Sloan accomplished at General Motors in the 1920's. His decentralization defined the "M-form" (multi-divisional) organization. Management Systems Research (MSR) materials have been prepared for internal education and awareness of the correct positioning of DIGITAL within the industry and in history.

Contrast With The Traditional "M-form" Organization:

DIGITAL's management philosophy and concepts seem unique in contrast to the traditional organization structure established by Alfred Sloan. The value of "bubble-up" ideas, employee self-direction and knowledge-based decision-making were unusual to say the least. In fact, to describe DIGITAL's organization as a matrix organization was simplistic. What we have discovered, years later, is that these origins of DIGITAL set in motion a new management system, which can be described as dynamic and multi-dimensional. The contrast with the traditional multi-divisional form is striking.

The move from the "M-form" to "D-form" is a paradigm shift, which is fundamental in the natural evolution of management. Given the dynamics of a world economy, the rapid advances in information technology and the increasing reliance on the human system for organizational effectiveness, optimizing the flow of knowledge is a challenge. It is especially difficult in a large scale traditional enterprise. The modern enterprise requires an infrastructure that systematically supports initiatives to maintain the creative, entrepreneurial juices that feed smaller organizations, without yielding to the pitfalls of autonomous units. "Value-creation"—through leveraging interdependent areas of world class expertise—is the essence of the knowledge based firm.

Note: A longer version of this internal memorandum circulated inside Digital Equipment Corporation in 1991.

Digital
THE STRATEGIC FAILURE

Peter DeLisi

In business as in war, defeat is deeply rooted in the organizational dimensions of the loser's strategy.
Joseph Bower,
Harvard Business Review

In this appendix I will argue that the collapse of Digital Equipment Corporation, as well as being a cultural failure, was fundamentally a strategic failure. This failure was rooted in DEC's lack of appreciation for the power of strategy, its reluctance to make strategic choices, its inability to redefine its identity and reposition itself when necessary, its frontal assault on a more dominant force, and its lack of success in capitalizing on emerging new markets. Before we begin the discussion of Digital's strategic failure, it is important that we discuss what strategy is and why it's important.

STRATEGY AND ITS IMPORTANCE

The handbook of strategic expertise defines *strategy* as "an approach to using resources within the constraints of a competitive environment in order to achieve a set of goals" (Hayden 1986). Much of our understanding of strategy comes from the military. Indeed, the strategic vernacular (terms such as *mission, goals, objectives, tactics*) almost entirely comes from the military. Viewing strategy within its military context provides us a wealth of experience, whereas our industrial experience with strategy dates back only to the 1960s. In the classic *The Art of War,* written by Sun Tzu over two thousand years ago, for example, we see already the importance of strategy. "All men can see the tactics whereby I conquer, but what none can see is the strategy out of which great victory is evolved."

If *strategy* is the employment of resources in support of the goals of the organization, then what are goals? *Goals* are the *whats* of success. Usually limited in number, they define the desired long-term destination for an organization. Typically, goals deal with financial attainments (profitability and growth), competitive results, people issues, marketplace emphasis, and the kind of organization one wants to build. If goals are the *whats* of success, then strictly speaking, strategies are the *how-tos* of success. From these definitions, we can make our first observation, that without clear goals, the employment of resources, and therefore organizational performance, becomes suboptimal. As the old expression goes, "If you don't know where you're going, then any road will do." Strategies take their meaning from the goals that they support. Without clear goals, the employment of resources tends to be misdirected, inefficient, and confusing.

There are other important reasons why strategy is important. Strategy is all about choices, and today there are more choices than ever to pick from. In strategic work with clients, we tell them that our job is to pose tough choices to the senior team. Many of these choices pose dilemmas for the organization. An example is "Do I want to be a product leader with a time-to-market imperative, or do I believe I can best compete by *not* being first to market, but rather by having a 100 percent quality product when it does reach the marketplace?" You can't do both and do them in an excellent manner.

A third argument for strategy is that only strategy can create sustainable advantage. Operational improvements, or best practices, can easily be copied by other companies. It is in our strategic deliberations that we reinvent the rules of competition and determine the uniqueness of our value proposition to our customers.

A fourth argument, and a very powerful one, is the need for strategy to inform the people in the organization. People need a sense of where the company is going and what their role in it is if they are to feel fulfilled and make a contribution to the strategic objectives of the company. Given a choice between this action or that action, how do employees select the action that will make the better contribution to the success of the company if there is either no strategy or if they do not understand the strategy?

DIGITAL'S FAILURE TO VALUE STRATEGY

Perhaps Digital's first strategic failure was its lack of appreciation for the importance and power of strategy, a failure that showed up most prominently as a reluctance to create a defining vision for the company when it was most needed. Although there were pockets of strategic thinking and strategic expertise, the company as a whole did not appear to value strategy. Here we need to distinguish between an overall corporate strategy versus a product strategy and between attempts to do strategic plans versus a real appreciation for the power of strategic thinking. Digital did indeed have product strategies and did engage in some strategic planning, but the company failed during its critical moments in the late 1980s to articulate a clear defining vision by answering such basic questions as "What business are we in?" and "How do we best position ourselves for competitive success?"

The best evidence of this failure comes from an exchange that I had with Ken Olsen in the aftermath of the Persian Gulf War in March 1991. Responding to recent events, I prefaced a long e-mail with the statement that "war is not pleasant, but can be a powerful study and model for examining business strategy.... Let me suggest some lessons that Digital can extract from this war." Later in the e-mail I focused on the importance of strategy and Digital's lack of it:

> It's perhaps inconceivable that one could wage a war without strategic moves.... Yet, within Digital, we are guilty of doing exactly that.
>
> I see no evidence of an existing or planned-for corporate, *business* strategy. Perhaps, it exists, but it's not obvious.

Having a product strategy is also only part of the answer. In the Persian Gulf War, there clearly was a U.S. strategy to have the latest and best products to use in the war, but no one would argue that these by themselves would have won the war.

In Digital, the values and the instructions from our superiors are present; *what appears to be lacking, is again an overall "win the war strategy."* (DeLisi, e-mail to Ken Olsen, 1991)

I concluded this discussion with the following statement, indicative once again of the strength of the Digital culture:

You have taught me . . . that it is alright to risk and to express yourself if you really feel strongly about something. It's been thirteen and a half years since I left IBM, but I still haven't forgotten how inappropriate and probably career-limiting such a memo would have been there. So, while I experience some anxiety, it is with the realization that this is still the greatest company in the world to work for. I hope my memo in some small measure makes a contribution to keeping it that way.

Ken Olsen's response, shown here in its entirety, was as follows:

Thank you for your long, thoughtful note. I am sure you are right, but I would come with a slightly different emphasis. First of all, in all the Armed Services the emphasis is on training, discipline, duty and competence. The Air Force, in particular, showed this in the skills and adaptability they continuously demonstrated.

There has been a major change in the military. This is partly the reason for the volunteer service and the tremendous emphasis on training.

It is interesting how the heroes from this war, particularly the General, the Secretary of Defense, and the Commander in Chief show no need for vain glory or aggrandizement, but skill, loyalty, and helpfulness while doing one's part.

Strategy is useless without a trained, organized, supplied and motivated Military. But the strategists of this war showed two very important characteristics, and they freely adapted these to the conditions as they found them.

They also freely probed, investigated, and tried things, and they adapted to what they learned. The leaders, who depended on many people, got information from everyone. But the strategy was not a participatory activity. It was clear where the responsibility [lay], and they needed no meetings, arguments, discussions or red tape to adapt to the conditions.

Thank you again for your note. (Ken Olsen, e-mail, personal communication, 1991)

As with so many Ken Olsen discourses, there was significant meaning here if we could only unravel it. Did he mean that Digital lacked a trained, motivated workforce, and therefore a strategy wouldn't work? Or was he saying that he had a strategy for the company and it was his responsibility to discharge it? Either interpretation does not make sense when you consider that Olsen created a culture that highly valued people and a culture in which strategy development would most likely have been a highly participatory activity. In any event, nothing resulted from the exchange.

DIGITAL'S RELUCTANCE TO MAKE STRATEGIC CHOICES

The second strategic failure of Digital was a very fundamental one. As a number of authors remind us, and as we indicated previously, strategy is all about making choices. Using business drivers as an example, when push comes to shove, is time, cost, or quality the most important determinant of success for the company? Will I push the product out the door because time-to-market is a competitive necessity, or will I hold on to it until it is 100 percent correct because quality is more important?

Digital failed repeatedly to make strategic choices. Indeed, it believed that if the company didn't know the right answer, let the marketplace decide. This is a clear formula for disaster.

Evidence of Digital's failure to make choices was everywhere. Even with the emergence of the personal computer, Digital didn't introduce one personal computer, it introduced three different ones: the Rainbow, DECmate, and Professional 350. Digital didn't support one operating system but at any given time would support a variety of them. Most controversial was the decision to support either VMS or UNIX as the primary platform.

When strategic choices are not made at the top of the organization, they inevitably default to people lower in the organization. As we discussed with the military example, do we really want everyone in the organization making strategic choices? Given a choice between this action or that action, how will employees know which one will contribute the most to corporate goals and, therefore, to corporate success? Part of good strategy practice is to establish boundaries. People need to know not only what is strategic but also what is off limits.

DIGITAL'S INABILITY TO REDEFINE ITS CORE IDENTITY

Perhaps most damaging was Digital's inability to choose among various options for its future core business. This leads us to a discussion of Digital's third strategic failure: its inability to redefine its core identity, or in marketing terms, its "brand." For years Digital had been known as "the minicomputer company," a space it dominated in the industry. But as the industry differentiated, Digital had used its product excellence to build respectable businesses in networking, software, and many other lines of business.

As Digital's lines of business proliferated, the company reached a point where it was confusing both its sales force and its customers about what it really was. I remember numerous discussions in those days with key customers who would ask, "What business is Digital in?" Unfortunately, Digital failed to take note of these repeated inputs, *but most devastating by far, was its failure to note the erosion of its core identity as "the minicomputer company."* Unnoticed by Digital, the computer market had differentiated, and Digital was no longer dominant in *any* segment of this differentiated market. At the time, you couldn't name one market segment in which Digital would be the first company to come to the minds of its customers. The company was in every segment you could imagine—mainframe, network, desktop, workstation, software, fault-tolerance, systems integration, management consulting, hardware repair, semiconductors—but sadly it was not dominant in any of them.

A memo I wrote to another sales executive within Digital highlights the above problem but also illustrates an earlier point that strategy was not valued within Digital. As a result, this memo, like so many other attempts to "get Digital moving on the right track" fell on deaf ears. Writing in May 1990, I compared the situation at Digital to the problems that Sears was experiencing at the time:

> As you know, Sears is having serious difficulties with its retail business—encroached on the low end by companies like Kmart and Wal-Mart, and on the high end, by premium retailers such as Nordstrom's. Throughout their product line, they're also besieged by very focused specialty retailers in electronics, hardware, appliances, etc. As a result of their failure to anticipate and respond to what was happening to their marketplace, Sears has lost its IDENTITY.
>
> It appears to me that Digital faces potentially the same fate, if we are not careful. Encroached on the low end by the desktop manufacturers and on the high end by the mainframe manufacturers, Digital is losing its distinctiveness and resulting IDENTITY in the marketplace.
>
> How do we build a business IDENTITY for the next 33 years? What business will Digital be in? The minicomputer business? The services business? The software business? The networking business? The computer business? It can't be the latter, because we'll fall into the same trap as Sears, who acted as if they were in "the retail business" and failed to see the need for a focused identity.

DIGITAL'S INABILITY TO REPOSITION ITSELF

Digital's fourth strategic failure was not repositioning itself when the need dictated. A strategic tool that illustrates this failure is the value discipline model of Michael Treacy and Fred Wiersema (1995). According to the research conducted by these two authors, excellent companies excel in one and only one of three value disciplines: product leadership, operational excellence, and customer intimacy. The *product leader company* is the one with the latest and greatest product and or technology or both. Time-to-market is its ultimate imperative. This company will obsolete its own products before its competitors do. The *operationally excellent company* provides good-quality products and services to its customers with the overall lowest cost of ownership. The cost of ownership includes the cost associated with the hassle, poor service, and so forth. Examples of operationally excellent companies are Wal-Mart, Southwest Airlines, and FedEx. A *customer-intimate company* will take its knowledge of customers to the next level. Its intimate knowledge of customer needs allows this company to define the segments it serves into narrower and narrower bands, until it reaches that hypothetical limit of one-on-one marketing. The customer intimate company tends to be very good at marketing and customer relationships.

I believe that I can safely say that historically Digital was a product leadership company. It had a strong passion for the latest and greatest technology and was very much engineering-driven.

While product leadership carried Digital for over three decades, the turning point was the years between 1986 and 1988. During those two years, Digital hired 26,800 people to go head-to-head with IBM. Looking back, we see that the growth that they anticipated did not materialize. Unbeknownst to anyone in the industry at the time, the computer business was entering a flat period of growth in anticipation of the future emerging client/server and networking-type businesses. Saddled with the increased cost of 26,800 people, Digital needed to cut costs and become much more efficient. In the value discipline scheme of Treacy and Wiersema, Digital needed to move the company from product leadership to operational excellence. It could also have reduced manpower, but in a no-layoff company, this was impossible.

DIGITAL'S INABILITY TO CAPITALIZE ON EMERGING MARKETS

A fifth Digital strategic failure was the company's inability to capitalize on emerging markets. As mentioned previously, Digital was in every conceivable market niche but was not able to emerge as dominant in any of them. Many reasons, such as cultural and political factors, could be given for this failure, but the strategic failure lies in not having an effective way to conduct environmental analysis and points again to overall weakness in strategy. In the classic strategic planning process, *environmental analysis* involves a detailed look at the outside environment and at trends, customers, the marketplace, and competition. When performed well, the environmental analysis provides good solid data from which the subsequent strategic choices are made. As we discussed earlier, Digital's approach was to let the marketplace decide. Driven by an empowered culture and the belief that "Truth is discovered through conflict," DEC suffered from lack of focus, an incredible range of products and services, significant duplication and overlap, and, as already discussed, great inefficiencies. Had Digital been better at this phase of the strategic planning process, it would have significantly narrowed its subsequent focus and, in the process, might have created a new core business and a new dominant niche for itself. Instead, it rode every horse to the detriment of the company and its people.

DIGITAL'S HEAD-TO-HEAD ATTACK ON IBM

The last strategic failure that we will identify was Digital's head-to-head attack against IBM. From military strategy, we learn the principle that one never goes head-to-head against a firmly entrenched, more dominant adversary. As mentioned previously, buoyed by overconfidence bordering on arrogance, Digital decided to hire 26,800 people in a two-year period and go after IBM's market share. In retrospect, this was a defining decision. Had Digital not done this, it might still be in business today. But as we have discussed, the decision started a downward spiral from which it never recovered. Excessive costs, with no commensurate growth, in a no-layoff company, with no efficiencies to deal with them is a sure recipe for disaster.

What might the strategic alternative have been? Continuing with military principles, Digital might have continued its guerrilla and flanking maneuvers into markets and spaces in which IBM was not dominant. Digital had done this quite successfully historically with penetrations into the engineering, scientific, and end-user communities. New growth markets such as client/server, desktop, and networks, were already on the horizon and could have represented Digital's next major opportunities. Indeed, Digital had already excelled in the server and networking markets. Instead, Digital chose to go head-to-head with IBM and will go down in history as yet one more example of defeat suffered at the hands of a more dominant force.

What Happened?

A POSTSCRIPT

Gordon Bell

Every time I meet a DEC alum whom I haven't seen for a decade or two, the talk quickly comes around to the inevitable question: What happened? This book gives a fine understanding based on Ed Schein's perspective of corporate cultures, especially Digital's. His observations, together with the various memos and reference interviews, stimulated me to state what *I believe* happened. I hope it will be a guide for other companies that will be tested and judged by these same laws that govern computing.

Although I left the company in 1983, I maintained communication with Digital and did consulting work, including reviewing its portfolio of failed start-up ventures. In 1986 while leading the government's effort to build what became the Internet, I encouraged Digital to compete for the contract to work on it (IBM and the University of Michigan won the first contract). In 1991, as an Intel consultant, I attempted to create a merger of the Alpha and Intel architectures, but unfortunately HP took on the role. In 1995 while keynoting the InternetWorld conference, I made and won a *never paid* $1,000 bet with Tom Richardson, marketing director of Digital's Internet business group (working for Vice President Rose Ann Giordano). The bet was that DEC would come in last behind Sun, HP, and IBM in Internet product sales, despite its research lead with tools, products, and services for the Web, including AltaVista. (An attempted spin-off of AltaVista failed in 1995 because AltaVista was a prized asset of the financially troubled DEC, which was in talks with Compaq. In June 1998 Compaq purchased DEC for $4.5 billion. In June 1999 Compaq sold AltaVista to CMGI for $2.3 billion, and in February 2003 CMGI sold AltaVista to Overtune for $140 million.) Internet products were perfect for DEC—it had all the pieces including servers, software, and networking. However, DEC didn't understand how to organize to engage in a new market.

Clayton Christensen invariably starts talks about his 1997 book, *The Innovator's Dilemma*, with DEC as his example of technology observation: DEC, *or more precisely its top leadership,* was found guilty of violating Moore's Law (Intel founder Gordon Moore's prediction that the number of transistors on a chip would double every eighteen months) and was sentenced to Compaq in 1998, and HP in 2002. The extraordinary price shift resulting from Moore's Law was clearly known in 1975 (see figure E.1), when VAX was planned; furthermore, this is the law that creates a new paradigm in computing about every decade! A common belief about DEC's failure was that the company failed "to get the PC." These explanations fail. Otherwise Sun, being tried by the same Moore's Law and events in 2003 on its twenty-first birthday (there are parallels between DEC in 1990–92 and Sun Microsystems in 2000–3) would have failed to get started. HP and IBM should have floundered.

It really was simply ignorance and incompetence on the part of DEC's top handful of leaders and, to some degree, its generally ineffective board of directors. Given the DEC culture of openness, honesty, letting the data decide, and taking personal responsibility, this straightforward explanation should suffice. The data clearly support the need to take individual responsibility for DEC's problems rather than believing that it was the "events and the culture that made us do it." (When former chairman and CEO Louis Gerstner arrived at IBM, the company was in the same relative position as when Olsen resigned from Digital; leaders can be responsible for the success or failure of a

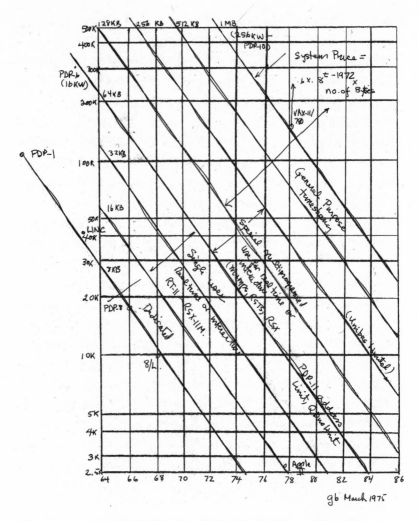

FIGURE E.1.   1975 Graph Showing the Decline in Price of Computers, 1966–1986

company.) These leaders lacked understanding of the nature of the computer industry in nearly every critical technology and product area:

- Moore's Law. In 1989 Olsen demonstrated his lack of understanding that a $300 CMOS NVAX microprocessor would equal and shortly exceed the $300,000 ECL Aquarius performance. Figure E.2 from 1981 shows that ECL would have a short life when I had proposed the purchase of a part of Trilogy. My 1982

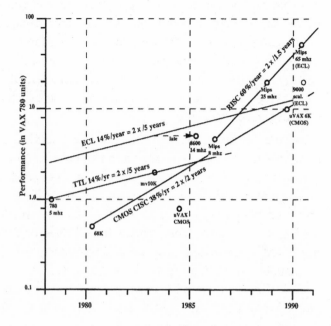

Notes:

Circuit Technologies

ECL	=	emitter coupled logic (bipolar semiconductor)
TTL	=	transistor-transistor logic (bipolar semiconductor)
CMOS	=	complementary metal oxide semiconductor (field effect)

Computer Architectures

CISC	=	complex (or complete) instructor-set computer
RISC	=	reduced instruction-set computer

FIGURE E.2. 1981 Graph Showing the Performance for Semiconductor and Processor Architectures in the Minicomputer Class. Source: C. Gordon Bell and John E. McNamara, *High-Tech Ventures: The Guide for Entrepeneurial Success* (Reading, Mass: Addison-Wesley, 1991).

optimism was a costly mistake that required killing the project. Not building an ECL computer was a clear and easy decision when the technology failed to materialize in a timely fashion. The market rejection confirmed the decision.

As Ed Schein shows in this book, Olsen loved having many options yet disliked killing projects implied by that—he was too much an engineer. (Although I refuse to believe that DEC lacked the money gene! The company's second rule after honesty was profitability. I personally wrote a program that analyzed sensitivity to cost, price, and schedule slips that product managers ran for all planned products.) Olsen's unilateral decision to continue the ECL project eroded the culture by going against the data and the technical community. In an earlier era when Olsen was a great CEO, data—not Olsen—would have made such an important and costly decision.

- Hardware × Software platform (the product of hardware and software versions), levels of integration and the resulting costs that structure the computing industry. Computers are built up in a layered fashion and include the following (ignoring the increased complexity when a database is added to a platform): hardware components (for example, microprocessor, disk), integrated hardware platform (for example, Macintosh, PC, System/360), operating system (for example, Palm O/S, Windows 2000, UNIX), generic and vertical applications (for example, Office XP, Acrobat, mySAP Business Suite), and finally user-specific customization, data, and content.

   Each hardware platform that hosts a specific operating system requires development, training, inventory, distribution, sales, support, customer knowledge, and *an implied commitment of eternal support*. Olsen's predilection for many alternatives and to "let the customer decide" is clearly impossible to profitably support. In 1992 Digital's VAX, MIPS, PC, and Alpha hardware and various versions of UNIX amounted to ten unique platforms. MIPS was adopted as an interim architecture and delayed but costly response to Sun. Cutler's Prism architecture had been delayed for two years by being reviewed to death. A subterranean version of Prism emerged from the semiconductor group as Alpha.

   By the mid-1980s DEC had become a classic well-run, vertically integrated company. By the mid-1980's, the industry had become fragmented and completely horizontally structured. Digital did not need to manufacture its own disks, tapes, and especially semiconductors and microprocessors! Bob Palmer built up substantial semiconductor facilities. The make-buy policy that I posited to prevent inventing and building everything was "Make what you sell, *not* what you buy." Alternatively, "If you make something it has to be competitive at that level of integration, otherwise buy it." DEC used its own components under a protective systems price umbrella.

- *Customers buy software solutions to their problems, not hardware.* What computing customers actually buy is solutions to problems, or application tools supplied by an independent software provider industry segmented by use (for example, small retailing, manufacturing). Few companies build their tools unless they sell them. Through a series of reorganizations, the DEC organization that focused on the acquisition of application software was eliminated, thereby cutting out exactly those products that customers buy. Who needs a computer that doesn't provide a solution to a problem?

- *Standards interconnect the components of each level of integration.* Building all computing systems requires the understanding that because of the legacy and always-increasing complexity of computing systems, standards are critical. As such, being able to invent a new standard or supply products that don't quite fit is risky. The policy I managed was "Either make the standard, or follow the standard." If you fail to make the standard, you usually get to develop the product twice. Alpha is an expensive example. Ethernet—a DEC-, Intel-, and Xerox-developed standard— allowed Sun to start up and to distribute the workstation and typifies DEC's role as a successful industry standards setter.

  While DEC is perpetually faulted for missing the PC, this was not the case. In 1982, when IBM, Intel, and Microsoft established the standard for the PC, DEC introduced *three* potential personal computers: a PDP-8 for word processing, a proprietary PDP-11 PRO (internal name, KO, for knockout) that was unable to be cloned (PDP-11 microprocessors weren't available because architecture was considered to be a corporate jewel, albeit an obsolete one that needed to be exploited or face its inevitable extinction), and an Intel 8088 that ran a version of DOS. The company tried but simply failed to establish the standard. Then it failed to follow the standards of the IBM PC established by Intel and Microsoft and was not a part of the resulting PC industry. In 1987 Olsen sent a DEC PC for me to test and use. It failed to run standard software, and even though its cabling was simple and elegant, it was "better" but incompatible. Was it arrogance or ignorance to believe that Digital could deviate from a well-established five-year-old standard?

Similar stories describe Digital's misunderstanding of exploiting its unique UNIX position.

- *Control based on comparable industry metrics.* Over time, every high-tech product protected by patents, know-how, or market position became a commodity. In this situation, cost structures are comparable across the industry. DEC's per-employee revenue was half that of its competitors in a horizontally integrated industry. Downsizing was long overdue. It wasn't the economy that initially masked the lack of revenue. Where was the CFO and his associates?

- *Overconfidence and belief in an omnipotent and omniscient VAX strategy.* The VAX strategy established a patent-protected proprietary product and marketing plan. This worked well for a decade. However, DEC's leadership didn't update the VAX strategy to include the transition to 64-bits. Instead, they ignored the problem after Dave Cutler left. (Cutler went to Microsoft and built Windows NT.)

    Just as bad, DEC ignored the computer industry's movement to UNIX. Olsen called UNIX "snake oil," believing that the VAX operating system, VMS, was far superior technologically. Perhaps he was right. Again DEC failed to recognize that customers wanted standards—albeit, in this case, a faux and fragmented standard—not a technically superior system.

    Why did Olsen and the other company leaders so love the VAX strategy even though it ran counter to Olsen's belief by putting all the eggs in one basket? The VAX strategy was simple and elegant because it allowed the whole company to focus in a single direction. The company didn't have to think about its direction! When proposed in 1979, it was one page, with six backup pages of tactics, including those regarding IBM and UNIX. The VAX strategy stated:

    > Provide a set of homogeneous, distributed-computing-system products so that a user can interface, store information, and compute, without reprogramming or extra work from the following computer sizes and styles:

- via [a cluster of] large, central (mainframe) computers or networks;

- at local, shared departmental/group/team (mini) computers [and evolving to PC clusters];

- with interfaces to other manufacturers and industry standard information processing systems; and

- all interconnected via the local area Network Interconnect [Ethernet] in a single area, with the ability of interconnecting the Local Area Networks (LANs) to form Campus Area and Wide Area Networks. (Bell and McNamara 1991, 37)

The strategy was simple and elegant, and focused a multibillion-dollar company around a single architecture. DEC's leadership was hooked, and it couldn't let go!

- *IBM understanding.* In 2002, about 50 percent of IBM's revenue came from service. This gives IBM complete control of corporate computing environments because customers pay for service from IBM personnel and that locks customers into unique software and continuing support. A direct attack on this ecosystem is doomed, especially based on hiring from the IBM sales organization that requires an extensive and expensive infrastructure. DEC had been successful in various markets such as R&D, manufacturing, and communications as a low-cost, high-performance technology-platform supplier. After DEC, HP and Sun took over this role.

In 1987, an IBM vice president told me that the VAX strategy had really eroded their midrange AS 400 business and was giving them heartburn in all fronts—just as we had planned. Within five years, while DEC was hiring IBM salespeople, who are generally unable to exist outside of the IBM environment, IBM established itself in DEC's traditional marketing-sales channels, especially the third-party software providers. Unlike the laissez-faire era of DEC product lines, every conceivable, often competing, channel of distribution was developed: OEMs, value-added resellers (VARs), independent software vendors (ISVs), systems integrators, retail stores, direct sales, and so forth. Jack Shields, who built DEC's service, was in charge. Service requires absolute

control and certainty, and the new sales and distribution
structure had to be under control and just one way.

- *Organizational complexity.* Ed Schein makes a strong point about
  the Digital organization. Prior to the PC, the Operations Committee had talked incessantly about divisionalizing the successful
  terminal business. No consensus could be reached because the
  revenue of each product line contained income from terminals
  and no one was willing to give that up. In addition, Olsen was
  fond of saying: "I don't trust anyone *left alone without checks and
  balances.*" Divisions implied making new, autonomous companies.

  The push in engineering was the opposite strategy, to simplify
  through autonomy: get the organization outside of Maynard to
  avoid new committees and task forces that impeded progress, reorganization, new plans, and perpetual reoptimization. Disk engineering and manufacturing went to Colorado, terminals were
  engineered and manufactured in Taiwan, and Dave Cutler went
  to Seattle (as discussed in chapter 12) in order to simplify yet
  formalize communication. Overall, Ed Schein has pointed out
  the failure of the organization to scale up, especially in interpret-
  ing rules like "Do the right thing." Did this mean rightness for
  self, supervisor, colleagues, department, company, customer, or
  shareholders?

FAILURE TO ACT ON OPPORTUNITIES

Was Digital's inevitable death caused by top-line failures or just errors
that affected present and potential earnings?

Various analyses, including this one, have enumerated failures: the
PC; creation of too many platforms, which confused sales and customers; misallocation of resources to support a mainframe; destruction of a marketing organization and the plethora of channels of distribution; replacement of one profit and loss responsibility dimension
with three (products, market segments, and field sales); the fatal
focus and direct attack on IBM; a costly, unsustainable semiconductor manufacturing organization (Bob Palmer had been allowed to
build a large captive facility); and so forth.

It is more positive to look at the missed opportunities that DEC's vast array of technology should have yielded to sustain and grow a technology company. DEC led all computer companies in the transition from other technologies to custom CMOS microprocessors, where the company maintained a lead (including over Intel) extending beyond 2003! In a similar vein, DEC's pre-PC terminal business included introducing one of the first laser printers—a business that HP ultimately claimed and that sustained its profits well into the early 2000s. With the introduction of the Ethernet, a communications products and services division could have exploited Digital's lead in distributed computing. DEC could have exploited its position with UNIX, as HP did in parallel with VMS, instead of being ambivalent and somewhat hostile.

THE LONG FINAL DAYS, 1992–1998

In 1992, Olsen resigned, and the board appointed Bob Palmer CEO. With no experience in computing or running a successful business, downsizing an out-of-control company was a no-brainer for a semiconductor manufacturing person. Unfortunately, Palmer provided no leadership for the critical top line, missing the biggest computing market of all time—supplying tools to build the World Wide Web (WWW). Palmer's severance from the acquisition by Compaq made him the first-prize winner. The board came in second. Employees, customers, and stockholders all lost.

As Digital's leadership continued to make bad, ill-informed decisions, they hired consultants and outsiders to advise. Instead, they only needed to look inward. DEC's talented employee base did have the answers—but no one was upstairs or listening. Digital Equipment Corporation employed some of computing's brightest and most motivated people, who came to work to design, manufacture, and market world-class products and services. Thus the greatest and fatal flaw was the failure to draw on its intellectual capital.

References

Amidon, D. M. 1997. *Innovation strategy for the knowledge economy: The KEN awakening.* Boston: Butterworth-Heineman.

———. 2003. *The innovation superhighway.* Woburn, Mass.: Butterworth-Heinemann.

Avolio, B. J., and T. C. Gibbons. 1988. Developing transformational leaders: A lifespan approach. In *Charismatic leadership: The elusive factor in organization effectiveness,* edited by J. A. Conger and R. N. Kanungo. San Francisco: Jossey-Bass.

Bass, B. M. 1985. *Leadership and performance beyond expectations.* New York: The Free Press.

Bell, C. G., and J. E. McNamara. 1991. *High-tech ventures: The guide for entrepreneurial success.* Reading, Mass.: Addison-Wesley.

Bennis, W. 1989. *On becoming a leader.* Reading, Mass.: Addison-Wesley.

Bennis, W., K. D. Benne, and R. Chin, eds. 1961. *The planning of change: Readings in the applied behavioral sciences.* New York: Holt, Rinehart and Winston.

Bennis, W., and B. Nanus. 1985. *Leaders: The strategies for taking charge.* New York: Harper and Row.

Burns, J. M. 1978. *Leadership.* New York: Harper and Row.

Christensen, C. M. 1997. *The innovator's dilemma: When new technologies cause great firms to fail.* Boston: Harvard Business School Press.

———. 2000. Meeting the challenge of disruptive change. *Harvard Business Review,* March/April 2000.

Davis, S., and P. Lawrence. 1977. *Matrix.* Reading, Mass.: Addison-Wesley.

DeLisi, P. S. 1998. A modern-day tragedy: The Digital Equipment story. *Journal of Management Inquiry* 7, no. 2 (June): 116–32.

Gibbons, T. C. 1986. Born vs. made: Toward a theory of development of transformational leaders. Ph.D. dissertation, The Fielding Graduate Institute.

Hayden, C. 1986. *The handbook of strategic expertise.* New York: The Free Press.

Kampas, P. J. 2003. Shifting cultural gears in technology-driven industries. *Sloan Management Review* 44, no. 2: 41–48.

Kanellos, M. 2002. Intel hyperthreading traced to DEC tech. *ZD Net,* October 10, 2002, <http://zdnet.com.com/2100-1103-961495.html> (April 25, 2003).

Kanter, R. M. 1983. *The change masters.* New York: Simon and Schuster.

Katz, R. 1993. Managing technological leaps: A study of DEC's Alpha design team. *Research in Organizational Change and Development* 7: 217–34.

Kimberly, J. R., R. H. Miles, and associates, eds. 1981. *The organizational life cycle.* San Francisco: Jossey-Bass.

Kunda, G. 1992. *Engineering culture: Control and commitment in a high-tech corporation.* Philadelphia: Temple University Press.

Lipnack, J., and J. Stamps. 1982. *Networking: The first report and directory.* New York: Doubleday.

———. 1986. *The networking book: People connecting with people.* New York: Routledge and Kegan Paul.

———. 1993. *The TeamNet factor: Bringing the power of boundary crossing into the heart of your business.* Essex Junction, Vt.: Oliver Wright.

———. 1994. *The age of the network: Organizing principles for the twenty-first century.* Essex Junction, Vt.: OMNEO Press.

Moore, G. A. 1991. *Crossing the chasm.* New York: HarperBusiness.

———. 1995. *Inside the tornado.* New York: HarperBusiness.

Pearson, J. P., ed. 1992. *Digital at work: Snapshots from the first thirty-five years.* Burlington, Mass.: Digital Press.

Rifkin, G., and G. Harrar. 1988. *The ultimate entrepreneur.* New York: Contemporary Books.

Roberts, E. B. 1991. *Entrepreneurs in high technology.* New York: Oxford University Press.

Savage, C. M. 1990. *Fifth generation management: Integrating enterprises through human networking.* Maynard, Mass.: Digital Press.

Schein, E. H. 1967, 1988. *Process consultation.* Vol. 1. 2nd ed. Reading, Mass.: Addison-Wesley

———. 1970. The role innovator and his education. *Technology Review* 73: 3–7.

———. 1987. *Process consultation.* Vol. 2, *Lessons for managers and consultants.* Reading, Mass.: Addison-Wesley.

———. 1992. *Organizational culture and leadership.* 2nd ed. San Francisco: Jossey-Bass.

———. 1996. Three cultures of management: The key to organizational learning. *Sloan Management Review* 38, no. 1: 9–20.

———. 1999a. *The corporate culture survival guide.* San Francisco: Jossey-Bass.

———. 1999b. *Process consultation revisited.* Reading, Mass.: Addison-Wesley.

Tichy, N. M. 1981. Problem cycles in organizations and the management of change. In *The organizational life cycle,* edited by J. R. Kimberly, R. H. Miles, and associates. San Francisco: Jossey-Bass, 164–83.

Treacy, M., and F. Wiersema. 1995. *The discipline of market leaders.* Reading, Mass.: Addison-Wesley.

Utterback, J. M. 1994. *Mastering the dynamics of innovation.* Boston: Harvard Business School Press.

Van Maanen, J., and S. R. Barley. 1984. Occupational communities: Culture and control in organizations. *Research in Organizational Behavior* 6.

Waldrop, M. M. 2002. The origins of personal computing. *Scientific American,* 85–91.

Zaleznik, A. 1977. Managers and leaders: Are they different? *Harvard Business Review,* May/June, 67–78.

Index

About the Author

ED SCHEIN is Sloan Fellows professor of management emeritus, a senior lecturer at the Sloan School at MIT, and a fellow of the American Psychological Association and the Academy of Management.

Besides his numerous articles Schein has authored fourteen books including *Organizational Psychology, Career Dynamics, Organizational Culture and Leadership, Process Consultation, Process Consultation Revisited,* and *The Corporate Culture Survival Guide.* He is the founding editor of *Reflections: The Journal of the Society for Organizational Learning,* and was also coeditor of the Addison Wesley Series on Organization Development.

At present he is devoted to connecting academics, consultants, and practitioners around the issues of knowledge creation, dissemination, and utilization. Among Schein's past and current clients are Digital Equipment Corporation, Ciba-Geigy, Apple, Citibank, General Foods, Procter & Gamble, ICI, Saab Combitech, Steinbergs, Alcoa, Motorola, Hewlett-Packard, Exxon, Shell, AMOCO, British Petroleum, Con Edison, the Economic Development Board of Singapore, and the International Atomic Energy Agency.

Professor Schein is married, has three children, and seven grandchildren. He and his wife, Mary, live in Cambridge, Massachusetts.